GETTING STARTED
WITH MARKSTRAT3

INSTALLING MARKSTRAT3

Follow the instructions in the table below to install MARKSTRAT3 on a stand-alone computer with the default options. To install MARKSTRAT3 in complex environments with network servers and/or remote workstations, please contact your instructor.

Windows 3.1	*Windows 95*
Insert the **Team** diskette in the disk drive.	
Select the **Program Manager** by pressing Alt-Tab a number of times until it appears.	Click on the **Start** button.
In the **File** menu, select **Run** . . .	In the **Windows 95** menu, select **Run** . . .
Type **A:SETUP** in the **Command line** box, and click on **OK.**	Type **A:SETUP** in the **Open** box, and click on **OK.**
In a short time, a dialog box will pop up to let you select your preferred language. Click on **OK** to proceed.	
A second dialog box with additional options will pop up. For a stand-alone installation, do not change the default options and proceed by clicking on **OK.**	
Insert the **Library** diskette when requested by the software. Click on **OK** to proceed.	
Congratulations! You have successfully installed MARKSTRAT3!	

STARTING MARKSTRAT3

Windows 3.1	*Windows 95*
Select the **Program Manager** by pressing Alt-Tab a number of times until it appears.	Click on the **Start** button.
In the **Window** menu, select **Markstrat3–By Strat*X.**	In the start menu, select **Programs.**
Double-click on the **MS3 Team** icon.	In the new pop-up menu, select **Markstrat3–By Strat*X** and, finally, **MS3 Team.**

DISCOVERING MARKSTRAT3

You are about to start a course using MARKSTRAT3. Before you begin working on the real data received from your instructor, you can get to know this simulation with a demonstration data file named PRACTICE. You can browse through the results of Firm E for the last seven years, and you can make decisions for year 8.

Firm E specializes in developing, manufacturing, and marketing the Sonite, a consumer durable good comparable to an electronic entertainment product. Recently it has diversified into a new product, the Vodite. Based on a technological breakthrough made in the space industry, Vodites satisfy an entirely different need than Sonites do.

To open the PRACTICE data file, please follow the steps below.

■ If you are still in front of the MARKSTRAT3 introduction screen, click on **OK.** With Windows 95, the **OK** button is partially hidden by the task bar.
■ Insert the **Team** disk in the drive.
■ In the **File** menu, select **Transfer results and default decisions from instructor.**
■ Select **practice.mre** in the left-hand side box; the boxes on the right will be filled in automatically, including the Password cell.
■ Click on **Transfer results & default decisions and open industry.**

You are now ready to analyze the results of Firm E. Before you start, it is important to understand that MARKSTRAT3 is organized in six main modules—**Decisions, Report, Newsletter, Market studies, Analysis,** and **Interface**—which you can activate by clicking on the buttons in the top bar.

For instance, click on the **Analysis** button. The menu below the top bar includes **Market, Performance, Benchmarking,** etc. Look at the **Market** graphs to get the big picture of the market evolution: size, growth, and price. Then use the **Performance** graphs to study the performance of the five competitors. You will see that Firm E is experiencing some difficulties in sales and market share.

The purpose of the other five modules is fully explained in the manual. You can print the current graph or data table at any time by clicking on the 🖨 button in the top right-hand corner. To print a complete company report, select the **Interface** module, click on the **Print** button, input 1 in the **Number of copies,** click on **Complete output,** uncheck **Excel files only,** and click on **Print.**

The manual will introduce you to the other features of MARKSTRAT3. We hope you enjoy your experience with MARKSTRAT3.

MARKSTRAT 3
THE STRATEGIC MARKETING SIMULATION

JEAN-CLAUDE LARRÉCHÉ
ALFRED H. HEINEKEN PROFESSOR OF MARKETING

INSEAD FONTAINEBLEAU, FRANCE

HUBERT GATIGNON
CLAUDE JANSSEN PROFESSOR OF BUSINESS ADMINISTRATION

AND PROFESSOR OF MARKETING

INSEAD FONTAINEBLEAU, FRANCE

SOUTH-WESTERN College Publishing

An International Thomson Publishing Company

PUBLISHER:	South-Western College Publishing, Cincinnati, Ohio
EDITOR-IN-CHIEF:	Valerie A. Ashton
PUBLISHING TEAM DIRECTOR:	John Szilagyi
ACQUISITIONS EDITOR:	Dreis Van Landuyt
DEVELOPMENTAL EDITOR:	Alice C. Denny
PRODUCTION EDITOR:	Judith O'Neill
PRODUCTION:	Lifland et al., Bookmakers
	Omegatype Typography, Inc.
	Pre-Press Company, Inc.
COVER DESIGN:	Tin Box Studio, Cincinnati, Ohio
COVER ILLUSTRATION:	Copyright Rob Colvin
MANUFACTURING COORDINATOR:	Sue Disselkamp
MARKETING MANAGER:	Steve Scoble

5   MZ   1

Printed in the United States of America

Package ISBN 0-538-88089-9

Library of Congress Cataloging-in-Publication Data

Larréché, Jean Claude.
    Markstrat 3 : the strategic marketing simulation / Jean-Claude
Larréché, Hubert Gatignon.
        p.   cm.
    Rev. ed. of: MARKSTRAT.
    Includes index.
    ISBN 0-538-86759-0 (paper)
    1. Marketing—Computer simulation.   2. Management games.
I. Gatignon, Hubert.   II. Larréché, Jean Claude. MARKSTRAT.
III. Title.
HF5415.125.L37   1997   97-7160
658.8'02—dc21   CIP

Software co-designed and developed by Strat*X, under the direction of Rémi Triolet.
Boston—London—Paris—Munich

I(T)P

International Thomson Publishing

South-Western College Publishing is an ITP Company. The ITP trademark is used under license.

CONTENTS

Getting Started with MARKSTRAT3   *iii*
The MARKSTRAT3 Simulation Software   *x*
Preface   *xi*

Chapter 1

Welcome to MARKSTRAT   *1*

Why a Simulation?   *1*
The MARKSTRAT Simulation   *2*
The MARKSTRAT Manual   *4*
The MARKSTRAT3 Software   *5*
    The Main Screen   *5*
    The Interface Module   *7*
Final Considerations   *8*
Chapter 1 Summary   *11*

Chapter 2

An Overview of the MARKSTRAT World   *13*

The Industry   *13*
Organization of the Firm   *14*
Market Structure and Its Environment   *16*
    Products   *16*
    Consumers   *18*
    Distribution   *19*
    Pricing   *20*
    Sales Force   *21*
    Advertising   *21*
    Market Research   *22*
    Research and Development   *22*
    Productivity Gains   *24*
    Economic Environment   *26*
Chapter 2 Summary   *27*

Chapter 3

Market Research   *31*

Consumer Survey   *32*
Consumer Panel   *34*

Distribution Panel   *35*
Semantic Scales   *35*
Multidimensional Scaling of Brand Similarities
    and Preferences   *39*
Competitive Advertising Estimates   *42*
Competitive Sales Force Estimates   *42*
Industry Benchmarking   *44*
Advertising Experiment   *45*
Sales Force Experiment   *45*
Market Forecast   *46*
Conjoint Analysis   *47*
Chapter 3 Summary   *49*

Chapter 4   **Operating Instructions   *51***

Decisions   *52*
    Brand Portfolio   *53*
    Production, Price, and Advertising   *56*
    Sales Force and Distribution   *58*
    Market Research Studies   *61*
    Research and Development   *62*
    Budget   *65*
    Changes in Available Financial Resources   *66*
    Summary   *68*
    Errors and Warnings   *70*
The Company Report   *71*
    Company Results   *72*
    Brand Results   *76*
    Research and Development Results   *78*
    Cumulative Results   *80*
    Messages   *80*
    Past Decisions   *82*
Newsletter   *82*
    Stock Market Information   *82*
    Economic Information   *84*
    Market Information   *85*
Chapter 4 Summary   *89*

Chapter 5   **Marketing Planning   *93***

Segment Sizes   *95*
Brand Sales or Brand Share Estimates by Segment   *95*
Distribution Mix   *96*
Projections   *97*

The Planning Process   *100*
Chapter 5 Summary   *102*

Chapter **6**   **Market Segmentation and Positioning**   **103**

Assessing Perceptions and Preferences   *103*
Optimal Brand Position   *105*
   Prediction of Ideal Points   *106*
   Forecasting Brand Demand   *108*
   Forecasting Brand Transfer Cost   *110*
   Matching Product Attribute with Position   *114*
Repositioning Strategies   *122*
Chapter 6 Summary   *126*

Chapter **7**   **The Marketing and R&D Interface**   **127**

Communication with the R&D Department   *128*
   Project Code Names   *128*
Product Physical Characteristics Requests   *130*
Unit Cost Request   *130*
Budget   *131*
R&D Department Responses   *132*
   Project Available Message   *132*
   Insufficient Budget   *133*
   Unrealistic Cost   *134*
Utilization of Completed R&D Projects   *134*
   Brand Introduction   *134*
   Brand Modification   *136*
   Keeping a Product for Future Use   *137*
   Multiple Brands with Same Physical
      Characteristics   *137*
R&D Strategies   *138*
   Cost Reduction Projects   *138*
   Feasibility Studies   *140*
   Sequential R&D Projects   *141*
   Planning R&D Activities   *142*
Conclusion   *145*
Chapter 7 Summary   *147*

Chapter **8**   **Consumer Analysis**   **149**

Category Purchase Decision   *149*
Brand Choice   *150*

Brand Awareness   *151*
Preference Formation   *152*
Brand Choice   *154*
Conclusion   *155*
Chapter 8 Summary   *156*

Chapter 9   **Competitive Strategies**   *157*

Competitive Analysis   *157*
Defining the Set of Relevant Competitors   *158*
Assessing the Intensity of Competition   *159*
Competitive Strategies   *163*
Basis of Competitive Advantage   *164*
Choice of Basis of Competitive Advantage   *166*
Entry Strategies   *168*
Pioneer Advantage   *168*
Entry Signaling   *169*
Marketing Mix   *170*
Scale of Entry   *170*
Defensive Strategies   *171*
Elements of Defensive Strategy   *171*
Determinants of Choice of Defensive Strategy   *172*
Conclusion   *173*
Chapter 9 Summary   *174*

Chapter 10   **Allocation of Resources**   *177*

Evaluation of Product/Market Portfolios   *177*
A Standardized Approach: The Growth/Share
Matrix   *177*
An Individualized Approach: The Attractiveness/Position
Matrix   *185*
Factors Affecting the Allocation of Resources   *190*
Evaluation of New Business Opportunities   *190*
Determinants of Allocation of Resources   *192*
The Effectiveness of Marketing-Mix Variables   *192*
Demand Synergies   *192*
Cost Synergies   *193*
Uncertainty and Risk   *193*
Conclusion   *193*
Chapter 10 Summary   *195*

Contents   **ix**

Appendix **A**   **Installing MARKSTRAT3**   *199*

Computer Requirements   *199*
Installing MARKSTRAT3   *199*

Appendix **B**   **Printing Documents**   *202*

Printing Team Reports   *202*
Printing Data Tables or Graphs   *204*
Printing Decision-Related Documents   *204*

Appendix **C**   **Software Configuration**   *205*

Index   *207*

THE MARKSTRAT3 SIMULATION SOFTWARE

The MARKSTRAT3 software was developed by and is distributed by Strat*X, a company specializing in strategic marketing training. The team disk provided with this book includes software that allows teams to access the MARKSTRAT results, to enter their decisions, and to make financial projections. It does not include the simulation model, which is available only to instructors.

Access to the MARKSTRAT simulation is available to colleges and universities and to corporations.

- *Colleges/universities.* Colleges/universities can obtain various licenses to use the MARKSTRAT3 software for undergraduate, graduate, and executive MBA programs and for publicly advertised open-enrollment executive programs.
- *Corporations.* Corporations can obtain a license to use the MARKSTRAT3 software for their internal programs.

To obtain more information on the MARKSTRAT3 simulation and how to obtain a license to use MARKSTRAT3, please contact

Strat*X International
222 Third Street
Cambridge, MA 02142
U.S.A.
Tel.: (617) 494–8282
Fax: (617) 494–1421

Strat*X S.A.
Tour Pacific
92977 Paris La Défense Cedex
France
Tel.: (33) (0) 1 64 45 87 53
Fax: (33) (0) 1 64 45 98 59

The MARKSTRAT3 software has been designed to be used in a class situation under the supervision of qualified instructors. Other simulations have been developed by Strat*X for specific sectors (industrial, pharmaceutical, services, etc.) and for individual use.

PREFACE

The MARKSTRAT simulation is widely used in business schools around the world as part of their graduate and executive development programs. A large number of companies have organized MARKSTRAT seminars for their executives. In total, more than 150,000 business students and executives in over 30 countries have used the simulation. This accumulated experience has shown that in today's increasingly competitive business world, the MARKSTRAT simulation is an effective tool for developing a strategic market orientation. It has also enabled us, in developing this version of MARKSTRAT, to benefit from the tests, comments, and suggestions of users.

MARKSTRAT3 incorporates a number of important innovations, many of which have been suggested over the years by users of MARKSTRAT. These innovations include a corporate scorecard, a stock market evaluation, a variable number of competing firms, multiple scenarios, a broad product portfolio, the possibility of bank loans, sales force allocation by channels and products, target segments for advertising, composite perceptual dimensions, selection of advertising objectives, brand awareness information per segment, multi-dimensional brand maps, conjoint analysis, competitive benchmarking, automated regression analyses, automated production of graphs, automated market share/market growth matrix representation, and the creation of data files compatible with regular spreadsheet programs. Furthermore, the MARKSTRAT3 software has been developed to operate in the Windows® and Windows 95® environments. It offers a level of user-friendliness and flexibility never before attained in marketing simulations, including an on-line help facility, a network configuration, and a clipboard to copy and paste tables and figures from the simulation into word-processing, spreadsheet, or presentation packages.

At the same time, MARKSTRAT3 retains the basic philosophy that has made MARKSTRAT distinctive: a design clearly focused on the learning, practicing, and testing of strategic marketing concepts. Compared with the more traditional marketing management games, its main advantages are

1. a longer-term perspective
2. an emphasis on strategic issues such as competitive analysis, product portfolio, market segmentation, and product positioning and repositioning
3. the opportunity to manage and expand the product line through the modification of existing brands and the introduction of new ones
4. the availability of a comprehensive set of marketing research studies, including the graphical representation of brand similarities and preferences through perceptual mapping, conjoint analysis, and competitive benchmarking

5. a more dynamic environment, reflected by different product/market life cycles, the creation of a new market, inflation, price controls, and changes in the level of productivity.

For maximum effectiveness, the MARKSTRAT simulation should be integrated into a course that emphasizes strategic marketing concepts. At the graduate level, the simulation is best suited for the end of a basic marketing management course or for more advanced marketing strategy courses. At the executive level, it can be a valuable component of marketing or general management programs. MARKSTRAT has been extensively used, with consistent success, in in-company training programs aimed at developing strategic marketing skills or a market-oriented culture.

The MARKSTRAT3 manual reflects the experience that we have gained since we first created the MARKSTRAT simulation. In particular, the present edition communicates necessary information more effectively. We separate the information that is required to start the simulation from additional information that becomes relevant only later in the simulation. Each chapter contains a number of figures displaying the exact screens that correspond to the subjects being discussed. From a conceptual standpoint, this edition further emphasizes the strategic orientation of MARKSTRAT. Starting with a concentration on the operational issues of the simulation in the early chapters, the manual moves progressively toward an emphasis on providing information on the strategic marketing concepts relevant to the simulation. These latter chapters are not intended to replace a text on these issues, but they should offer a better perspective on and a greater opportunity to investigate strategic concepts that are illustrated during the course of a MARKSTRAT simulation.

To facilitate the student/instructor interface with the simulation, we have augmented this manual with diskettes containing the team software. As explained in the manual, this software is used especially to enter decisions, display results, and transfer data between participants and the instructor, but it also has many other uses. The software checks for inconsistent decisions at the time of data entry so that all types of mechanical errors are greatly reduced, and it allows participants to use a password so that data files left on the hard disks of publicly available computers cannot be accessed by competing teams. Further, the diskettes contain a data file representing the situation of an industry called PRACTICE at an advanced stage of a simulation. As its name suggests, the purpose of this data file is to allow participants to get acquainted with MARKSTRAT before the beginning of the course.

We originally developed the MARKSTRAT simulation in a three-year project undertaken at the European Institute of Business Administration (INSEAD) and at the European Center for Continuing Education (CEDEP) in Fontainebleau, France. Since 1984, the rights to the MARKSTRAT software and trademark have been transferred to Strat*X, a company specializing in design and delivery of strategic marketing training programs for clients worldwide and industry/client-specific simulation development. Strat*X is now responsible for the licensing of the simulation worldwide. The development of the MARKSTRAT3 software has been a major project under the dynamic leadership of Rémi Triolet, director of R&D. Strat*X is committed to continuously improving the simulation, providing related products, and supporting the implementation of MARKSTRAT management development programs.

Over the years, the MARKSTRAT simulation has benefited from the comments of many of our colleagues around the world: Erin Anderson, Reinhard Angelmar, Philip Parker, Christian Pinson, Vikas Tibrewala, Wilfried Vanhonacker, Charles Waldman, and David Weinstein at INSEAD; Gert Assmus at Dartmouth College; Harper W. Boyd Jr. at the University of Arkansas; Thomas C. Kinnear at the University of Michigan; Gary Erickson and Reza Moinpour at the University of Washington; David B. Montgomery at Stanford University; Victor Cook and Edward C. Strong at Tulane University; Barton A. Weitz at the University of Florida; Marian Moore at Duke University; Philippe Naert at Tilburg; Sam Gillespie and Chris Miller at Texas A&M; David Lambert at Suffolk University; John Antil and Carter Broach at the University of Delaware; Aydin Mudderisoglu at Babson College; Stephen Achtenhagen at San Jose State University; Noel Capon at Columbia University; Christopher Gale at the University of Virginia; Michael Hyman at New Mexico State University; Peter Palij at the University of South Carolina; Richard Leininger at Saginaw Valley State University; Deepak Agrawal at Purdue University; Sridhar Moorthy at the University of Rochester; and Peter Fader and Barbara Kahn at the Wharton School of the University of Pennsylvania.

Strat*X's MARKSTRAT3 development and licensing team, led by Rémi Triolet, consists of Christophe Pottier, Julia Downs, and Elizabeth Imm. All have been instrumental in bringing this product to market through their great dedication. In addition, Laurent Bonnier, Carole Cavaye, Jim Ciuca, Kevin Dolgin, Scott Imperatore, Joe Leah, Niall McDonagh, Rhonda Smith, James Thorne, and Don Whyte have contributed to improving the simulation based on their extensive experience with in-company executive training programs.

Mandakini Arora has provided first-class editing of the manual. Sylvaine Imbert, Ruth Lewis, Micheline Lumb, Claudine Veillet Lavallée, and Monique Soubiran have all contributed very effectively to the preparation of the manuscript.

Finally, thousands of enthusiastic business executives and students from around the world have given us constructive feedback on successive versions of the simulation. We have tried to listen to them.

To all of the above we would like to express our gratitude.

Jean-Claude Larréché
Alfred H. Heineken Professor
of Marketing

Hubert Gatignon
Claude Janssen Professor
of Business Administration
and Professor of Marketing

INSEAD
Fontainebleau
France

Welcome to MARKSTRAT

Whenyou enter the MARKSTRAT world, you are immediately immersed in a dynamic competitive situation. Given the complexity of strategic decision making in marketing, the MARKSTRAT simulation offers you a unique but realistic learning experience that you probably could not get from traditional learning tools alone.

In the simulation, participants form teams, each of which manages a company. Your company faces a competitive environment in which four other firms operate similarly. Management is especially concerned with marketing strategy, so long-term strategic issues of product and brand portfolio, product design, distribution, pricing, advertising, and sales force are the basis of each firm's actions. You will make decisions under uncertainty as to market conditions, including competitors' moves.

Many years of activity are simulated in a short time, and you get rapid feedback on all decisions. You learn through trial and error and through the accumulation of information. Since the behavior of competitors affects your company's results, you must take it into account in making strategic decisions. Teamwork is critical in MARKSTRAT; you must learn to cooperate with other members of your "management" team.

As you progress in the game, you will quickly discover that the process of learning through a simulation can be stimulating and enjoyable. Compared with the traditional case-study method widely used in business education, a simulation offers a more dynamic situation that allows you to test and, if necessary, modify your actions. At the same time, compared with real-life experience, a simulation satisfactorily reproduces the main aspects of reality while providing faster feedback at lower cost and risk.

WHY A SIMULATION?

In general, a simulation aims to allow you to test alternative actions without incurring the cost or the risk of implementing them in real settings. A simulation requires a model that is a simplified representation of reality. Although models can be expressed in several forms (such as physical, graphical, and verbal), they are most frequently represented by mathematical relations. The structure of the model, the mathematical equations used, and the values of its parameters are defined by data relevant to the situation being modeled.

It would be impractical and technically difficult to include in a model all of the variables interacting in a social or business situation—even when they can be defined. So the art of modeling lies in selecting only the most important variables in a given process and defining their relationships. The resulting model can then be programmed and run on a computer to economically test alternative actions and to answer "what if" questions.

Simulation models have been extensively developed in marketing. They are, by definition, incomplete representations of reality and cannot incorporate unexpected competitive actions or drastic changes in the environment. Yet they are empirically based and have high enough predictive validity that a satisfactory plan, tested on a good simulation model, may be successfully implemented in a real situation.

Pedagogical games are a particular type of simulation that allows participants to learn and practice concepts, techniques, and decision-making processes. Games have been developed for such diverse areas of application as political science, economics, history, psychology, sociology, and business. The simulation model used in a business game represents a business situation in such a way that the concepts, techniques, and decision-making processes learned can be applied to real business situations. But a game, as opposed to a decision-making simulation model used in a company, does not have to be based on specific empirical data. A game can simulate a fictitious industry and use synthetic data, so although the numerical results from playing it cannot be transferred to real-life situations, it can illustrate concepts and enhance the learning process.

In a typical business game, several companies—each managed by a group of participants—are in competition in a given industry. Each group makes decisions about various aspects of its company's management for a given period of "simulated time," which may run from one month to one year. When all groups have independently made their decisions, the decisions are entered into a computer-based simulation model. The results for each company are returned to it. Often a company may purchase information, including information on competitors. The game is therefore played over several simulated periods in which each team tries to maximize its objectives (for instance, sales, market share, or profits). The objectives are, of course, achieved much more systematically and successfully when concepts previously developed in lectures are considered and applied.

THE MARKSTRAT SIMULATION

As an educational simulation, MARKSTRAT has the following characteristics:

1. *It is a simplification of reality.* The computerized model used in MARKSTRAT contains a set of relationships that simulate real business phenomena, particularly strategic marketing phenomena. However, in order to maximize its effectiveness as a learning tool, it includes only the main elements of those phenomena.

2. *It represents a specific business environment: the MARKSTRAT world.* This environment has its own characteristics in terms of products, market sizes, distribution channels, etc. Accordingly, you should base decisions solely on information gathered in MARKSTRAT and not on data obtained from real markets or products, which might not be compatible with the situations modeled in MARKSTRAT.

3. *It provides a realistic learning setting.* In MARKSTRAT, you can test various propositions gathered through prior business education or practice. The experience you gain during the course of the simulation can then be transferred to real business situations. The MARKSTRAT simulation has been used by a large number of corporations around the world, and thousands of business executives have found it to represent a realistic learning environment.

MARKSTRAT is different in several respects from other business games that you may know. It has been designed primarily to apply and test marketing strategy concepts. Because of the availability of essential, strategically relevant information, MARKSTRAT gives you an opportunity to experience the marketing strategy development process. Participants have available to them all the information necessary to do a strategic marketing analysis using tools that they have been acquiring in accompanying lectures and readings or tools that they have acquired previously. The result of that analysis is a thorough evaluation of the various possible strategy alternatives. Here again the various strategy evaluation approaches, such as portfolio analysis or empirical methods, can be applied.

MARKSTRAT goes beyond strategy formulation, since the strategic plan needs to be implemented through decisions at the tactical level. This is in itself a challenge typically not provided by traditional pedagogical methods. In particular, the possibility of assessing the success or failure of marketing implementation over time is an important benefit of MARKSTRAT. Specifically, MARKSTRAT focuses on the various marketing functions of the firm and on the elements of the environment that have the greatest impact on these functions. It particularly emphasizes the main elements of marketing strategy: segmentation and positioning. Other analyses that should be done to assess strategic opportunities and evaluate alternative strategies are (1) consumer analysis, (2) competitive analysis leading to defensive or offensive strategies, (3) analysis of the dynamics of productivity as markets evolve, and (4) environmental analysis. Decisions on the allocation of resources across products/markets are enhanced by product/market portfolio analysis. Marketing mix allocation is made more effective by evaluating individual marketing variables and their synergies. Product, distribution, price, advertising, and sales force policy are all considered as means of implementing an overall marketing strategy that is formulated at the corporate level.

This emphasis on strategy is supported by the length of the simulated periods, which correspond to one year. The simulation is usually run over six to ten periods in order to provide the longer time horizons needed to adequately test marketing strategies. Other functions of the firm (such as finance, production, and R&D) intervene only as support for or constraints upon the firm's marketing strategy.

The MARKSTRAT simulation also incorporates a large number of market research studies, which the competing companies may purchase as aids to decision making. In addition to classical studies—such as consumer surveys, consumer panels, distribution panels, and market forecasts—MARKSTRAT offers more sophisticated information—such as perceptual maps, conjoint analysis, sales force experiments, and advertising experiments.

THE MARKSTRAT MANUAL

The general setting of MARKSTRAT is described in Chapter 2 on the MARKSTRAT world. Chapter 3 presents the information that can be obtained through market research. Chapter 4 describes in detail how to operate one of the MARKSTRAT companies, how to report decisions, and how to interpret yearly results. Chapter 5 focuses on the marketing planning process and the development of the marketing plan with the formulation of pro forma income statements. Finally, Chapters 6 through 10 introduce strategic concepts in marketing and discuss how they are integrated in MARKSTRAT. Chapter 6 discusses segmentation and positioning strategies and illustrates several examples of segmentation strategies that can be used in MARKSTRAT. The interface between marketing and research and development is discussed in Chapter 7, which covers communicating with the R&D department and presents strategic concepts involving new product development. Chapter 8 deals more specifically with understanding how consumers behave in the MARKSTRAT world. The role of each element of the marketing mix in influencing consumers' decisions to buy in the product category and to choose among competing brands is examined. Chapter 9 introduces concepts of competitive strategies. It discusses how to assess the competition in a given market, and the implications of various strategies in different competitive environments are illustrated with vivid examples from MARKSTRAT simulations. Chapter 10 covers making decisions about which market(s) and product(s) the firm should put its resources into. This chapter integrates many of the strategic marketing issues examined in previous chapters from the perspective of the markets/products portfolio of the firm.

Each chapter gives many examples of situations that firms face in the context of competitors' strategies. These examples enhance the experience gained in using MARKSTRAT because participants become better able to anticipate certain types of competitive behavior. Consequently, they can more thoroughly examine the competitive environment and understand market behavior. This manual is the only text that presents sets of marketing strategy principles within the same environment. Typically, each principle is illustrated by analyzing different industries with different characteristics that are determinants of behavior according to that principle. By using a simulation that can reproduce different market conditions depending on competitive behavior, participants are able to gain a better understanding of the principles because the comparison across competitive behaviors is easier, given that everything else is constant. As a result, this manual can be used as a reference for an inventory of marketing strategy principles.

You do not need to read the manual in its entirety before starting the MARKSTRAT simulation. In fact, only the first five chapters are essential to making decisions for the first period. You can then read Chapters 6 and 7 before making the next decisions. Chapters 8 through 10 can be used as the game progresses, to enhance marketing strategy decision making.

THE MARKSTRAT3 SOFTWARE

The MARKSTRAT3 team disk, enclosed in this book, contains the software that allows you to display and print the results of your simulated MARKSTRAT firm, to enter your decisions, and to project the financial implications of these decisions. You cannot use this software directly from the diskette but must install it on the hard drive of a computer using the simple, standard install procedure described in Appendix A, Installing MARKSTRAT3 (page 199). To illustrate the issues discussed in this manual and to help you familiarize yourself with MARKSTRAT, a sample industry named PRACTICE has been provided. You can follow the manual with this example to get acquainted with MARKSTRAT.

The MARKSTRAT3 team disk does not, however, contain the model that, based on your decisions and those of competing firms for a given period, simulates the competitive market activities and generates the results for the period. The MARKSTRAT instructor keeps that part of the software, and participants do not have access to it. After you have made your decisions for a given period, you submit these to the instructor either on a team diskette (which will be handed out by the instructor at the beginning of the simulation) or via the computer network. The instructor then runs the simulation model and returns the results via the same team diskette or via the network. This process is repeated for each period of the MARKSTRAT simulation.

You will find that using the MARKSTRAT3 software is easy and does not require any specific computer knowledge. Read the following instructions carefully, but after a little practice with the sample industry included in the book diskette, you should find the software self-explanatory.

The Main Screen

The main screen appears when you launch the MARKSTRAT software. The screen is composed of four parts, as indicated in Figure 1.1: the Menu Bar, the Selection Bar, the Tool Bar, and the Module Window.

The Menu appears in the top bar of the screen and has six buttons, labeled **Decisions, Report, Newsletter, Market Studies, Analysis,** and **Interface.** A button to exit the software is on the right corner of the Menu Bar. The first five buttons are described in the following chapters. The **Interface** button is described in the next section.

The left half of the area below the Menu Bar is the Selection Bar. Its contents will change, depending on the module being used. The Selection Bar can be blank (for instance, before a data file has been selected), or it can allow you to choose a period number or a product category.

Figure 1.1   The MARKSTRAT Main Screen

Menu Bar

Tool Bar

Selection
Bar

Module
Window

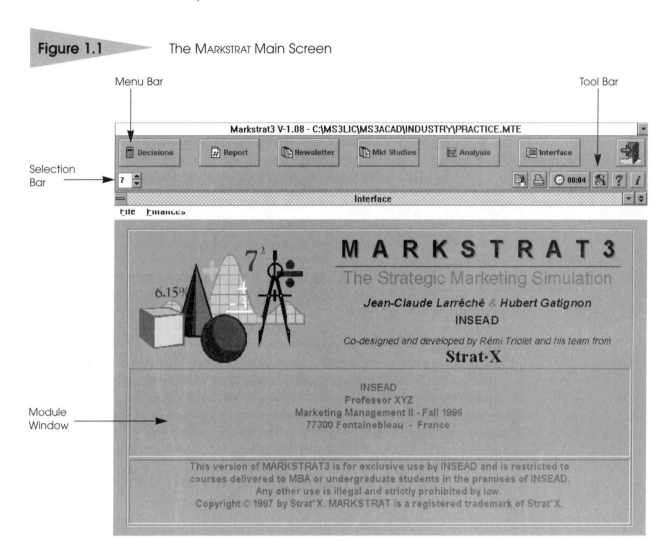

The right half of the area below the Menu Bar is the Tool Bar. The Tool Bar can also contain a variable number of buttons such as **Clipboard, Print, Configuration,** and **Help.** The **Clipboard** button enables you to copy information into the clipboard for pasting into another document. For example, you can paste the content of the clipboard into a word-processing document as an image or insert it into a spreadsheet for easy data processing and graphing.

The **Print** button gives you the capability of sending any of the MARK-STRAT3 documents into a file in an Excel®-compatible format or to a printer as defined in Windows. Appendix B, Printing Documents (page 202), describes the Print dialog box in detail.

The **Configuration** button, represented by a tool box, defines the language used in the software and the location of the files used by the software. The default configuration assumes that the MARKSTRAT3 files are located in the folder used when the software was installed on the hard disk. This enables a team to practice with a sample industry in order to get acquainted with the simulation. A different configuration will be necessary depending on whether or not the simulation set up uses network facilities. Appendix C,

Software Configuration (page 205), describes the Configuration dialog box in detail.

The **Help** button provides help on many topics, which can be selected from a standard Help topic search dialog box. The **Help** button, represented by a question mark, is probably the most important one at the start, when you may have many questions.

When relevant, the Tool Bar also contains two icons of hands, one pointing left and one pointing right, which you can use to move to the previous or the next menu item (screen), respectively.

The Module Window may contain a menu of options or information on the option chosen directly from the main menu. Such options can be, for example, the different types of decisions to be made each period. These options are described in the following chapters.

The Interface Module

The **Interface** module is designed for communication with the instructor. It concerns two types of communication: file exchange and financial changes. As shown in Figure 1.1, the options are **File** and **Finances** (**Finances** is discussed in detail in Chapter 4).

The **File** menu allows you to manage the file used by the MARKSTRAT3 team software. Such a file is called an **Industry,** as it contains all the past results of the simulation plus your own past decisions. The specific options in the **File** menu include the following.

- **Open industry:** to access your data file, once it has been saved on your hard disk.
- **Change industry password:** to change your password.
- **Save and close industry:** to inform MARKSTRAT3 that you do not wish to work with the current industry any longer.
- **Save and back up industry:** to save your file on the hard disk or on a diskette as a backup. This procedure compresses the file so that it can fit on a diskette and allows you to transport it from one computer to another one.
- **Restore industry:** to load your backup file from a diskette to the hard disk.
- **Transfer decisions to instructor:** to save your decisions on a diskette, which the instructor will then use to run the simulation.
- **Transfer results and default decisions from instructor:** to load the last simulated results from the diskette given to you by the instructor or the hard disk.

To access the information from the last period simulated by the instructor, you first need to transfer the data file from the team diskette. For the sample provided with the software, the file is named PRACTICE. You open it by clicking on the **Transfer results & default decisions from instructor** option of the **File** menu. A dialog box like the one in Figure 1.2 appears, and you have to click on the name of the selected file—PRACTICE, in the sample case. A password is usually necessary as protection against accessing of the data

Figure 1.2   Transfer Results & Default Decisions from Instructor Dialog Box

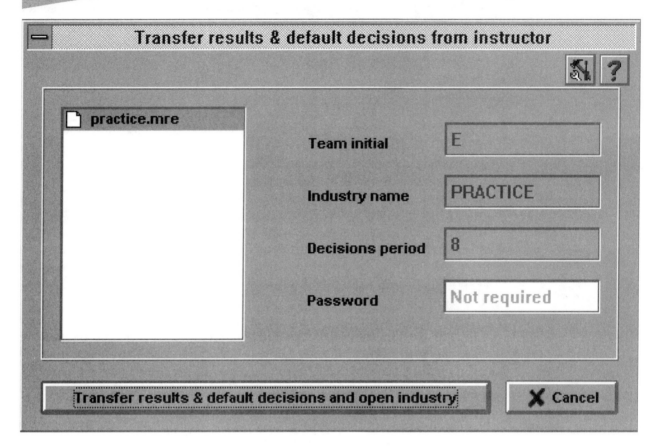

by competitors. This is not the case for the PRACTICE file, which is available to all teams. As you transfer results of the PRACTICE industry, the file is automatically opened and you now have access to all the main menu modules: **Decisions, Report, Newsletter, Market Studies,** and **Analysis.** You are in a position to use the MARKSTRAT3 team software with the PRACTICE sample, which represents the situation of an industry in Period 7 and when decisions have to be made for Period 8. This sample case will allow you to get familiar with the simulation and the software before joining your team and managing a real firm in the MARKSTRAT world.

FINAL CONSIDERATIONS

After you read Chapters 1 through 5, you will be ready to participate in the MARKSTRAT simulation. You certainly will not yet have assimilated all the information in these chapters, and the main purpose of the first decisions is to make you familiar with the MARKSTRAT world and the mechanics of the simulation. At the beginning of the simulation exercise, you are assigned to a firm, and you receive a Company Report representing the situation of your firm and of the market you are active in at this time. You are able, from the Company Report and the information in this manual, to evaluate the relative market strength of your firm compared to that of your competitors. Even though you have a fair amount of information, there are still many uncertainties. These will decrease as you acquire more specific market research data and make decisions and as your competitors make their moves. Hence, you should not take inconsiderate risks for your first decisions.

For your first set of decisions, concentrate on the management of your existing brands. In the process of reaching decisions for the first period, you should analyze the actions of your firm's previous management team. It is unwise at this stage to drastically change your advertising, pricing, sales force, and production policies, since you are probably not yet in a position to make a sound decision about the direction and degree of any change. On the other hand, you might consider purchasing market research studies, which will be made available for your next set of decisions.

While making the first set of decisions, it is essential that you rapidly develop good working relationships within your group. Every member of your group should be involved in the discussion of all issues and should develop a grasp of the overall situation, in order to avoid the natural tendency for each member to concentrate on his or her area of expertise. Later in the simulation—when everybody has a common understanding of the strategic issues and the management of the firm becomes more complex in terms of the number of brands, the R&D interface, the market developments, and the intensity of competition—some specific problem areas can be delegated to individuals. In this way, the group should learn to work efficiently, and all members should benefit equally from the MARKSTRAT experience.

In previous administrations of the MARKSTRAT simulation, the following advice has proved to be useful:

- **Emphasis on strategic issues.** Concentrate your efforts on strategic issues and long-term planning. The simulation purposely does not consider short-term activities such as promotions or the design of advertising research studies. In addition, adjustments are automatically made within a simulated period to relieve you of the burden of some operational problems, such as production planning.
- **Importance of analysis.** Before making decisions, be sure that you understand the behavior of the market. Do not jump to the first explanation or conclusion that you reach when faced with a problem—it may be incomplete. Be aware that at various points in the simulation, as the warning about railroad crossings has it, "one train may hide another one." A detailed analysis of market research studies, of your own situation, and of past competitive behavior should help you reach more robust decisions.
- **Group time allocation.** Allocate your discussion time sensibly among problem areas. You will be under pressure to submit decisions by a given deadline, and you should avoid making hasty, last-minute decisions. Do not waste time discussing a $100,000 issue if this will force you to rush through other decisions where millions are at stake.
- **Administrative errors.** Your team will have to bear the consequences of administrative errors made in inputting your decisions using the MARKSTRAT software. These errors cannot be corrected retroactively.

Although the MARKSTRAT software performs automatic checks as information is entered, some errors cannot be detected systematically. In particular, be careful to state your decisions in the specified units and to provide the MARKSTRAT instructor with the final decisions you intended to make.

■ *Artificial accuracy.* Avoid artificial accuracy in quantifying your decisions. All decisions should be in rounded numbers. For instance, the impact of a price of $546.15 will certainly not be substantially different from that of a price of $546.00. Artificial accuracy may give you a feeling of false confidence or draw your attention too much toward the numbers themselves, when, in fact, the main issues are the strategic options that lie behind the numbers.

■ *Role of the instructor.* The MARKSTRAT instructor does not manipulate the simulation parameters in the course of the game. The simulation has been designed to automatically generate some environmental changes. However, the markets will evolve mainly according to the actions of the competing firms, and the instructor will not interfere in favor of or against any firm. You should feel entirely responsible for your firm's performance.

In the final analysis, even though extensive marketing information is available to allow you to systematically analyze market situations, you will soon realize that your judgment plays an important role in making decisions. As is true of most real cases, there is no single specific solution to any of the problems you will encounter. There are, however, alternatives that will clearly appear inferior after thorough analysis of the situation. There are other alternatives that will appear satisfactory, but whose relative merits depend mainly on the uncertainties of competitive actions. You will, in that case, have to exercise your judgment of competitive behavior and make choices under uncertainty. Over a series of decisions, sound analysis and good judgment will inevitably bear fruit.

We hope that participating in the MARKSTRAT simulation will give you a better understanding of marketing strategy concepts and that you will enjoy this learning experience. We wish you success in managing your firm!

CHAPTER 1 SUMMARY

Effective Pedagogical Simulations

- Are a simplification of reality
- Represent a specific business environment
- Provide a realistic and dynamic setting for learning

MARKSTRAT's Main Characteristics

- It focuses on marketing strategy concepts.
- Each simulated period corresponds to one year.
- The objectives of the firm are long term.
- Marketing acts as a profit center.
- Firms operate in a competitive environment.
- Marketing strategy is designed around basic segmentation and positioning concepts.
- Marketing mix decisions are secondary to strategic decisions.

Main Menu Modules

- Decisions
- Report
- Newsletter
- Market Research Studies
- Analysis
- Interface

Interface Module Menu

- File
- Finances

An Overview of the MARKSTRAT World

The MARKSTRAT simulation does not claim to accurately represent a particular industry or market. It is based on an artificial community of approximately 250 million inhabitants whose monetary unit is the MARKSTRAT Monetary Unit (MMU), symbolized by $. This MARKSTRAT world behaves globally like most markets, and all general marketing principles that you have learned from experience or from marketing textbooks are relevant. However, MARKSTRAT, like any specific country, market, or industry, also has its own peculiarities. It is therefore important to read carefully the description of the MARKSTRAT world that follows and to interpret the information you receive in the course of the simulation concerning the features of the products you are about to manage and the environment in which you are to operate. This chapter describes the MARKSTRAT world based on the MARKSTRAT classic scenario. Several other scenarios with different parameters are also available, and your instructor has selected one of them for your class. The environment that you will face may be somewhat different; if it is, your MARKSTRAT instructor will give you a description of the exact scenario you face. Whatever the specific characteristics of different scenarios, they will have some commonalties with the classic MARKSTRAT scenario.

THE INDUSTRY

The MARKSTRAT world typically consists of competing companies that manufacture and market a consumer durable good comparable to an electronic entertainment product. Each firm is managed by a team. Your team is taking over the management of one of these firms at a point in time that will be referred to as Period 1. At the beginning, each firm markets a number of brands that can be modified or withdrawn from the market. New brands can be introduced as the simulation evolves. In any given year, a company may commercialize up to five brands in each of the markets. Each firm may start from a different initial situation in terms of market share, consumer awareness level, or distribution coverage of its brands. The marketing strategy of each firm should be adapted to its particular situation within the industry. Because of their differing situations, the performance of the companies over successive periods should be compared not in absolute terms but, more appropriately, with respect to their initial situation. In spite of differences in the characteristics of the firms, none has a systematic advantage over the others. Each company has the opportunity to develop an appropriate strategy that will lead to successful performance.

ORGANIZATION OF THE FIRM

The marketing department of each firm is considered to be a profit center, responsible for the design and implementation of marketing strategy as well as for marketing operations. In this privileged situation, the marketing department is responsible for the overall orientation of the company to its markets, and it must interact with other departments of the firm. In each period, it must ask the production department to attain a certain level of production for each brand. The quantities requested and produced are charged to the marketing department at an internal transfer cost that corresponds to the production cost and includes a profit margin for the production department, which also operates as a profit center. The marketing department is also responsible for inventory holding costs incurred by over-production. Similarly, the marketing department may ask the R&D department to work on specific projects, the costs of which are charged to the marketing department's budget.

The performance of the marketing department as a profit center is appraised as its *net contribution,* represented in Figure 2.1. This net contribution is defined as total revenues from sales, minus the cost of goods sold (based on transfer costs), inventory holding costs, and R&D, advertising, sales force, and market research expenditures. Inventory holding costs are taken out of the net contribution because the quantity to be produced—and therefore the level of inventory—is seen in MARKSTRAT as a strategic marketing decision. Marketing managers must make a tradeoff between the likelihood and amount of lost sales and the risk of incurring additional costs due to holding inventory.

The marketing department is given a budget for the following period—that is, the next year—to cover R&D, advertising, sales force, and market research expenditures. If total spending exceeds the budget for a period, expenses will be automatically cut, starting with advertising expenditures. The budget is allocated automatically, based partly on the net contribution in the preceding period, but a firm may sometimes negotiate changes with the instructor, on the basis of a well-defined marketing plan. The marketing department's budget allocation is linked to the success of the department—the budget for a given year is a straight 40% of the net contribution for the previous year. Beyond a maximum level, however, resources are reallocated to other businesses of the company under a different management organization.

A minimum budget is always provided in case of insufficient performance. Because of these resource allocation decision rules, a firm may be given a much larger budget than it really needs to maximize its performance. In such a situation, the firm certainly should not automatically spend its en-

Figure 2.1

The Marketing
Department as
a Profit Center

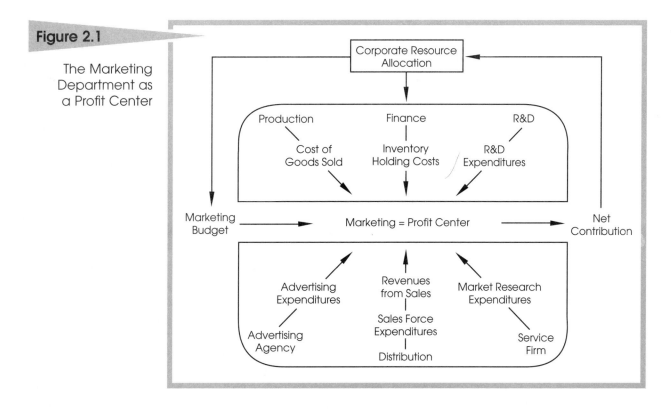

tire allocated budget. Theoretically, it should spend additional MMUs only if the return is at least equal to the MMUs spent. Note, however, that if the whole allocated budget is not spent in the current period's move, the leftover is not added to next year's budget. The MMUs that are not spent will increase the firm's net contribution (or, at least, will not be an expense deducted from revenues). Consequently, the budget for the following period will be higher than if the entire budget had been spent without increasing net contribution by an equal or greater amount.

The marketing departments in MARKSTRAT have considerable influence on the general strategy of their firms. They can give directives to other departments—such as production and R&D—but are also responsible for any inefficiencies that may result. They are not concerned with other activities of the firm such as credit management, capital investments, financial reporting, purchasing, and plant management. These services are performed by other departments, also acting as profit centers. For instance, increases in production capacity are made by the production and finance departments, according to the requirements of the marketing department. The net contribution is used at the corporate level to cover these activities, as well as fixed costs, financial charges, and profits. For the marketing department, the net contribution represents only a measure of performance; its yearly budget represents available funds that can be used freely to attain self-assigned objectives. Consequently, MARKSTRAT companies should take into consideration the cash flow over time associated with the strategies they develop. Growth strategies that entail large resources and only a long-term payback might not be feasible because of the decreased budget that would result in the short term.

Because of this organizational structure, some agreements have been made between the firm's various departments regarding their interaction and internal profit computations. A particularly important agreement has been made between the marketing and production departments concerning two issues: the magnitude of possible adjustments of production schedules and transfer pricing.

The requested production level is automatically adjusted during a given year, according to the potential sales of the brand during that year. These adjustments are, however, limited to plus or minus 20%. Anything beyond this level would overly disrupt the organization of the production department and is not allowed.

The marketing and production departments have agreed to transfer units of products at a transfer cost according to the following rules:

1. Transfer costs benefit from the experience gained in production. This means that, discounting for inflation, the unit cost of a product decreases as the firm gains more experience in manufacturing it.
2. Only the units sold are charged to the marketing department. These are charged on a "first in, first out" basis.
3. Although in the case of over-production the transfer cost benefits from the total accumulated production experience, the finance department charges inventory holding costs. The surplus will be transferred during succeeding years at the current transfer cost, which is subject to inflation.
4. The base cost agreed upon by the production, R&D, and marketing departments for a new product represents the average unit cost for an initial batch of 100,000 units. When a smaller first batch is produced, fixed costs have to be allocated among fewer units. Consequently, the actual transfer cost, in constant MMUs, will be higher than the base cost until accumulated production reaches 100,000 units.
5. The transfer cost increases with inflation.

MARKET STRUCTURE AND ITS ENVIRONMENT

The MARKSTRAT market has grown consistently over the last twenty years. In the course of its history, there have been several significant technological breakthroughs and the products have increasingly appealed to a wider audience. Recently, when all competitors redesigned their products, the market achieved an even greater rate of growth. It is now a well-structured market with a set of principal competitors and established channels of distribution. Over the years, the firms have acquired an understanding of consumer behavior, industry practices, and characteristics of the environment similar to the information presented in this manual. In the classic scenario, the number of competing firms is five.

Products

The product currently available in the MARKSTRAT market is the Sonite, a consumer durable good comparable to an electronic entertainment product. It is relatively sophisticated technically, but, in contrast to what has occurred in the last twenty years, no major technological changes are expected in the future. Sonite brands are differentiated mainly in terms of five physical characteristics, and only these characteristics will be considered in the course of the simulation. They are

1. Weight (kg)
2. Design (index)
3. Volume (dm^3)
4. Maximum frequency (1000 Hz)
5. Power (W)

These five characteristics can be measured for a given Sonite, either by standard measurement instruments or by well-defined procedures. The level of accuracy considered is in integer numbers of the specified units. A product is identified by these five characteristics as well as by its base cost. The base cost characteristic of a given Sonite is the average unit transfer cost of its first production run, assuming a production batch of 100,000 units.

In the MARKSTRAT classic scenario, each firm currently markets two brands. The ten Sonite brands available at the start of the simulation and their characteristics are listed in Table 2.1, which presents extracts from the Newsletter. It is easy to recognize the origin of the brands from their names. Each brand name is made up of four characters: the first letter is S, for Sonite; the second letter, A, E, I, O, or U, identifies the firm (in a scenario with six firms, Y identifies the extra firm); the last two characters are letters or numbers selected by each firm to generate different brand names. It is, for instance, easy to recognize that brands SIRO and SIBI in Table 2.1 are Sonites marketed by Firm I.

It is generally thought that the MARKSTRAT firms will modify their brands and introduce new ones in the coming years to better meet the needs of

Table 2.1

Physical Characteristics of Brands Commercialized at the Start of the Simulation

			Physical Characteristics					Base	Retail
Firm	Brand	New or Modified	Weight (kg)	Design (Index)	Volume (dm^3)	Max. Freq. (1000 Hz)	Power (W)	Cost ($)	Price ($)
A	SAMA	No	18	5	70	15	10	92	260
	SALT	No	15	4	35	20	30	117	420
E	SEMI	No	13	7	40	40	75	194	495
	SELF	No	15	4	40	45	90	214	550
I	SIRO	No	20	3	70	10	12	51	210
	SIBI	No	19	8	60	15	20	97	340
O	SOLD	No	13	7	45	30	75	184	510
	SONO	No	17	4	90	48	95	189	395
U	SUSI	No	18	3	75	25	12	71	225
	SULI	No	14	7	50	35	70	194	520

the market segments. These changes will represent variations in the five physical characteristics and the base cost. Brand improvements and the introduction of new brands depend, naturally, on the willingness and ability of the firms to launch R&D projects. All new Sonite brand names should follow the conventions previously described (the first letter should be S, the second letter should identify the company, and the last two letters can be freely selected, as long as all brands have different names). The selected name has no influence on the market response to the brand.

Recently, there has been talk in the industry about a completely new product, the Vodite. The idea for the product comes from a technological breakthrough made in the space industry, under government contracts. The MARKSTRAT industry, because of its technological and marketing expertise, is certainly the most likely to manufacture and distribute the Vodite.

Although the scientific bases are known, substantial R&D efforts are still required for the development of a Vodite brand. Preliminary information indicates that its main physical characteristics would be

1. Autonomy (m)
2. Maximum frequency (1000 Hz)
3. Diameter (mm)
4. Design (index)
5. Weight (g)

The Vodites would satisfy an entirely different need from that satisfied by the Sonites, and there would be no interaction between the two types of products at the sales level. They could be distributed, however, through the same channels, although the appropriateness of each channel differs for the Sonite and Vodite markets. If a Vodite brand is developed and launched, the reaction of the market to this new product, the rate of adoption, and the equilibrium level of sales remain entirely unknown at the present time (although development of the Vodite market may be similar to the historical development of the Sonite markets). Vodite brand names follow the same convention as Sonite brand names, except that the first letter is V, for Vodite.

Each MARKSTRAT firm has the capacity to market a maximum of five brands of Sonite and five brands of Vodite per year. It could, for example, have four Sonites and three Vodites or five Vodites and no Sonites. The number of brands marketed varies over time as a function of the strategy of the firm and according to its R&D activity. MARKSTRAT firms should market at least one brand. A firm is not allowed to disappear completely from the market, even for only a limited period. The minimum allocation rule for the budget guarantees the survival of the business because the market opportunities are worth the investment from the corporate management perspective.

Consumers

The target markets in the MARKSTRAT classic scenario are households and individuals generally over 18 years of age. The opinion of experts, confirmed by several studies undertaken by the firms, is that in the Sonite market one can distinguish five segments with different characteristics and significantly different purchasing behavior.

- *The Buffs* are people who are enthusiastic and very knowledgeable about the products. They are primarily concerned with quality and technical features.
- *The Singles* are people who live alone. Although they are less technically competent than the Buffs, they demand good performance from a product that they may use more often than the average consumer does.
- *The Professionals* are people who have a high level of education and high incomes. They tend to be independent in their occupation and to engage in many social activities. In buying the product, they are partially motivated by considerations of social status.
- *The High Earners* are people who have high incomes but do not possess the high level of education or occupational independence of the Professionals.
- *Others* are people who do not belong to any of the above groups. This segment represents the largest proportion of the population, but in the past it has demonstrated a significantly lower penetration of Sonite products than have other segments.

The order in which these groups are listed corresponds to the priority of attribution of an individual to a segment. For instance, the people in the High Earners group are those who have high incomes but do not qualify as members of the three preceding segments, the Buffs, the Singles, or the Professionals. The resulting segmentation is thus mutually exclusive and exhaustive.

The Buffs currently constitute the largest segment in terms of Sonite unit sales and represent approximately 30% of the market. They are followed by the Professionals (20%), the Others (19%), the High Earners (16%), and the Singles (15%). It is, however, common knowledge in the industry that the five segments are at different stages in their development. This is partly reflected by their different growth rates. While the overall Sonite market has grown at an average rate of 35% over the last three years, the Buffs segment has been stagnant, the Singles and Others segments have grown at 25–30%, and the Professionals and High Earners segments have grown at twice that rate.

It is not certain that the above segmentation of the Sonite market will be equally applicable to the Vodite market whenever it is actually developed by the MARKSTRAT firms. Market research studies will then have to be done to investigate the most appropriate segmentation of this new market.

Distribution

All products can be directly distributed through three channels:

- *Specialty stores.* An important proportion of their sales is Sonite-type products, and they provide specialized services.
- *Department stores.* They handle a wide variety of merchandise and may have a department carrying Sonites.
- *Mass merchandisers.* They carry Sonites only as one of the many product categories they distribute.

In Period 0 of the MARKSTRAT simulation, there are approximately 30,000 specialty stores, 15 department stores representing 6,000 points of sale, and 10,000 mass merchandiser outlets grouped into eight chains. All of these can potentially distribute the Sonite and Vodite brands. Each of the channels differs in terms of penetration of Sonite brands and attraction of different types of clientele. There are differences in the margins received by the stores in each of the three channels, largely due to differences in the service levels and the quantities bought. These margins, expressed as a percentage of the recommended retail price, are approximately constant across brands for a given channel type. Their values are 40%, 30%, and 30% for specialty stores, department stores, and mass merchandisers, respectively. These margins represent an equilibrium that has evolved over the years, which neither distributors nor Sonite manufacturers have any interest in disrupting.

The distribution channels also use different merchandising strategies. Because the space devoted to a single product category in mass merchandising outlets is limited and turnover is essential, the number of brands that the store management decides to offer is smaller than in the other distribution channels. Obviously, because of their general strategy, the specialty stores typically carry the broadest product lines. Because of the visibility of the products in the distribution outlets, consumers' knowledge about the brands can be improved by a substantial level of distribution.

Pricing

The MARKSTRAT companies provide recommended retail prices for each of their brands. The specialty and department stores generally respect these list prices except during promotions, which do not last long and account for only a small proportion of sales. In these channels, the average retail price in any one year is therefore close to the recommended retail price. Mass merchandisers typically sell all brands at the same discount rate of 10% off the list price. So a brand sold at a list price of $100 in specialty and department stores is sold at $90 in discount stores. Because the percentage margin applies to this discounted price, mass merchandisers' actual margins are typically lower than those of the other channels. In the Sonite and Vodite product categories, mass merchandisers do not want to initiate price wars, because their credibility depends on their ability to carry the brands favored by the market that shops in their stores. Therefore, the 10% discount rate has been and is expected to remain stable. In fact, over the last three years, prices of Sonites have increased regularly and have followed inflation.

If the recommended retail price becomes very high compared to the unit cost of a given product, consumers and consumer unions may react negatively. Indeed, consumers realize when they are sold a lower quality product at a premium price. A sudden large price increase or decrease could provoke the same negative reactions. Although consumers may react strongly to an excessive price increase, distributors may react as strongly when their margins are about to be cut because of a significant decrease in the price of a brand. In the past, such problems have arisen with price changes of more than 30% in a given year. This applies whether or not the product marketed under that brand name is modified. If a team decides to increase or decrease prices by more than 30% using the MARKSTRAT software, it will receive a warning. If the team ignores the warning, the recommended retail price is automatically adjusted to limit the negative effect of these adverse reactions.

Sales Force

The sales force of a MARKSTRAT company is organized around markets, not products. Specifically, the sales force is organized by channel type in order to better meet the specific needs of each channel. Each salesperson represents the company's entire line of brands. A company may, naturally, change the size of its sales force at a cost covering hiring, training, firing, and salary expenses. These costs are provided each period in the Newsletter. Changes in the number of salespeople are expected to have an influence on the distribution coverage of the company's brands. Also, each year a company can modify the allocation of its sales force to specific distribution channels without incurring significant expenditures, since all salespeople are knowledgeable about all of the company's products.

In addition to organizing the sales force by channel, management instructs salespeople on how to allocate their time among the various brands that they sell. It could be, for example, that, during their visits to distributors, salespeople allocate a disproportionate amount of their time to a new brand. Salespeople are responsible for obtaining and entering orders and for supporting the distributors.

Advertising

The practice in the MARKSTRAT industry is to advertise specific brands, rather than the company name. So even though a firm might market several brands, possibly even to the same segment, these brands do not benefit from the company's identity and image. Advertising is primarily used as a communication device to make consumers familiar with a brand name and the characteristics of the brand. Brand awareness is therefore directly related to advertising expenditures. A firm's advertising strategy should be consistent with its marketing strategy, and advertising is typically targeted at specific consumer segments. In the absence of advertising, consumers tend to forget about a brand. Because of the competitive nature of the market, this also happens if a brand is withdrawn from the market. Advertising has substantial persuasive power in MARKSTRAT, as it is used to communicate specific product features. Brands are thus positioned and repositioned by manufacturers to better fit consumers' needs and wants.

Advertising can also develop primary demand for a whole product class. As potential consumers learn more about the products and their characteristics, they are more likely to buy these products. The size and growth rate of specific market segments and of the total market are consequently influenced by the amount spent by the industry on advertising. Furthermore, advertising can have an impact on motivation of the sales force and on decisions made by distributors, and it creates barriers to entry by competitors.

Advertising expenditure for Sonite brands is of two types. The bulk of the advertising budget is devoted to the purchase of media space and time. The rest is spent on advertising research. On average, the MARKSTRAT companies spend 6% of their sales on advertising, 5% of which is earmarked for advertising research, carried out by their advertising agencies and concerned mainly with creative work, media selection studies, and copy testing. A company may try to adjust the budget allocation for media expenses and research expenditures in an effort to improve advertising effectiveness. The greater the advertising research, the more likely it is that the message will be clearly communicated to the targeted audience with minimal miscomprehension.

Market Research

The MARKSTRAT companies can buy 12 different types of studies from outside marketing service firms. The studies deal with the Sonite market, the Vodite market, and the firms competing in both markets; the studies are described in the next chapter. When a firm orders a study, the study is done during the simulation period and the results are made available at the end of the period, providing information for the next period's decisions. The industry Newsletter lists the costs of these studies every period.

Research and Development

The marketing department of a firm may ask the R&D department to develop specific projects either to improve existing brands or to introduce new ones. Although a complete coverage of R&D strategies and procedures is included in Chapter 7, an overview is given here in order to illustrate the extent of the marketing department's control in developing and implementing a marketing strategy.

A request to the R&D department consists of a project name, a budget, values of the physical characteristics that the researched product should have, and the base cost targeted for the product.

The names of R&D projects are made up of five characters. The first character is always the letter P, for Project. The second character identifies the type of product being developed: S for Sonites and V for Vodites. The last three characters can be selected by the firms to identify specific projects; PSETA and PVOTE are, for instance, valid names for a Sonite and a Vodite project, respectively. There is no need for the name of an R&D project to correspond to the name of an existing or planned brand. Current and past R&D projects must have different names. So an R&D project name is structured as follows:

P				

P	Product type:	Freely chosen
for	S = Sonite	letters or numbers
Project	V = Vodite	to identify the project

An example of an R&D project code name is

P	V	O	X	3

This R&D project is a Vodite. The last three characters identify the project according to the team's wishes. So the letter following the product type (letter O in this example) does not mean that this project is developed by Firm O, as is the case for brand names.

In the past, in the MARKSTRAT classic scenario, each firm successfully completed two R&D projects corresponding to the brands marketed at the beginning of the simulation. Their names are made up of the letter P followed by the corresponding brand name. For example, the R&D project for the existing brand SAMA is called PSAMA.

The budget for a given project represents the investment that marketing is ready to make in the R&D department's trying to develop that specific product in the coming year. This expenditure will be subtracted from the marketing budget, since the marketing department uses the R&D output to implement its strategy. Therefore, the performance of the marketing department depends on its effective use of the R&D department. Note that the R&D effort does not concern fundamental research but instead involves specific products.

In specifying the physical characteristics of the desired product, the marketing department should, obviously, evaluate the market opportunities for alternative offerings. The values of the physical characteristics for R&D projects must be given in integer numbers of the relevant units. The feasible ranges for the five product characteristics determining the specification of a product are indicated in Table 2.2.

For both Sonites and Vodites, the base cost (the next to last column of Table 2.1) represents the average unit production cost of manufacturing the first 100,000 units of the new product. Its lowest level depends on the five physical characteristics of the product. The unit cost increases with the specification levels of design, maximum frequency, power, and autonomy; it decreases with the specification levels of weight, volume, and diameter. A request for an R&D project indicates the unit cost that the R&D department must use as a target. The R&D department must then determine the feasibility of such a product at such a cost, within the budget it has been given.

Table 2.2		*Physical Characteristic*	*Feasible Range*
Feasible Ranges of the Physical Characteristic Values for Sonites and Vodites	Sonites	Weight (kg)	10–20
		Design (index)	3–10
		Volume (dm^3)	20–100
		Maximum frequency (1000 Hz)	5–50
		Power (W)	5–100
	Vodites	Autonomy (m)	5–100
		Maximum frequency (1000 Hz)	5–20
		Diameter (mm)	10–100
		Design (index)	3–10
		Weight (g)	10–100

The R&D department not only has to develop a product with the given physical characteristics; it also has to find the raw materials and technology to allow production at the specified cost. Obviously, the more stringent this economic constraint, the more difficult it will be for the R&D department to develop the product. If the product is eventually marketed, the original (i.e., launching period) transfer cost will be determined on the basis of this cost, which is associated with the completed project. If the team waits several periods to launch the brand, the base cost can be expected to increase with inflation. After the brand is introduced, its cost may vary as a function of the quantities produced because of experience curve effects as well as inflation.

Up to five projects for each market (five Sonite projects and five Vodite projects) may be given to the R&D department simultaneously during a given year. If a project is not successfully completed in one year, the R&D department will indicate this in a message. If a project is not successfully completed for lack of funds, the R&D department will supply an estimate of the additional budget it will need to complete the project. An R&D project that is not successfully completed in one year may be continued in the following periods. The likelihood of the success of a project depends primarily on the cumulative cost and the degree of similarity between the desired product and the firm's existing ones. The R&D department is a profit center and will therefore use all funds provided to it in the course of the year.

Conceptually, R&D project expenses include not only the cost of developing the prototype but also the cost of researching and evaluating components and potential suppliers, making technical evaluations, providing production line planning, and producing prototypes. In Period 1, a successful R&D project for a Sonite would generally cost between $100,000 and $1,000,000, depending on the degree of difference between the desired characteristics of the project and the characteristics of existing products. To develop a Vodite, industry experts believe that it will be necessary to spend a minimum of $2,000,000 on R&D.

The R&D on-line query allows a firm to communicate with the R&D department more often than once a simulated year, and at any point, a team can check on the feasibility of a product with specific characteristics. The R&D department will respond immediately to such a request with the estimated minimum base cost and with an estimate of the budget required to complete such a project. This information is provided at no cost, but, because of fixed capacity constraints in the R&D department, each team is allowed only five on-line queries per period. Because the R&D department responds quickly to on-line queries, it provides its best estimates without doing a thorough, costly investigation. Based on its experience, the R&D department provides reliable answers in the sense that it would not commit itself if it were not convinced that it could deliver what it promises. However, its responses include an over-estimation factor to cover any surprises it may encounter if the project is implemented.

Productivity Gains

The manufacturing costs of the products tend to decrease as a result of productivity improvements gained through experience, although this effect may be offset by inflation. Firms can further reduce manufacturing costs by undertaking appropriate R&D projects, for which it is necessary to change only the cost characteristic of an otherwise unmodified product. Both of these effects are represented conceptually in Figure 2.2.

Point *A* in Figure 2.2 indicates the previous base cost for the initial batch of 100,000 units. As cumulative production increases, resulting productivity gains cause transfer cost to decrease to point *B*. The curve on which points *A* and *B* are found is the original experience curve for that product. The R&D department might, however, complete a project with identical product characteristics, but at a lower cost. This is represented in Figure 2.2 by point *C*, which reflects an initial base cost lower than the original cost (point *A*) but higher than the unit cost previously obtained through experience effects (point *B*). In this example,

- the unit cost has been reduced through experience (*a* is negative)
- the R&D project has reduced the unit cost for the same experience basis (*b* is negative)
- but the immediate effect of the R&D project for an initial 100,000 units of production is to increase unit cost (*c* is positive).

The experience curve corresponding to the new R&D project is represented in Figure 2.2 by the lower line. The actual transfer cost for the product resulting

Figure 2.2

Productivity Gains

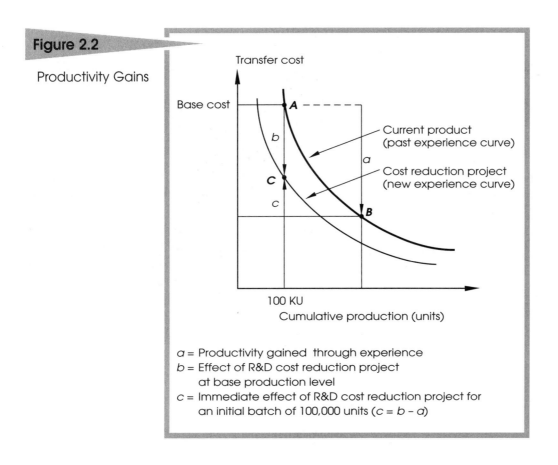

a = Productivity gained through experience
b = Effect of R&D cost reduction project
   at base production level
c = Immediate effect of R&D cost reduction project for
   an initial batch of 100,000 units ($c = b - a$)

from the new R&D project will be somewhere on that curve, according to the production schedule of that product.

Economic Environment

The MARKSTRAT industry operates in an economy that currently has an average inflation rate of 2%. Inflation affects the manufacturing, advertising, sales force, R&D, and market research costs of the firms. In addition, if it were to reach much higher levels in the future, the government could impose price controls on all brands to try to reduce inflation.

The gross national product (GNP) gives management information about trends in the MARKSTRAT economy. In the recent past, the entire economy has been growing at a rate of 4%.

In summary, each MARKSTRAT team must manage the marketing mix, including the product portfolio, prices, advertising, sales force, and distribution, and is responsible for market research, research and development, production forecasts, and inventories. The marketing department in MARKSTRAT is *not* responsible for credit management, capital investment, financial reporting, purchasing, or plant management.

Management Responsibilities of a MARKSTRAT Team

- Brand portfolio
- Production forecast
- Price
- Advertising
- Sales force and distribution
- Market research
- R&D
- Inventory

Activities the Marketing Department Is Not Responsible For

- Credit management
- Capital investment
- Financial reporting
- Purchasing
- Plant management

Budget Expenditures

- Advertising
- Sales force
- Market research
- R&D

Contribution after Marketing

	Retail sales (unit retail price × units sold)
minus	Distribution margins
equals	Company revenues
minus	Cost of goods sold (unit transfer cost × units sold)
minus	Inventory holding cost
minus	Advertising expenditures
minus	Sales force expenditures
equals	**Contribution after marketing**

Net Contribution

	Contribution after marketing
minus	Market research expenditures
minus	R&D expenditures
minus	Interest paid
minus	Exceptional cost or profit
equals	**Net contribution**

Brand Naming Conventions

■ Brand names consist of four characters:
— The first letter is S for a Sonite and V for a Vodite.
— The second letter identifies the company.
— The last two characters may be freely chosen by a company when it launches a new brand, as long as all brands commercialized by the company have different names.

■ The brand name should have the following structure:

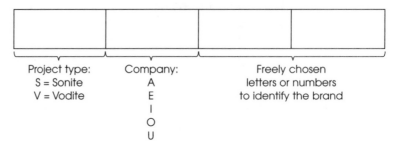

Project type: Company: Freely chosen
S = Sonite   A   letters or numbers
V = Vodite   E   to identify the brand
                      I
                      O
                      U

■ Thus,

S	A	R	C

is a Sonite produced and marketed by Firm A.

R&D Project Naming Conventions

■ R&D project names consist of five characters:
— The first character is always the letter P.
— The second character identifies the type of product that is sought (S for Sonite and V for Vodite).
— The last three characters may be freely chosen by a firm, as long as all of its projects (current and past) have different names.
— The R&D project name bears no relationship to the commercialized brand name. Thus, PSUZZ may be a project to improve existing brand SULI or to create a new brand, SUZI.

■ An R&D project name should be structured as follows:

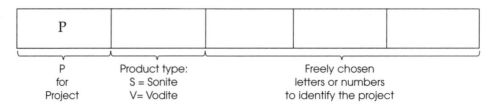

P   Product type: Freely chosen
for   S = Sonite   letters or numbers
Project   V= Vodite   to identify the project

■ Thus, the R&D project

P	V	O	X	3

is a Vodite. The last three characters identify the project, so the letter following the product type (O in this example) does not mean that this project is developed by Firm O.

General Background Information

■ Average annual inflation rate over the last three years: 2%
■ Average annual price increases in the Sonite market over the last three years: 3%
■ Percent of Sonite unit sales by segment in the last year:

Buffs:	30%
Singles:	15%
Professionals:	20%
High Earners:	16%
Others:	19%

■ Average annual increases of Sonite unit sales over the last three years:

Buffs:	5%
Singles:	25%
Professionals:	50%
High Earners:	60%
Others:	30%
Total:	35%

■ Total number of potential retail outlets for Sonites or Vodites:

Specialty stores:	30,000
Department stores:	6,000
Mass merchandisers:	10,000

■ Average margins of distributors as a percentage of retail price:

Specialty stores:	40%
Department stores:	30%
Mass merchandisers:	30%

■ Average advertising expenditures as a percentage of sales over the last three years: 6%
■ Average advertising research expenditures as a percentage of total advertising expenditures over the last three years: 5%

Market Research

To design and implement a marketing strategy, you need to gather information on the competitive market situation. You can do this in several complementary ways. The first is by carefully reading and assimilating the information in this manual, particularly in the first five chapters. The second is by trying out various marketing actions in succession and learning through experience. This corresponds to experimenting in the marketplace in order to improve knowledge and reduce uncertainties. The third way is by buying market research information from outside marketing service firms.

Given some knowledge of market structure and behavior, you can design a marketing strategy by repositioning existing brands and positioning new brands with respect to the five customer segments. Action must then be taken at the level of marketing mix elements, R&D projects, and production planning to implement the marketing strategy. It should be clear from this three-stage process—gathering of information, design of a marketing strategy, and implementation of this strategy—that the management of the marketing mix should not be an end in itself but only a means of achieving a strategy. However, management needs to understand consumer behavior, measure the impact of marketing mix actions, and evaluate past actions, so market research should provide management with information from different types of analyses, performed at various times during the decision process, whether at the strategy design or strategy implementation stage.

The companies in the MARKSTRAT industry may buy a number of market research studies concerning their market (either Sonite or Vodite) in one annual period. These studies are done by major market research houses that make their reports available to all the competitors in the industry. Examples of costs for these studies in the initial period are given in Figure 3.1; these costs are expected to increase with inflation in the course of the simulation. The results from these studies have different levels of error attached to them, according to the methodology applied and the sample size. The reports for the studies concern the information at the end of the period for which the decisions have been made—that is, at the end of the simulated period.

The studies listed in Figure 3.1 are organized in the **Market Studies** menu under the following headings: **Consumer,** for the consumer survey and the

Figure 3.1   Initial Costs of Market Research Studies

COST OF MARKET RESEARCH STUDIES NEXT PERIOD
(all numbers in K$)

Study	Market covered by study		
	All markets	**Sonite**	**Vodite**
Industry benchmarking	31		
Consumer survey		62	42
Consumer panel		104	73
Distribution panel		62	52
Semantic scales		10	10
Multidimensional scaling		36	36
Market forecast		21	21
Competitive advertising		31	31
Competitive sales force		16	16
Advertising experiment		26	26
Sales force experiment		36	36
Conjoint analysis		36	36
Total market	31	440	379
Total if all studies ordered	850		

consumer panel; **Distribution,** for the distribution panel; **Semantic,** for the semantic scale survey; **MDS,** for the multidimensional scaling analysis; **Intelligence,** for information about competitive advertising expenditures and competitive sales forces and for the benchmarking study; **Projections,** for the advertising and sales force experiments and the market forecast study; and **Conjoint,** for the conjoint analysis study.

CONSUMER SURVEY

The consumer survey is a survey questionnaire administered to 3,000 individuals during the simulated period. It gives brand awareness levels, purchase intentions, and shopping habit data for each segment in the product category. The brand awareness figures (Figure 3.2) represent the proportion of individuals in the segment who have unaided recall of a brand's name. The report gives the information for each brand currently on the market. The purchase intentions figures (Figure 3.3) represent the proportion of individuals who would select a brand as their first choice if they were buying within a year. These figures are given for each brand currently on the market and correspond to the situation during the year in which the study is done. They do not necessarily represent purchase intentions for the following year. The shopping habit data (Figure 3.4) represent, for each channel type, the proportion of individuals in each segment who would choose that channel when shopping for a Sonite.

Figure 3.2 Consumer Survey Example for the Sonite Market: Brand Awareness

CONSUMER SURVEY - BRAND AWARENESS BY SEGMENT

Firm	Brand	Buffs	Singles	Pros	HiEarners	Others	Total
A	SAMA	47.8%	53.0%	46.3%	48.9%	63.8%	55.2%
	SALT	45.6%	57.5%	42.4%	44.5%	34.2%	44.5%
	SAND	23.7%	17.2%	58.9%	31.9%	15.6%	24.4%
E	SEMI	56.8%	49.3%	75.9%	56.9%	39.2%	50.6%
	SELF	41.2%	34.7%	51.2%	41.0%	23.4%	33.9%
	SEBU	69.7%	24.8%	30.5%	27.5%	19.1%	26.8%
	SERT	31.3%	24.7%	30.3%	66.5%	23.3%	30.5%
I	SIBI	50.4%	66.1%	46.4%	47.7%	37.5%	49.6%
	SIPE	24.7%	21.6%	26.4%	25.7%	48.3%	32.8%
	SICK	22.6%	44.9%	21.9%	20.6%	15.8%	26.6%
O	SOLD	60.6%	55.7%	59.5%	77.8%	49.7%	57.0%
	SONO	53.3%	43.2%	73.4%	45.7%	34.8%	45.1%
	SODU	34.6%	58.4%	33.5%	31.5%	26.5%	38.4%
	SODE	57.6%	11.8%	16.8%	14.2%	9.5%	15.0%
U	SUSI	41.8%	48.5%	46.2%	47.7%	65.7%	54.0%
	SULI	59.6%	51.0%	77.3%	59.5%	41.6%	52.7%
	SUBF	11.5%	19.1%	10.8%	10.2%	7.9%	12.3%

Figure 3.3 Consumer Survey Example for the Sonite Market: Purchase Intentions

CONSUMER SURVEY - PURCHASE INTENTIONS

Firm	Brand	Buffs	Singles	Pros	HiEarners	Others	Total
A	SAMA	0.1%	0.4%	0.0%	0.1%	22.7%	8.0%
	SALT	0.4%	7.2%	0.1%	0.3%	1.1%	2.8%
	SAND	0.3%	0.0%	5.2%	0.3%	0.1%	0.8%
E	SEMI	0.8%	0.1%	30.0%	0.7%	0.1%	4.4%
	SELF	0.4%	0.1%	8.2%	0.4%	0.1%	1.3%
	SEBU	52.8%	0.2%	0.3%	0.6%	0.1%	4.0%
	SERT	0.5%	0.1%	0.2%	26.5%	0.1%	3.1%
I	SIBI	0.3%	45.0%	0.1%	0.2%	1.1%	15.3%
	SIPE	0.1%	0.2%	0.0%	0.1%	44.0%	15.3%
	SICK	0.2%	6.0%	0.0%	0.1%	0.6%	2.2%
O	SOLD	1.2%	0.2%	0.5%	68.8%	0.3%	8.0%
	SONO	0.8%	0.1%	29.0%	0.6%	0.1%	4.2%
	SODU	0.2%	39.7%	0.0%	0.2%	0.7%	13.4%
	SODE	40.9%	0.1%	0.2%	0.3%	0.1%	3.1%
U	SUSI	0.1%	0.3%	0.0%	0.1%	28.5%	10.0%
	SULI	0.8%	0.1%	26.1%	0.7%	0.2%	3.9%
	SUBF	0.1%	0.3%	0.0%	0.0%	0.1%	0.1%
Total		100.0%	100.0%	100.0%	100.0%	100.0%	100.0%

Figure 3.4   Consumer Survey Example for the Sonite Market: Shopping Habits

CONSUMER SURVEY - SHOPPING HABITS

Segment	Specialty stores	Depart. stores	Mass Merchandis.	Total
Buffs	59.1%	22.3%	18.6%	100.0%
Singles	34.5%	34.5%	30.9%	100.0%
Professionals	41.8%	27.3%	30.9%	100.0%
High earners	30.9%	50.0%	19.1%	100.0%
Others	14.5%	34.5%	51.0%	100.0%
Total	29.3%	34.6%	36.0%	100.0%

CONSUMER PANEL

The consumer panel study (an example of which is shown in Figure 3.5) gives the market shares, based on units sold, by segment for each brand in the product category. The unit product category sales for the industry are also supplied by segment.

Figure 3.5   Consumer Panel Study Example for the Sonite Market

CONSUMER PANEL - MARKET SHARES BASED ON UNIT SALES

Firm	Brand	Buffs	Singles	Pros	HiEarners	Others	Total
A	SAMA	0.2%	0.7%	0.1%	0.2%	37.7%	14.1%
	SALT	0.0%	0.0%	0.0%	0.0%	0.0%	0.0%
	SAND	0.0%	0.0%	0.1%	0.0%	0.0%	0.0%
E	SEMI	1.1%	0.2%	37.7%	0.8%	0.2%	5.3%
	SELF	0.0%	0.0%	0.3%	0.0%	0.0%	0.0%
	SEBU	62.6%	0.2%	0.3%	0.5%	0.1%	4.4%
	SERT	0.8%	0.1%	0.4%	43.0%	0.2%	5.5%
I	SIBI	0.5%	64.5%	0.1%	0.3%	1.3%	20.4%
	SIPE	0.0%	0.1%	0.0%	0.0%	15.7%	5.8%
	SICK	0.1%	3.0%	0.0%	0.1%	0.2%	1.0%
O	SOLD	1.0%	0.2%	0.4%	53.4%	0.2%	6.7%
	SONO	0.9%	0.1%	30.4%	0.5%	0.1%	4.3%
	SODU	0.2%	30.1%	0.0%	0.1%	0.5%	9.5%
	SODE	31.4%	0.0%	0.1%	0.2%	0.0%	2.2%
U	SUSI	0.1%	0.5%	0.0%	0.2%	43.6%	16.3%
	SULI	1.0%	0.1%	30.0%	0.7%	0.1%	4.3%
	SUBF	0.1%	0.2%	0.0%	0.0%	0.1%	0.1%
Total		100.0%	100.0%	100.0%	100.0%	100.0%	100.0%
Total sales (U)		133 100	605 100	261 800	238 200	722 200	1 960 400
Total sales (% Total)		6.8%	30.9%	13.4%	12.2%	36.8%	100.0%

DISTRIBUTION PANEL

The distribution panel study provides the market shares, based on units sold, by channel for each brand in the product category (Figure 3.6). The product category sales in the industry are also supplied by distribution channel, in thousands of units. The extent to which each brand is carried by the channels of distribution appears in the distribution coverage table (Figure 3.7).

SEMANTIC SCALES

The semantic scales study provides a map of brands based on a semantic differential questionnaire administered to a sample of 600 individuals. Several semantic scales (such as the following one for weight), corresponding to the physical characteristics of Sonites, were presented to the respondents:

Lightest   1 2 3 4 5 6 7   Heaviest

Respondents were asked to rate each brand according to the way they perceived the brand on that characteristic. They were also asked to indicate their

Figure 3.6   Distribution Panel Study Example for the Sonite Market: Market Shares

DISTRIBUTION PANEL - MARKET SHARES BASED ON UNIT SALES					
Firm	Brand	Specialty stores	Depart. stores	Mass Merchandis.	Total
A	SAMA	6.5%	15.2%	21.6%	14.1%
	SALT	0.0%	0.0%	0.0%	0.0%
	SAND	0.0%	0.0%	0.0%	0.0%
E	SEMI	8.1%	3.9%	3.9%	5.3%
	SELF	0.1%	0.0%	0.0%	0.0%
	SEBU	10.2%	1.9%	1.1%	4.4%
	SERT	5.2%	8.4%	1.9%	5.5%
I	SIBI	24.9%	20.0%	15.8%	20.4%
	SIPE	1.7%	5.9%	10.4%	5.8%
	SICK	1.2%	1.0%	0.8%	1.0%
O	SOLD	6.1%	10.4%	2.8%	6.7%
	SONO	7.3%	2.8%	2.7%	4.3%
	SODU	12.0%	9.0%	7.2%	9.5%
	SODE	5.4%	0.7%	0.4%	2.2%
U	SUSI	4.0%	17.6%	28.7%	16.3%
	SULI	7.2%	2.9%	2.6%	4.3%
	SUBF	0.1%	0.1%	0.1%	0.1%
Total		100.0%	100.0%	100.0%	100.0%
Total sales (U)		658 700	729 700	571 500	1 959 900
Total sales (% Total)		33.6%	37.2%	29.2%	100.0%

Figure 3.7   Distribution Panel Study Example for the Sonite Market: Distribution Coverage

Firm	Brand	Specialty stores	Depart. stores	Mass Merchandis.
A	SAMA	47.0%	51.1%	34.4%
	SALT	0.0%	0.0%	0.0%
	SAND	0.0%	0.0%	0.0%
E	SEMI	52.0%	41.7%	28.0%
	SELF	0.0%	0.0%	0.0%
	SEBU	51.1%	25.9%	13.2%
	SERT	44.6%	50.4%	22.1%
I	SIBI	39.4%	33.8%	19.3%
	SIPE	25.5%	40.5%	31.0%
	SICK	15.8%	13.5%	7.9%
O	SOLD	44.5%	53.4%	27.1%
	SONO	48.0%	30.3%	19.5%
	SODU	44.2%	34.4%	20.8%
	SODE	34.1%	13.2%	5.2%
U	SUSI	20.2%	45.6%	35.2%
	SULI	53.6%	35.0%	20.6%
	SUBF	24.3%	31.3%	15.5%
Total number of outlets		27 273	6 638	12 603

DISTRIBUTION PANEL - DISTRIBUTION COVERAGE BY CHANNEL

preferred (or "ideal") point on each scale. The reported results are the mean values for each brand (Figure 3.8) and for the segment ideal points (Figure 3.9) on each scale.

Figure 3.8   Semantic Scales Study Example for the Sonite Market: Brand Perceptions

SEMANTIC SCALES - BRAND PERCEPTIONS (1 TO 7)

Firm	Brand	Weight	Design	Volume	Max Freq	Power	Price
A	SAMA	5.59	3.04	5.84	3.08	2.69	2.09
	SALT	5.50	4.52	4.95	4.73	4.43	2.95
	SAND	3.54	1.87	3.43	5.61	5.89	6.06
E	SEMI	3.17	2.81	2.99	5.81	5.89	6.24
	SELF	3.63	2.01	2.79	6.03	6.00	6.27
	SEBU	2.71	4.60	2.44	5.77	5.55	4.83
	SERT	2.70	4.69	3.16	4.37	4.07	5.84
I	SIBI	6.45	5.66	4.00	5.04	4.69	2.65
	SIPE	6.50	4.30	4.86	2.23	2.72	2.05
	SICK	6.45	5.66	4.00	4.74	4.27	2.78
O	SOLD	3.26	4.59	2.35	4.36	4.18	5.58
	SONO	3.32	2.72	3.14	5.84	5.83	6.13
	SODU	4.68	4.92	5.20	5.16	4.67	2.62
	SODE	3.91	4.43	2.49	5.57	5.72	4.97
U	SUSI	5.37	3.22	6.17	3.35	2.52	2.10
	SULI	3.37	2.42	3.17	5.79	5.80	6.19
	SUBF	5.31	1.63	4.46	5.12	5.22	3.09

Figure 3.9   Semantic Scales Study Example for the Sonite Market: Ideal Values

SEMANTIC SCALES - IDEAL VALUES (1 TO 7)

Segment	Weight	Design	Volume	Max Freq	Power	Price
Buffs	2.37	4.24	1.85	6.23	6.48	3.86
Singles	5.65	4.63	6.01	4.99	4.85	4.47
Pros	4.57	5.00	5.09	4.80	2.26	4.35
HiEarners	5.27	4.24	5.15	5.26	2.80	5.90
Others	6.37	1.95	6.18	2.21	5.31	3.38
Importance of characteristic (1)	4	2	4	10	4	7

(1) On a scale from 1 to 10 - 1 = Not important - 10 = Very important

The bottom line of Figure 3.9 also contains importance ratings attributed to each characteristic by consumers participating in the study. These numbers are averaged across all segments. In the MARKSTRAT3 environment, consumer segments naturally differ on the exact importance ratings attributed to the characteristics, but they tend to agree on the rankings of the scales (that is, on their relative importance). This is why only average values of these importance ratings are reported. The differences between segments are much more significant in terms of ideal points (the *level* desired of each characteristic) than in terms of the *relative importance* of each characteristic. These two concepts are often confused, as it is common in everyday life to associate a "difficult" level requirement (for instance, low price or high reliability) with strong importance and an "easy" level requirement (high price or low reliability) with weak importance. For instance, it may appear irrational that all segments perceive price to be important and that consumers in one of these segments desire a high price level. It is true that "price is important" is associated with "price must be low" in many market segments, as it is in popular wisdom. High importance may be given simultaneously to price and the need for a high price level, however, for a variety of reasons, such as to guarantee quality, to ensure that the product is not used by many others, to differentiate the product, to bestow prestige, or to express the value of a gift. For those convinced of the universality of the "economically rational man," these situations are most difficult to understand. They illustrate the high variety present in human behavior, the risk of personal biases in the absence of market research, and the need for a deep understanding of different groups of consumers.

Maps representing consumers' perceptions based on the semantic scales can be obtained for each pair of attributes (Figure 3.10). When no brand is available on the market, such as in the Vodite market in the early periods of the simulation, this study gives the perception of ideal values on the semantic scales for each segment, which would be used primarily in R&D planning. The graph of the evolution of the preferences (ideal points) over time is also displayed (this is illustrated in Figure 3.11 for Period 4 of a simulation) in order to capture the dynamics of the needs of the various segments.

The semantic scales study is particularly useful in positioning brands, and its third component (Figure 3.12) helps determine the relationships between

Figure 3.10   Semantic Scales Study Example for the Sonite Market: Brand Map

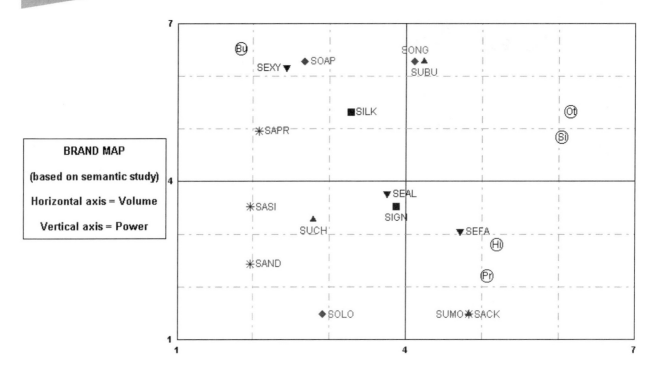

BRAND MAP

(based on semantic study)

Horizontal axis = Volume

Vertical axis = Power

Figure 3.11   Semantic Scales Study Example: Ideal Value Evolution

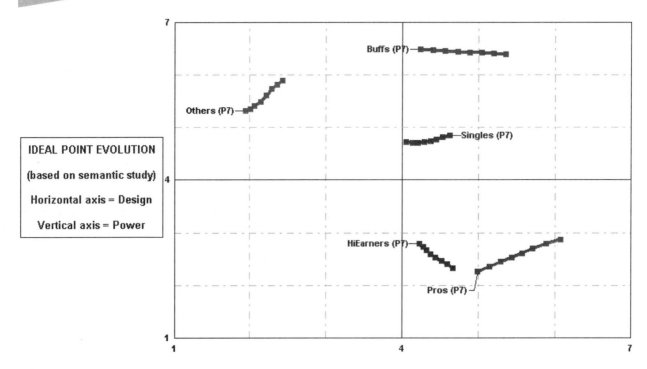

IDEAL POINT EVOLUTION

(based on semantic study)

Horizontal axis = Design

Vertical axis = Power

Figure 3.12   Semantic Scales Study Example: Relationship between Characteristic and Perception

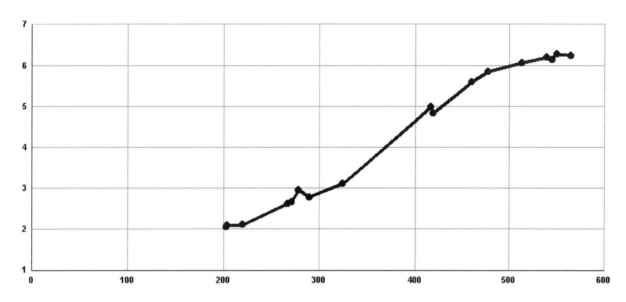

Relationship between PRICE and perceived PRICE

product characteristics and perceptions. A number of options are available in the **Analysis** module to help address these issues in greater depth. These options are not presented now but are described in detail in Chapter 6.

MULTIDIMENSIONAL SCALING OF BRAND SIMILARITIES AND PREFERENCES

The multidimensional scaling study provides a joint space configuration obtained by non-metric multidimensional scaling. It relies on similarity and preference data on the complete set of brands available in the market. These data are obtained through interviews with a sample of 200 individuals. The study gives the minimum number of dimensions that were sufficient to provide a good fit to the data, as well as a likely interpretation of the axes based on semantic scale responses. It then provides the graphical representation of the perceptual positioning of the Sonite brands and the segments' ideal points (Figure 3.13). Further details on such a perceptual map and its interpretation are given in Chapter 6. This study differs from the semantic scales study in that the respondent is not provided with criteria on which to evaluate the brands. Instead, the criteria are discovered by the methodology, which is based on global assessments of similarities of pairs of brands. This is a complex task, requiring the inclusion of a number of brands in order to derive a solution. The study thus will not be available for the Vodite market until it includes a significant number of competitors. A table like the one in Figure 3.14 gives the coordinates of the brand positions on the perceptual map, on a scale

Figure 3.13   Example of Multidimensional Scaling Study: Perceptual Map

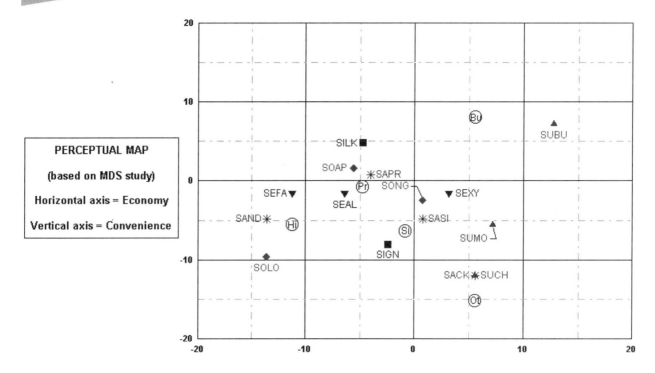

Figure 3.14   Example of Multidimensional Scaling Study: Brand Perceptions

Firm	Brand	Economy	Performance	Convenience
A	SACK	5.3	-9.2	-12.2
	SAND	-13.5	-1.1	-4.7
	SAPR	-3.9	14.7	0.5
	SASI	1.2	-0.6	-4.7
E	SEAL	-6.4	7.5	-1.3
	SEXY	2.9	12.7	-2.0
	SEFA	-11.4	4.2	-1.3
I	SIGN	-2.8	-3.7	-8.1
	SILK	-5.1	4.3	4.9
O	SOAP	-5.5	10.2	1.6
	SONG	0.5	13.0	-2.0
	SOLO	-13.3	12.8	-9.3
U	SUCH	5.2	1.6	-12.4
	SUMO	6.9	-12.7	-5.5
	SUBU	12.5	14.6	7.0

MULTIDIMENSIONAL SCALING - BRAND PERCEPTIONS (-20 TO +20)

from –20 to +20. The ideal point coordinates are provided in a separate table (Figure 3.15), and the evolution of these ideal values over time is plotted (Figure 3.16). An indication of the influence of product characteristics in determining perceptual dimensions is also provided (Figure 3.17) to help you interpret the perceptual dimensions that were derived from the study. For example, you can see that economy is moderately related to both the power and the price of the product, whereas performance is strongly related to the maximum frequency of the product.

The multidimensional scaling study is useful in positioning brands. Further, it can be used to investigate the relationships between product characteristics and perceptions (Figure 3.18). As with the semantic scales study, a number of options are available in the **Analysis** menu to address these issues further. They are described in detail in Chapter 6.

Figure 3.15   Example of Multidimensional Scaling Study: Ideal Values

MULTIDIMENSIONAL SCALING - IDEAL VALUES (-20 TO +20)			
Segment	Economy	Performance	Convenience
Buffs	5.6	14.7	8.1
Singles	-0.5	1.6	-6.4
Pros	-5.1	2.2	-0.6
HiEarners	-11.3	4.4	-5.5
Others	5.5	-12.6	-15.2

Figure 3.16   Example of Multidimensional Scaling Study: Evolution of Ideal Values

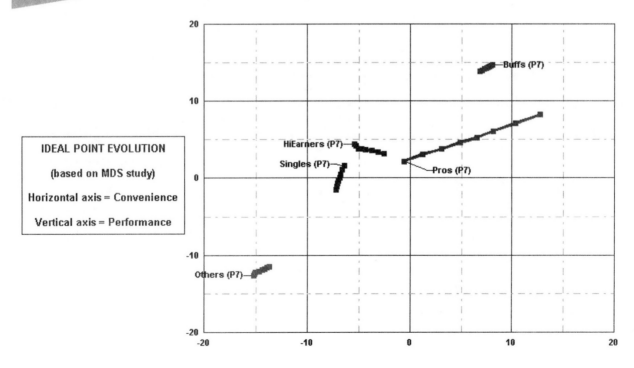

Figure 3.17 ▶ Example of Multidimensional Scaling Study: Influence of Product Characteristics

MULTIDIMENSIONAL SCALING INFLUENCE OF PRODUCT CHARACTERISTICS ON MDS DIMENSIONS	Weight (Kg)	Design (Index)	Volume (Dm3)	Max Freq (KHz)	Power (W)	Price ($)
Economy	Slight	Slight	Slight	Slight	Moderate	Moderate
Performance	Slight	Slight	Moderate	**Strong**	Slight	Slight
Convenience	Moderate	Moderate	Slight	Slight	Slight	Slight

Figure 3.18 ▶ Example of Multidimensional Scaling Study: Relationship between Characteristic and Perception

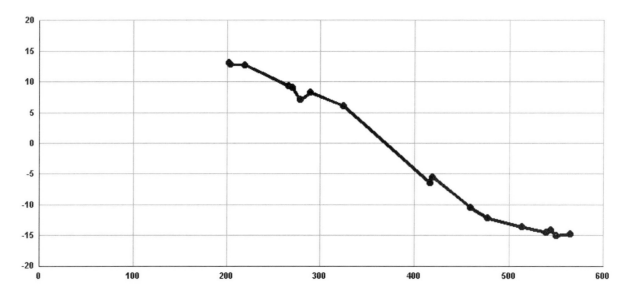

Relationship between PRICE and perceived ECONOMY

COMPETITIVE ADVERTISING ESTIMATES

An advertising research firm gives estimates of the total advertising expenditures for each competitive brand (see the example in Figure 3.19). Estimates are also given for the brands of the company requesting the study, as a reference to control for estimation errors.

COMPETITIVE SALES FORCE ESTIMATES

Companies can get estimates of the size of the sales force of competitors and their breakdown by channel of distribution from a specialized market re-

Figure 3.19 Competitive Advertising Estimates Study Example

COMPETITIVE ADVERTISING - ESTIMATED TOTAL EXPENDITURES
(all numbers in K$)

Firm	Brand	Buffs	Singles	Pros	HiEarners	Others	Total
A	SAMA	150	150	150	150	1 000	1 600
	SALT	0	50	0	0	0	50
	SAND	0	0	50	0	0	50
	TOTAL	**150**	**200**	**200**	**150**	**1 000**	**1 700**
E	SEMI	300	300	2 050	300	300	3 250
	SELF	0	0	0	0	0	0
	SEBU	1 400	200	200	200	200	2 200
	SERT	250	250	250	1 700	250	2 700
	TOTAL	**1 950**	**750**	**2 500**	**2 200**	**750**	**8 150**
I	SIBI	200	1 350	200	200	200	2 150
	SIPE	150	150	150	150	1 250	1 850
	SICK	0	50	0	0	0	50
	TOTAL	**350**	**1 550**	**350**	**350**	**1 450**	**4 050**
O	SOLD	200	200	200	1 450	200	2 250
	SONO	150	150	1 100	150	150	1 700
	SODU	200	1 500	200	200	200	2 300
TOTAL		**4 500**	**6 250**	**6 450**	**5 250**	**5 650**	**28 100**
AVERAGE BY BRAND		265	368	379	309	332	1 653
AVERAGE BY FIRM		900	1 250	1 290	1 050	1 130	5 620

search firm (see Figure 3.20 for an example). The estimates are given for each brand in salespeople equivalents, reflecting the effort of the sales force for each brand. Estimates are also given for the sales force of the company requesting the study, as a reference to control for estimation errors.

Figure 3.20 Competitive Sales Force Estimates Study Example

COMPETITIVE SALES FORCES - ESTIMATED SIZES
(in number of salespeople)

Firm	Brand	Specialty stores	Depart. stores	Mass Merchandis.	Total
A	SAMA	28	33	34	95
	SALT	0	0	0	0
	SAND	0	0	0	0
	TOTAL	**28**	**33**	**34**	**95**
E	SEMI	32	20	22	74
	SELF	0	0	0	0
	SEBU	25	9	7	41
	SERT	18	31	13	62
	TOTAL	**75**	**60**	**42**	**177**
I	SIBI	12	13	10	35
	SIPE	9	20	27	56
	SICK	3	3	2	8
	TOTAL	**24**	**36**	**39**	**99**
O	SOLD	16	38	19	73
	SONO	20	11	10	41
	SODU	16	12	10	38
TOTAL		**225**	**238**	**215**	**678**
AVERAGE BY BRAND		13	14	13	40
AVERAGE BY FIRM		45	48	43	136

INDUSTRY BENCHMARKING

The industry benchmarking study provides general information obtained from annual reports about each of the competitors. This information includes income statement data on revenues and expenses for each competitor at the level of the firm (Figure 3.21) or within one market (Figure 3.22).

Figure 3.21   Industry Benchmarking Study Example—Overall Performance

BENCHMARKING - ESTIMATED OVERALL PERFORMANCE	Unit	A	E	I	O	U
Sales						
Retail sales	K$	54 288	319 047	133 645	421 421	203 733
Revenues	K$	37 020	208 844	88 553	278 648	137 813
Production						
Cost of goods sold	K$	-20 080	-96 150	-64 440	-121 407	-64 108
Inventory holding cost	K$	-175	-2 729	-57	-361	-1 009
Inventory disposal loss	K$	0	-997	-823	0	0
Contribution before marketing	K$	16 765	108 968	23 232	156 880	72 697
Marketing						
Advertising expenditures	K$	-1 696	-14 406	-3 710	-12 204	-8 887
Advertising research expenditures	K$	-89	-1 425	-440	-1 657	-879
Sales force	K$	-2 360	-7 401	-2 604	-6 395	-4 214
Contribution after marketing	K$	12 620	85 736	16 478	136 624	58 717
Other expenses						
Market research studies	K$	-565	-1 018	-621	-1 018	-720
Research and development	K$	0	-100	-2 510	-3 075	0
Interest paid	K$	-332	0	0	0	0
Exceptional cost or profit	K$	0	0	0	0	0
Net contribution	K$	11 723	84 618	13 347	132 531	57 997
Next period budget	K$	8 700	24 850	8 700	24 850	23 200

Figure 3.22   Industry Benchmarking Study Example—Performance by Market

BENCHMARKING - ESTIMATED PERFORMANCE IN SONITE MARKET	Unit	A	E	I	O	U
Sales						
Retail sales	K$	54 288	144 616	133 645	171 239	111 722
Revenues	K$	37 020	93 803	88 553	111 658	74 886
Production						
Cost of goods sold	K$	-20 080	-42 816	-64 440	-54 183	-31 454
Inventory holding cost	K$	-175	-1 073	-57	-144	-628
Inventory disposal loss	K$	0	-997	-823	0	0
Contribution before marketing	K$	16 765	48 917	23 232	57 331	42 804
Marketing						
Advertising expenditures	K$	-1 696	-7 211	-3 710	-6 697	-5 742
Advertising research expenditures	K$	-89	-713	-440	-1 074	-568
Sales force	K$	-2 360	-4 534	-2 604	-4 210	-3 563
Contribution after marketing	K$	12 620	36 458	16 478	45 350	32 932

ADVERTISING EXPERIMENT

An advertising experiment is conducted by increasing the advertising budget in a selected regional test market. The results of the experiment are used to project the level of brand awareness and the share of market for each of the company's brands, by segment, if the advertising budget had been increased for each brand by the indicated percentage over the actual expenditure (see Figure 3.23). The experiment tests only the size of the media budget and not changes in other parts of advertising strategy such as advertising research or positioning objectives. It also estimates the net change in contribution after marketing due to the increase in advertising expenditures.

SALES FORCE EXPERIMENT

A sales force experiment is set up by increasing the number of salespeople per channel in a regional test market. The results (an illustration is given in Figure 3.24) are then used to estimate the number of distributors and market share that each of the firm's brands would have had in the entire market if the sales force directed to each channel had been increased as indicated. The experiment uses the allocation of effort of the salespeople as defined in the decisions for the period. The net change in contribution after marketing due to the increase in the number of salespeople is also estimated.

Figure 3.23   Advertising Experiment Study Example

ADVERTISING EXPERIMENT EXPECTED RESULTS WITH INCREASED ADVERTISING BUDGET				
	SEMI	SELF	SEBU	SERT
Change in awareness (%)				
Buffs	0.8%	0.0%	1.7%	1.1%
Singles	0.3%	0.0%	0.3%	0.4%
Professionals	1.3%	0.0%	0.7%	1.0%
High earners	0.5%	0.0%	0.6%	1.8%
Others	0.3%	0.0%	0.3%	0.3%
Change in market share (%)				
Buffs	0.0%	0.0%	0.7%	0.1%
Singles	0.0%	0.0%	0.0%	0.0%
Professionals	0.7%	0.0%	0.0%	0.0%
High earners	0.0%	0.0%	0.1%	0.7%
Others	0.0%	0.0%	0.0%	0.0%
Change in contribution after marketing (K$)	**18**	**0**	**-25**	**25**

Notes.

These results would have been achieved by a given brand if its advertising budget had been increased by 20% and if competitive actions had remained unchanged.

Figure 3.24 Sales Force Experiment Example

SALES FORCE EXPERIMENT
EXPECTED RESULTS WITH INCREASED SALES FORCE

	SEAL	SEXY	SEFA
Change in number of distributors (U)			
Specialty stores	678	467	610
Depart. stores	194	98	216
Mass Merchandis.	249	193	276
Change in market share (%)			
Specialty stores	1.0%	0.6%	1.5%
Depart. stores	0.6%	0.2%	1.7%
Mass Merchandis.	0.3%	0.4%	0.6%
Change in contribution after marketing (K$)	**1 704**	**357**	**4 246**

Notes.

These results would have been achieved if the number of salespeople had been increased by 10 in each channel and if competitive actions had remained unchanged.

MARKET FORECAST

The market forecast study provides an estimate of the expected market size (in thousands of units) and market growth (as a percentage) for the product category as a whole. These forecasts are for the next period and are broken down by segment (Figure 3.25). The study relies on market extrapolation and assumes stable marketing actions by the competitors, so it would not reflect any change in competitors' strategies or in market conditions.

Figure 3.25 Market Forecast Example

MARKET FORECAST - SEGMENT SIZES AND GROWTH RATES

Segment	Buffs	Singles	Pros	HiEarners	Others	Total
Segment sizes in KU						
Actual size this period	232	467	36	731	138	**1 604**
Forecasted size next period	215	505	34	829	135	**1 717**
Forecasted size in five periods	159	690	25	1 366	123	**2 363**
Relative segment sizes in %						
Actual size this period	14.5%	29.1%	2.3%	45.6%	8.6%	**100.0%**
Forecasted size next period	12.5%	29.4%	2.0%	48.3%	7.8%	**100.0%**
Forecasted size in five periods	6.7%	29.2%	1.1%	57.8%	5.2%	**100.0%**
Forecasted growth rates in %						
Next period	-7.3%	8.2%	-7.3%	13.3%	-2.1%	**7.0%**
Total over next five periods	-31.5%	48.0%	-31.5%	86.7%	-10.3%	**47.3%**
Average over next five periods	-7.3%	8.1%	-7.3%	13.3%	-2.1%	**8.1%**

When no brand is available in the market—such as in the Vodite market in the early periods of the simulation—this study will give a forecast of the potential market for the next period if a brand were to be introduced. This forecast is based on declared likelihood of purchase obtained from a sample of individuals. It should be noted that here the market forecast obviously does not rely on history and tends to be less accurate and generally somewhat optimistic.

CONJOINT ANALYSIS

The conjoint analysis study enables firms to estimate the relative importance of—and the utility attached by the consumers to—the price and features of a product category. The utilities are represented graphically for four values of each of the four characteristics perceived as most important. Figures 3.26, 3.27, and 3.28 are examples of a Conjoint Analysis study. In Figure 3.26, each point of the graph for a characteristic represents the utility attached to a product with this level of the characteristic. By comparing the various utilities attached to different levels (see Figure 3.27), it is possible to infer the main drivers of what individuals prefer (i.e., the relative importance of each characteristic). Figure 3.28 summarizes the estimated importance of each characteristic for all the segments.

Figure 3.26 Example of Conjoint Analysis: Utility Graph

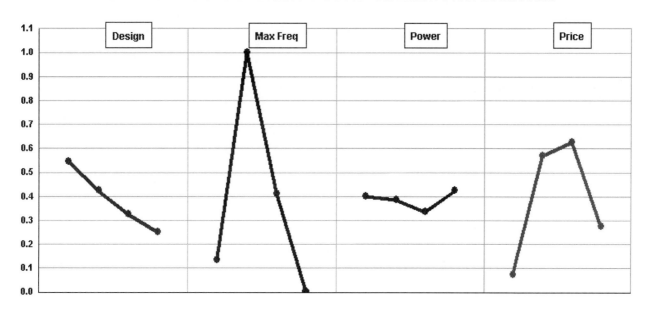

CONJOINT ANALYSIS - UTILITY GRAPHS - SEGMENT PROFESSIONALS

Figure 3.27   Example of Conjoint Analysis: Utilities

CONJOINT ANALYSIS - UTILITIES - SEGMENT PROFESSIONALS

		Unit	1	2	3	4	Importance
Design	Level	Index	7	8	9	10	15.2%
	Utility	[0,1]	0.55	0.42	0.33	0.25	
Max Freq	Level	KHz	22	30	38	46	51.7%
	Utility	[0,1]	0.13	1.00	0.41	0.00	
Power	Level	W	5	21	37	53	4.5%
	Utility	[0,1]	0.40	0.38	0.34	0.42	
Price	Level	$	244	327	410	493	28.6%
	Utility	[0,1]	0.07	0.57	0.63	0.27	

Figure 3.28   Example of Conjoint Analysis: Importance

CONJOINT ANALYSIS - RELATIVE IMPORTANCE OF CHARACTERISTICS

Segment	Design	Max Freq	Power	Price	Total
Buffs	7.2%	51.2%	5.2%	36.4%	100.0%
Singles	18.8%	53.4%	2.1%	25.7%	100.0%
Pros	15.2%	51.7%	4.5%	28.6%	100.0%
HiEarners	19.7%	55.0%	3.5%	21.7%	100.0%
Others	23.8%	44.6%	5.9%	25.7%	100.0%

CHAPTER 3 SUMMARY

Market Research Studies

- Consumer survey
  - Brand awareness for each brand
  - Purchase intentions by segment for each brand
  - Shopping habits by channel for each segment
- Consumer panel
  - Market shares based on unit sales, total and by segment, for each brand
  - Industry sales by segment
- Distribution panel
  - Market shares based on unit sales, total and by channel, for each brand
  - Industry sales by channel
  - Distribution coverage by channel
- Semantic scales
  - Brand map
  - Average evaluation of each brand on perceived product characteristics
  - Ideal values of each segment on the three most important product characteristics
  - Evolution of ideal values
  - Relationship between product characteristics and perceptions
- Multidimensional scaling of brand similarities and preferences
  - Perceptual map
  - Average position of each brand on multidimensional perceptual space
  - Ideal values of each segment on multidimensional perceptual space
  - Evolution of ideal values
  - Influence of characteristics
  - Relationships between product characteristics and perceptions
- Competitive advertising estimates—Estimated total advertising expenditures for each brand
- Competitive sales force estimates—Estimated number of salespeople, by channel, for each firm
- Industry benchmarking
  - Performance and cost structure of competitors
  - Overall performance of firms
  - Performance of firms by market
- Advertising experiment—Expected awareness and market share, by segment, for each brand if the advertising budget had been increased by a specified percentage

■ Sales force experiment—Estimated number of distributors and expected market share, by channel, for each brand if the sales force had been increased in each channel by the specified number
■ Market forecast
  — Expected market size, by segment, for the next period for the product category as a whole
  — Expected market growth, by segment, for the next period for the product category as a whole
■ Conjoint analysis
  — Utility graphs for each segment in each product category
  — Utilities associated with levels of product characteristics
  — Relative importance of product characteristics

Operating Instructions

Each of the MARKSTRAT companies is managed by a team that can organize itself as it likes. It is, however, recommended that your team elect a chairperson, or a coordinator, to facilitate communications with the instructor. For each period, a deadline will be set for your team to submit a decision—electronically, via a network or on a microcomputer diskette—representing the firm's decisions for the current simulated year. These decisions are entered with the MARKSTRAT3 software, and the decisions for all the companies are used as inputs to the MARKSTRAT computerized simulation model. Each team then receives its results either via a network or on computer diskette. The results are communicated in three types of documents: the Company Report, the Newsletter, and market research studies.

The Company Report contains (1) eventual messages, (2) the results for the firm overall, as well as by product category (Sonite and Vodite markets), for the period, (3) results for each brand marketed by the firm, (4) feedback from the R&D department, (5) cumulative results since the beginning of the simulation, and (6) a summary of the firm's decisions. The Newsletter contains general market information. The market research studies that were requested follow the descriptions in the previous chapter.

These four modules—decisions, Company Report, Newsletter, and market research studies—correspond to the buttons found on the menu bar of the MARKSTRAT3 main screen, as shown in Figure 4.1

The MARKSTRAT simulation is usually played over six to ten simulated years. At the beginning of the simulation, each team receives the Company Report corresponding to Period 0 operations, which represents its company's initial situation. Thus, its first decisions deal with Period 1.

Figure 4.1   Modules on the MARKSTRAT3 Software Module Bar

Following is a description of how to use the MARKSTRAT3 software to enter the firm's decisions. Then, the contents of the Company Report and of the Newsletter are presented. The market research studies were described in Chapter 3.

DECISIONS

When you are in the **Decisions** module, the number of the Decisions period is shown on the main MARKSTRAT3 screen in the selection bar. For example, in Figure 4.1 the number 7 indicates that results are available for Period 6 and the decisions will be entered for Period 7. (The number 6 will appear when you are in a module other than **Decisions**.) Although you can access decisions made in prior periods, only changes made to decisions of the current period will be considered in the simulation.

The **Decisions** module in the MARKSTRAT3 software has five main sections, each represented by a button in the **Decisions** module window of the screen, as shown in Figure 4.2: (1) **Brand Portfolio**, (2) **Production, Price, & Advertising**, (3) **Sales Force & Distribution**, (4) **Market Research Studies**, and (5) **Research & Development.** Four additional buttons appear at the bottom of the screen: (1) **Error & Warnings**, (2) **Summary**, (3) **Budget**, and (4) **Marketing Plan.** We first discuss the main five components of the **Decisions** module and then describe the **Budget, Summary,** and **Errors &**

Figure 4.2   Decisions Module Main Window

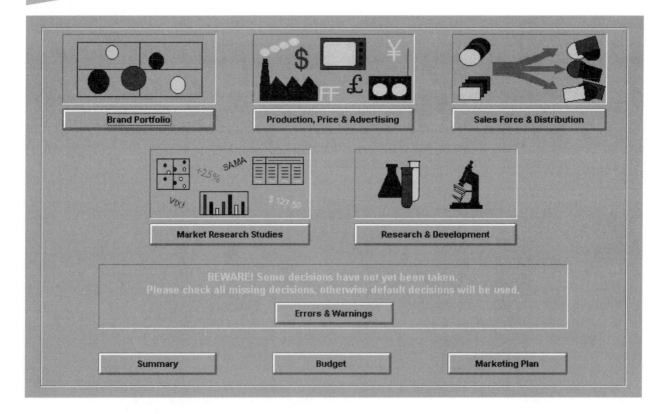

Warnings buttons. The **Marketing Plan** sub-module is presented in the next chapter.

This section does not attempt to present an exhaustive list of possible decisions, but rather provides a general discussion of the type of information typically entered on these different screens. The following chapters offer a more detailed description of alternative decision options with a series of examples referring back to the **Decisions** module.

Brand Portfolio

The **Brand Portfolio** module allows you to maintain, modify, or withdraw existing brands, as well as introduce new ones. When you click on the **Brand Portfolio** button, the module presented in Figure 4.3 appears on the screen. In the top left-hand corner of the window, buttons appear for the two markets in the MARKSTRAT world—S for Sonites and V for Vodites. Click on the market button of your choice. The button is lowered and appears in lighter grey than the other button, which is raised.

The brands to be marketed next period are displayed in the top table of the window. When you retrieve this screen the first time after a period has been simulated, the brands that are currently available in the market appear in the first column, as can be seen in Figure 4.3. You can change the brand portfolio simply by using the buttons on the right side of the screen. You may introduce new brands, modify existing brands with new product

Figure 4.3　　　Brand Portfolio

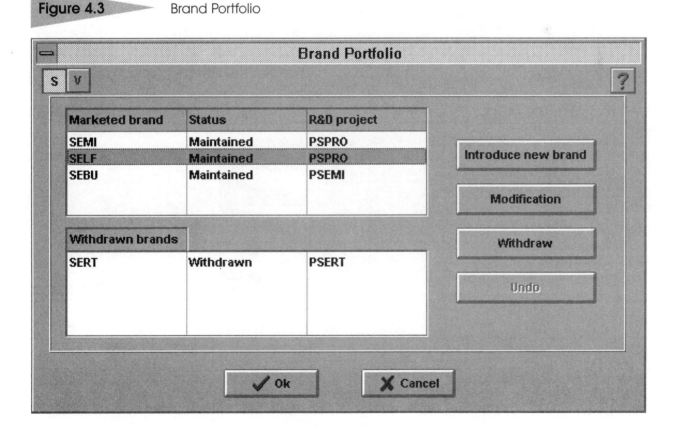

specifications, and withdraw brands from the market. The status of a brand—new, modified, or maintained—is indicated in the second column of the top table in Figure 4.3. The third column displays the name of the R&D project used as the prototype for the brand. For each market, up to five brands can be marketed in a given period. This allows each firm to market a total of ten brands at a single point in time. The minimum size of the portfolio is one brand, which can be a Sonite or a Vodite.

Introducing a New Brand. If there are already five brands in a given market (Sonites or Vodites), it is no longer possible to introduce a new brand in that specific market, and the corresponding button on the right-hand side of the window is grey. If the number of brands in the market is less than five, clicking on the **Introduce new brand** button gives you access to a dialog box (see Figure 4.4).

First, you must enter the name of the new brand, following the rules laid out in Chapter 2. The first two letters, corresponding to the market and the firm, respectively, appear automatically. You need to enter only the last two letters of the brand name.

Enter the name of the R&D project, giving the prototype specifications for producing the brand, on the line "Base R&D project." Again, you must follow the naming conventions (the first letter is P for project, and the second letter indicates the market, Sonite or Vodite). The list of available R&D projects is provided for your information, and you can get the detailed specification of each project by clicking on the **View R&D report** button. You can select the name of the R&D project to be used as the prototype by clicking on it in the list of available projects. Obviously, for a brand to be introduced in a given period, the corresponding R&D project must have been successfully

Figure 4.4   Brand Introduction Dialog Box

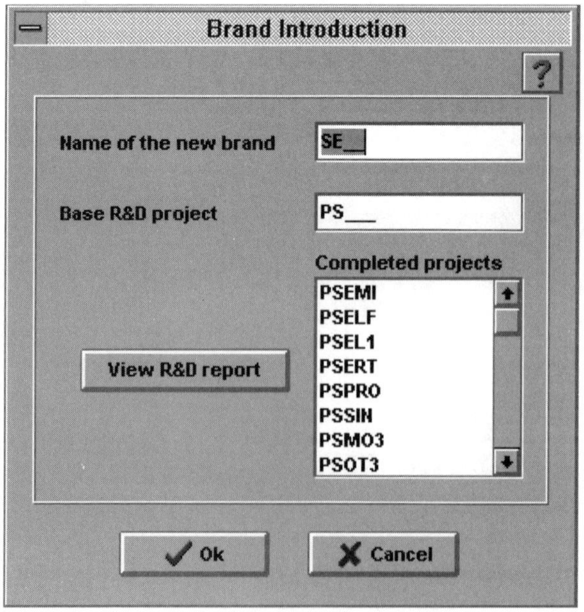

completed in a previous period. A project requested from the R&D department is never available for commercialization before the beginning of the following period.

You can use the **Undo** button in the **Brand Portfolio** window to remove a new brand that you added to the portfolio with the **Introduce new brand** button. Just select the brand and click on the **Undo** button; the new brand is removed from the "Marketed brand" list.

Modifying an Existing Brand. When you select a line in the "Marketed brand" table, the **Modification** and **Withdraw** buttons become operational. A dialog box, similar to the one just described for introducing a new brand, appears when you click on the **Modification** button (Figure 4.5). You must select the R&D project name corresponding to the new product specification from among the available R&D projects completed in prior periods. Of course, the name of the brand cannot be changed, since this would be a brand introduction.

The **Undo** button in the **Brand Portfolio** window can be used to cancel the changes you made to a brand using the **Modification** button. Just select the modified brand and click on the **Undo** button; the old brand specification (based on the prototype used in the prior period) replaces the changes you had made.

Withdrawing a Brand. The **Withdraw** option removes a brand that was marketed last period from the market for the following period. You first select the brand to be removed by clicking on it (anywhere on the line) in the upper table of the **Brand Portfolio** window, shown in Figure 4.3. Then, clicking on

Figure 4.5 Brand Modification Dialog Box

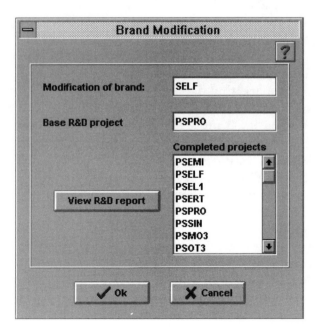

the **Withdraw** button moves the brand into the lower table of the **Brand Portfolio** window.

The **Undo** option enables you to reinsert a brand you have moved to the "Withdrawn brand" table. Just click on the brand that you no longer wish to have withdrawn from the market; this brand name will be highlighted. Then click on the **Undo** button, and the brand name will reappear in the "Marketed brand" table above.

If inventories remain when the brand is withdrawn from the market, they are sold to a trading company at 80% of the transfer cost, and the 20% loss is written off as an extraordinary cost. A brand that was marketed and then withdrawn from the market in the past may not be reintroduced later in the simulation.

Production, Price, and Advertising

In the **Production, Price, and Advertising** section of the **Decisions** module, you choose the market the same way you did in the **Brand Portfolio** section—by clicking on S or V. The brands to be marketed during the next period appear on tabs at the bottom of the screen (see Figure 4.6). Click on the tab of the brand to be displayed. You can now enter decisions on production, price, and advertising for that brand.

Production. The production level you request is based on your expectations of sales in the coming period. To respond to the real demand, the production department can adjust the quantity requested up to a limit of 20% (plus or minus) without incurring extra costs. So, if the initial inventory was zero and you had requested 100,000 units and demand was 130,000, production would automatically be adjusted upward to 120,000 units. Because of this flexibility in production, 100,000 units would be a good plan if actual demand were to fall between 80,000 units and 120,000 units. In this case, there would not be any inventory left at the end of the simulated period. However, if sales were to be 70,000 units (with a requested production level of 100,000 units), the ending inventory would be 10,000 units. The older stocks are sold first, and the inventory is evaluated using the first in, first out (FIFO) method.

It is possible to cut production completely by requesting zero production. The production department manages such requests without charging fixed costs to the marketing department. Note that for a new product, if the production level is low, the transfer cost may be above the base cost specified in the prototype R&D project. Indeed, until accumulated production reaches 100,000 units, fixed costs have to be allocated to fewer units than anticipated in the base cost estimate.

Normally, the inventory can change only with sales of the brand within the MARKSTRAT world. When an existing brand is modified, the old inventory is automatically sold to a trading company. The trading company offers less than production cost; specifically, old inventories are sold at 80% of the current transfer cost. This creates a loss of 20% of the transfer cost per unit for the company, which will appear as an extraordinary cost. In this case, the line labeled "Inventory sold to trading Co." (in Figure 4.6) will show the number of units for the obsolete product. In the "Brand production level"

Figure 4.6 Production, Price, and Advertising Window

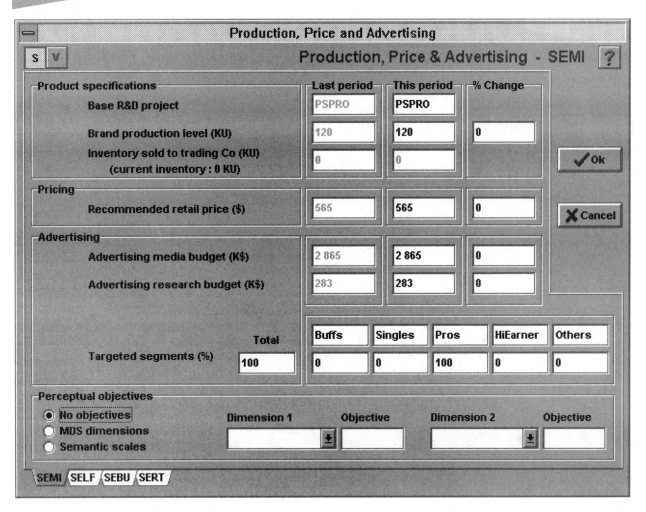

line, enter the number of units of the product with the new specifications to be produced.

If you have abnormally high inventory for one brand, you may decide to dispose of part of it. Your team can then decide the amount of inventory to sell to the trading company according to the pricing agreement described above (80% of the transfer cost). You might decide to sell none, in which case the remaining inventory will be sold through the market, or you might prefer to sell only a portion of the inventory. The number representing the quantity of inventory sold to the trading company is in thousands, so, for example, an entry of 100 indicates a quantity of 100,000.

Price. The recommended retail price of the brand is entered in MARK-STRAT Monetary Units, or MMUs ($). This is the list price for the consumer, and it corresponds to the price usually paid by consumers except in the case of short-term promotions and in the mass merchandiser channel, as discussed in Chapter 2.

Advertising. The advertising budget has two parts: the advertising media budget and the advertising research budget. These are defined in Chapter 2. The amount to spend on advertising research depends on the nature of the advertising message, so it can change depending on the maturity of the product or market, the awareness of a brand at a particular time, or the difficulty of the positioning task requested. Both budgets—media and research—are entered in thousands of MMUs ($), so an entry of 100 indicates an expenditure of $100,000.

In addition to the budget for advertising, an essential team decision concerns the target of this mass communication program. Your team can allocate its advertising budget among the various market segments. The entry in the "Targeted segments" line (in Figure 4.6) gives the proportion of the budget allocated to each segment. These proportions are used by media planners to allocate the media budget to communication vehicles targeting the appropriate segments.

Perceptual Objectives. When trying to reposition a brand through advertising, you need to indicate to the advertising agency what the desired perceptual objectives are. If your intent is just to raise brand awareness, without any perceptual objective, simply check the **No objectives** option.

Perceptual objectives can be provided either in terms of semantic scales (such as perceived weight, design, or volume) or in terms of the scales derived from the multidimensional scaling study (such as economy, performance, or convenience); just click on the scale of your choice. Objectives may be chosen on two communication dimensions. The choice of objectives to communicate depends on your scale choice. The appropriate dimensions will be displayed if you click on the arrow of the boxes for Dimensions 1 and 2. Once you have chosen a dimension, the objective level must be entered. For the scales based on the multidimensional scaling study, these numbers should be between +20 and –20, the maximum and minimum coordinates of the axes. For the semantic scales, the range is from 1 to 7.

These perceptual objectives convey information primarily of a qualitative nature (for example, how much the lightness of the product should be stressed) for the design of the advertising platform and copy, as well as for the selection of media compatible with the message. The numeric representation of these perceptual objectives is used only for communication purposes.

Communication may be on a single objective (a unique selling proposition). Note that the list box for Dimension 2 has **None** as an option in the list. The box should not remain blank; pick **None** to indicate that the communication is made on the single objective indicated in the objective box for Dimension 1.

Sales Force and Distribution

As discussed in Chapter 2, the sales force in the MARKSTRAT companies is organized by channel of distribution. Therefore, the primary sales force decision concerns the number of salespeople to assign to each channel. As Figure 4.7 indicates, you make an entry for the sales force size in each of the three channels. The sales force cost is shown in the right column.

Figure 4.7 Sales Force and Distribution Window

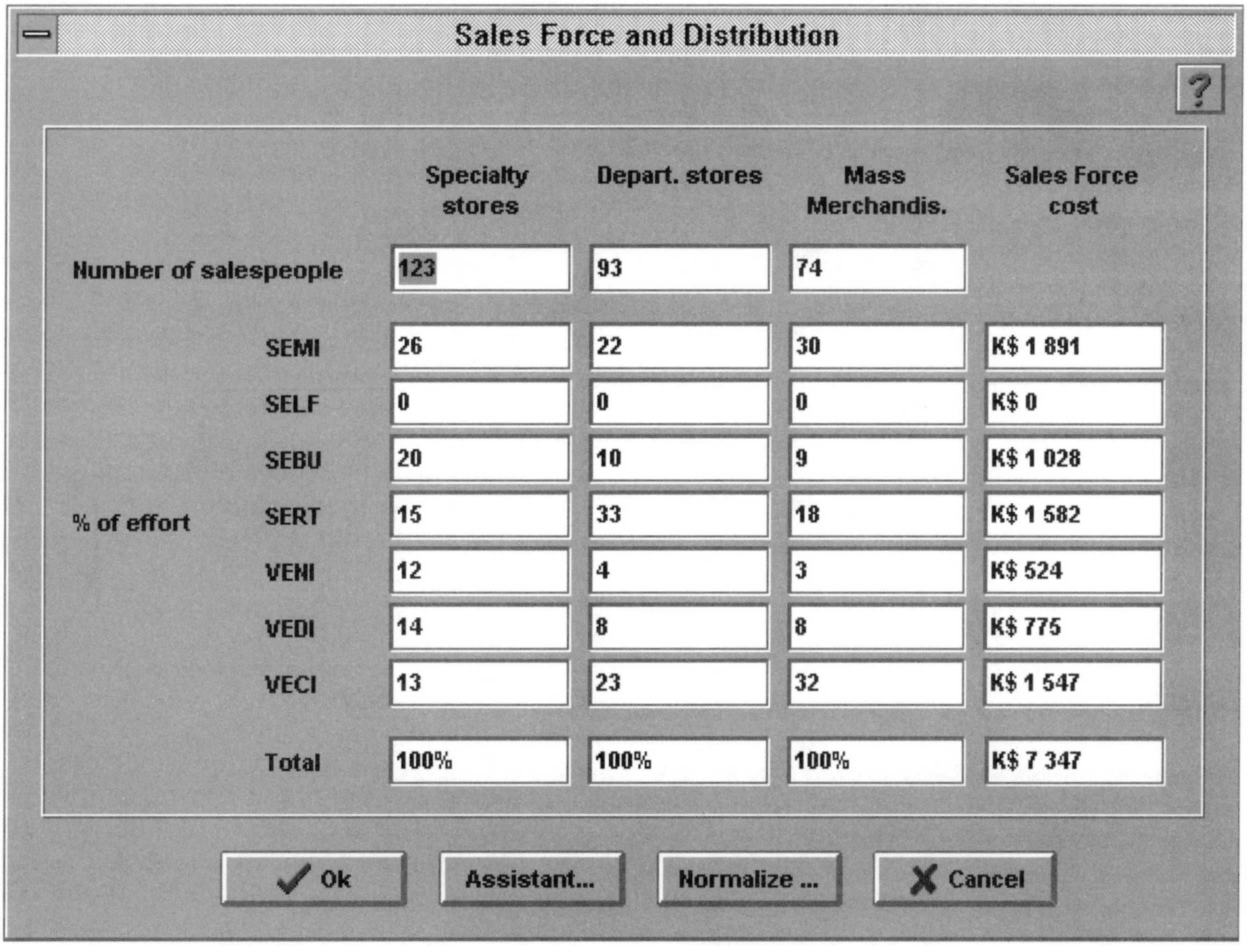

	Specialty stores	Depart. stores	Mass Merchandis.	Sales Force cost
Number of salespeople	123	93	74	
SEMI	26	22	30	K$ 1 891
SELF	0	0	0	K$ 0
SEBU	20	10	9	K$ 1 028
SERT	15	33	18	K$ 1 582
VENI	12	4	3	K$ 524
VEDI	14	8	8	K$ 775
VECI	13	23	32	K$ 1 547
Total	100%	100%	100%	K$ 7 347

% of effort (row label for SEMI–VECI)

| ✓ Ok | Assistant... | Normalize ... | ✗ Cancel |

Typically, the time and effort devoted by the sales force to the various brands offered by the firm should not be identical across channels. Some brands are specifically targeted at segments that are more likely to make their purchases in certain channels of distribution. An important sales force management decision concerns the allocation of time and effort to each of the brands. Each team can indicate how this effort should be allocated within a channel. For example, you could ask the salespeople in the specialty store channel to devote 25% of their time to the SAMA brand and 75% to the SALT brand. These are major guidelines, which the sales force will make every reasonable effort to follow. You just enter numbers that represent the desired relative sales effort for each brand and then click on the **Normalize** button so that the numbers are automatically re-estimated to add up to 100%. The resulting allocation of the sales force cost, by brand, is shown in the right-hand column of Figure 4.7, computed based on the percentage of time spent by the salespeople on each brand.

Allocating time is a complex decision, especially when information is limited. You can get help by clicking on the **Assistant** button, which generates automatic allocation options through a dialog box such as the one in Figure 4.8.

The "Decisions preview" table at first contains the decisions that were entered before you selected the **Assistant** option. Clicking on **Cancel** will restore these original values. Four options are proposed in automatic mode. The first option, **Equal allocation across all brands,** allocates an equal amount of effort to each brand within a channel. The second option, **Proportional to last period's unit sales,** allocates the effort in the proportions of the unit sales of each brand during the previous period; no effort is allocated to new brands that will be introduced during the current period. Obviously, these proportions will need to be changed so that some effort is devoted to new brands if there are any. However, this option serves as a starting point. The third option offers a similar rule but is based on the retail sales value instead of unit sales. The fourth option, **Proportional to last period's contribution,** uses the contribution after the marketing of each brand as a starting point for the effort allocation. Again, no effort is allocated to new brands. When you select an option, the resulting allocation is displayed in the "Decisions preview" table. If you click on **OK,** the dialog box will close and

---

Figure 4.8   Distribution Assistant Dialog Box

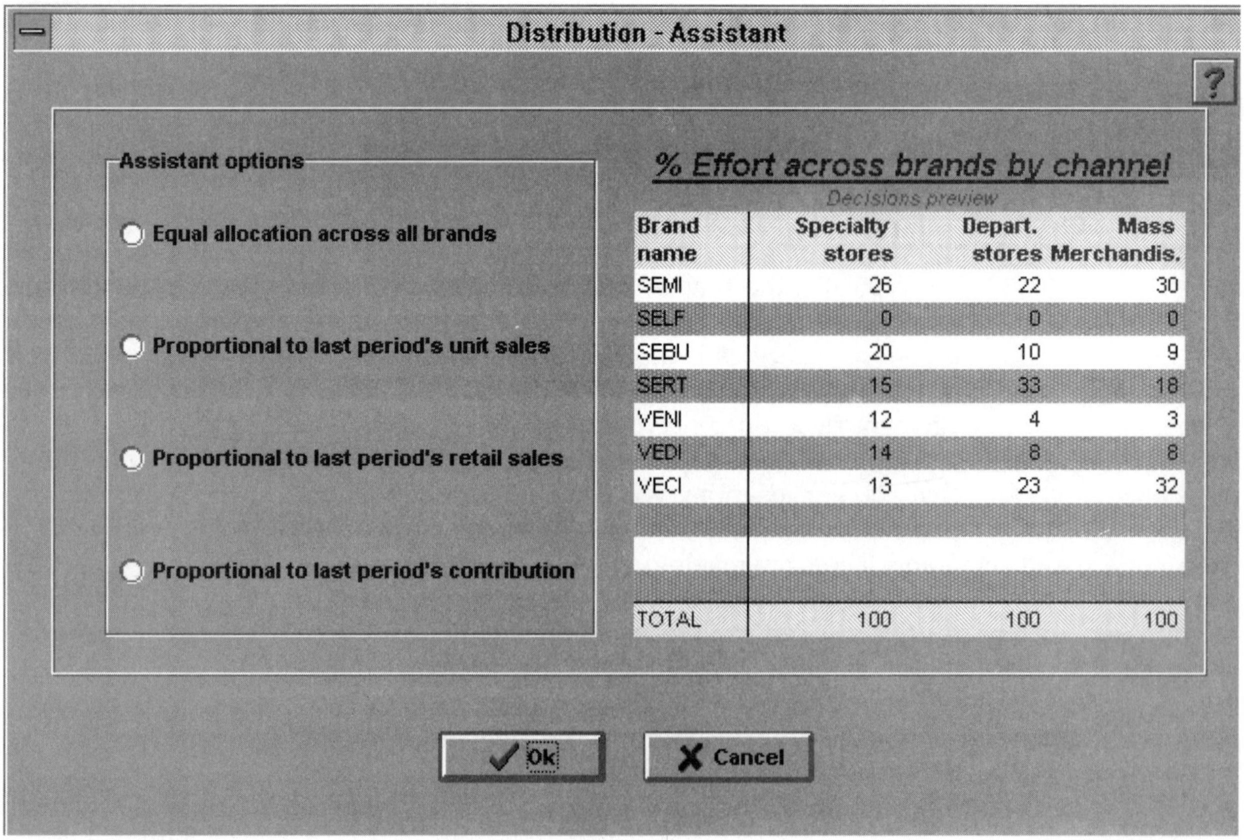

Distribution - Assistant

Assistant options

○ **Equal allocation across all brands**

○ **Proportional to last period's unit sales**

○ **Proportional to last period's retail sales**

○ **Proportional to last period's contribution**

% Effort across brands by channel

Decisions preview

Brand name	Specialty stores	Depart. stores	Mass Merchandis.
SEMI	26	22	30
SELF	0	0	0
SEBU	20	10	9
SERT	15	33	18
VENI	12	4	3
VEDI	14	8	8
VECI	13	23	32
TOTAL	100	100	100

✓ Ok   ✗ Cancel

the selected option will be displayed on the **Sales Force and Distribution** screen. You can still modify it before moving on to the next task.

Market Research Studies

You may request market research studies simply by checking the box for each of the studies you want (see Figure 4.9). Two buttons at the bottom of the screen allow you to order all studies or none at all. The cost of these studies appears as the boxes are checked. Some of the studies may apply only if there are brands marketed during the period (e.g., the consumer panel for the Vodite market). It may be difficult to anticipate whether competitors will launch new brands; however, you can order a study with the expectation that it will contain relevant information. If it does not, your firm will not be charged for the study. Nevertheless, the cost of the study has to be included in the budget.

Figure 4.9   Market Research Studies Window

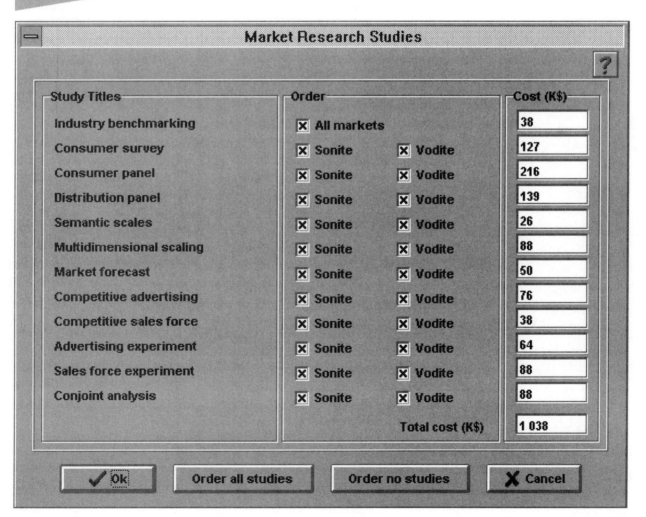

Research and Development

You may specify up to five R&D projects in one period for each of the two MARKSTRAT markets (five Sonite projects and five Vodite projects).* Name R&D projects according to the conventions described in Chapter 2. The name of an R&D project does not have to correspond to the name of an existing or planned brand, although all current and past R&D projects must have different names. Clicking on the S or V button retrieves the information on the Sonite or Vodite market, respectively. For example, in Figure 4.10, Firm E requests one R&D project in the Sonite market (the S button has been selected): PSOT1. This project name is shown at the bottom of the window. Use the buttons at the bottom of the window to start new R&D projects, to shelve a current project, or to continue a project that had been temporarily abandoned. You can also access the R&D report directly from this window. Information about a project appears in the upper section of the screen, which is divided into two parts: **Project Specifications** and **Response from R&D for ongoing project.**

For each project, list the values of the five physical characteristics for the desired product in the top row of the **Project Specifications** section of the window. The technically feasible ranges of these physical characteristics for Sonites and Vodites were indicated earlier, in Table 2.2 (see Chapter 2).

The requested base cost is the unit cost for the product that would be charged to the marketing department for a production batch of 100,000 units. Specify this cost once you have information about the feasibility of the product at a certain cost with a given R&D budget. In the absence of such information, you can, by checking the corresponding box, request that the R&D department search for the minimum transfer cost that is technically feasible. Although the completion of a project at a minimum cost is certainly advantageous to the firm, the budget requested based on this search may be higher than the allotted budget, delaying the introduction of a new brand or the modification of an existing brand. So, it is not advisable to always request the lowest cost possible.

The amount to spend in the current period is the budget allocated to the project during the current period.

In the case of a feasibility study, the corresponding box should be checked. The R&D department will reply with the minimum cost at which the product could realistically be produced and the R&D budget required to guarantee the completion of the project in the next period. This information is provided in the following period in the section titled **Response from R&D for ongoing project.** The numbers indicated by the R&D department for the minimum transfer cost and the budget required for completion are adjusted for inflation and guarantee the completion of the project if entered in the **Project Specifications** section for the next period's decisions.

On-Line Query. Clicking on the **On-line query** button opens a window titled **R&D on-line query** (see Figure 4.11). For the project specified in the **Project Specifications** section of the screen, the R&D department provides

---

*A maximum capacity of twenty Sonite and twenty Vodite projects applies over the simulation.

Figure 4.10 Research and Development Window

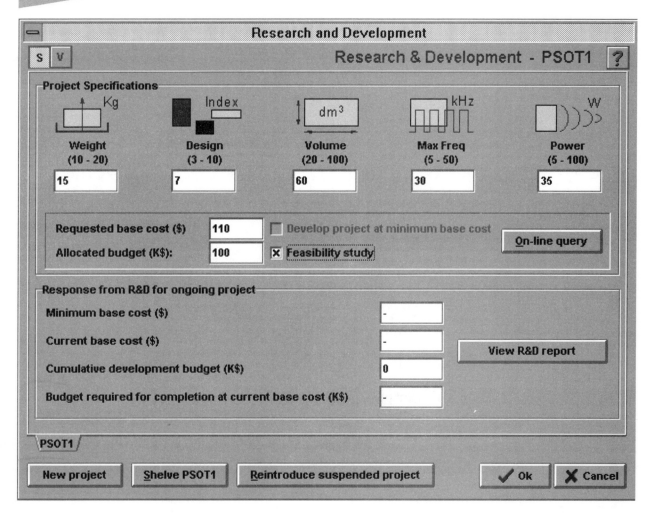

the minimum base cost and the budget required to complete the project. This information is also a guarantee from the R&D department that it will complete the project. However, given the short lead time for each request, the R&D department incorporates a safety margin. These figures, are, therefore, the minimum MMU ($) amounts that it guarantees but not the minimum that are feasible; a feasibility study done over the simulation period will provide more accurate estimates. These R&D on-line queries are informal dialogs with the R&D department that are considered part of the normal responsibilities of R&D and, as such, are free of charge. There is, however, a limit of five such on-line queries per period.

New Project. The **New Project** button generates a dialog box (see Figure 4.12) to facilitate the entry of information.

After you have assigned a name to the new project, check the box provided in order to use an existing prototype as a basis for the new project. An existing prototype can be selected from the list of available projects that your

Figure 4.11 ▸ R&D On-Line Query

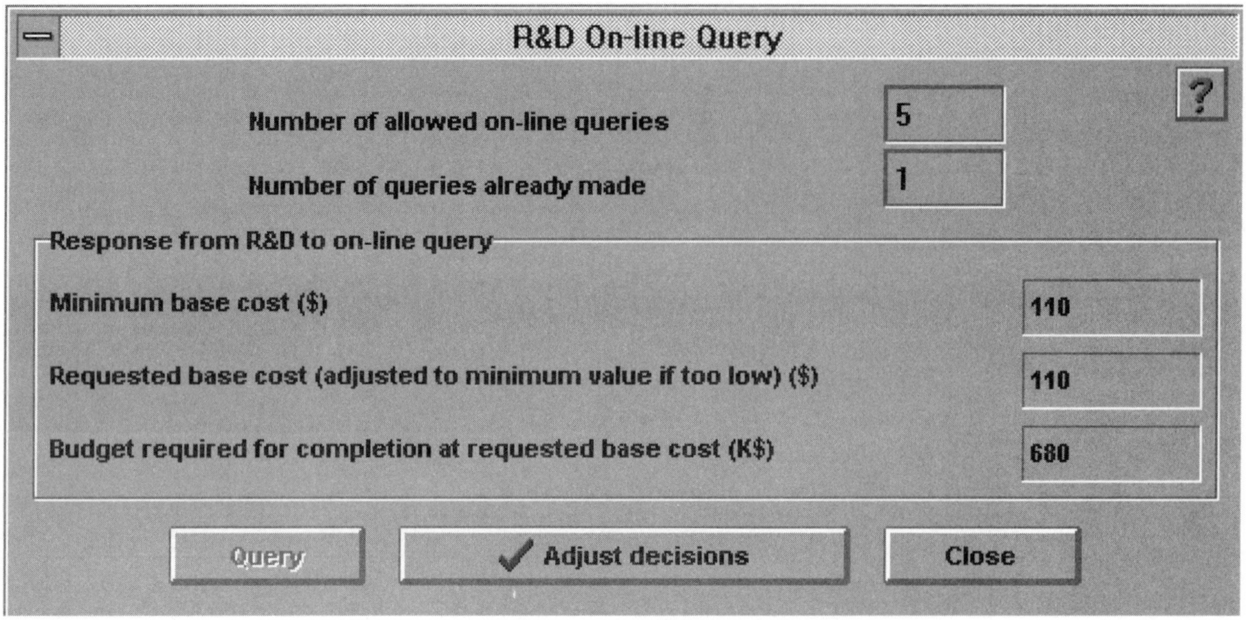

firm has launched in the past. You can get details about the specifications of these projects by clicking on the **View R&D report** button. For a cost reduction project, the physical characteristics specification of the old prototype will be used. Otherwise, the physical characteristics specification of the project selected can be used as a basis on which modifications will be made in the appropriate boxes after the new project has been created by clicking on the

Figure 4.12 ▸ New Project Dialog Box

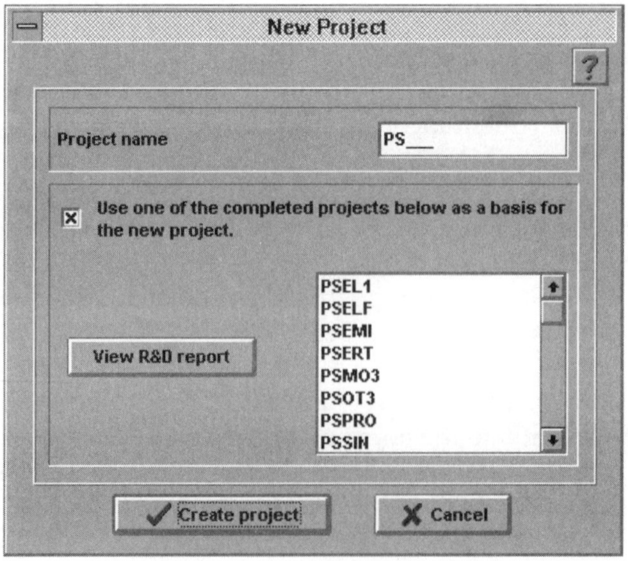

New project button. This avoids the need to re-enter values identical to those for an existing prototype. If a project is selected to serve as a basis for entering the physical characteristics specification of a new project, this does not mean that the R&D department will ignore the experience built from other R&D projects. Indeed, the R&D department will use the experience it has gained from all the activities it has pursued until the current period. This selection of a project is purely for the convenience of entering the values of the physical characteristics of the new project.

Shelve Project. The **Shelve** button displays the name of the currently selected project as a precaution against deleting an incorrect project. Clicking on the button removes the project from the current set of projects that the R&D department has been asked to research. (Note that when you are entering specifications for a new project this button is labeled **Delete** instead of **Shelve**.)

Reintroduce Suspended Project. You can use the **Reintroduce suspended project** button to recall a project that was started in prior years but abandoned (at least temporarily) in process. A list of such projects appears on the screen, as shown in Figure 4.13, and you can select a project from it. The **Project Specifications** section discussed above is then automatically completed.

Budget

The **Budget** button in the **Decisions** module window provides a financial recapitulation of all decisions. This information is divided into three parts, shown on tabs at the bottom of the screen: **Overall budget, Brand budget,** and **R&D budget** (see Figure 4.14).

Figure 4.13   Reintroduce Suspended Project Dialog Box

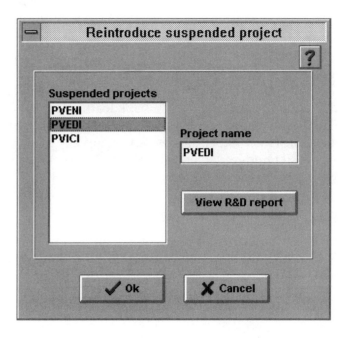

Figure 4.14   Overall Budget Section of Budget

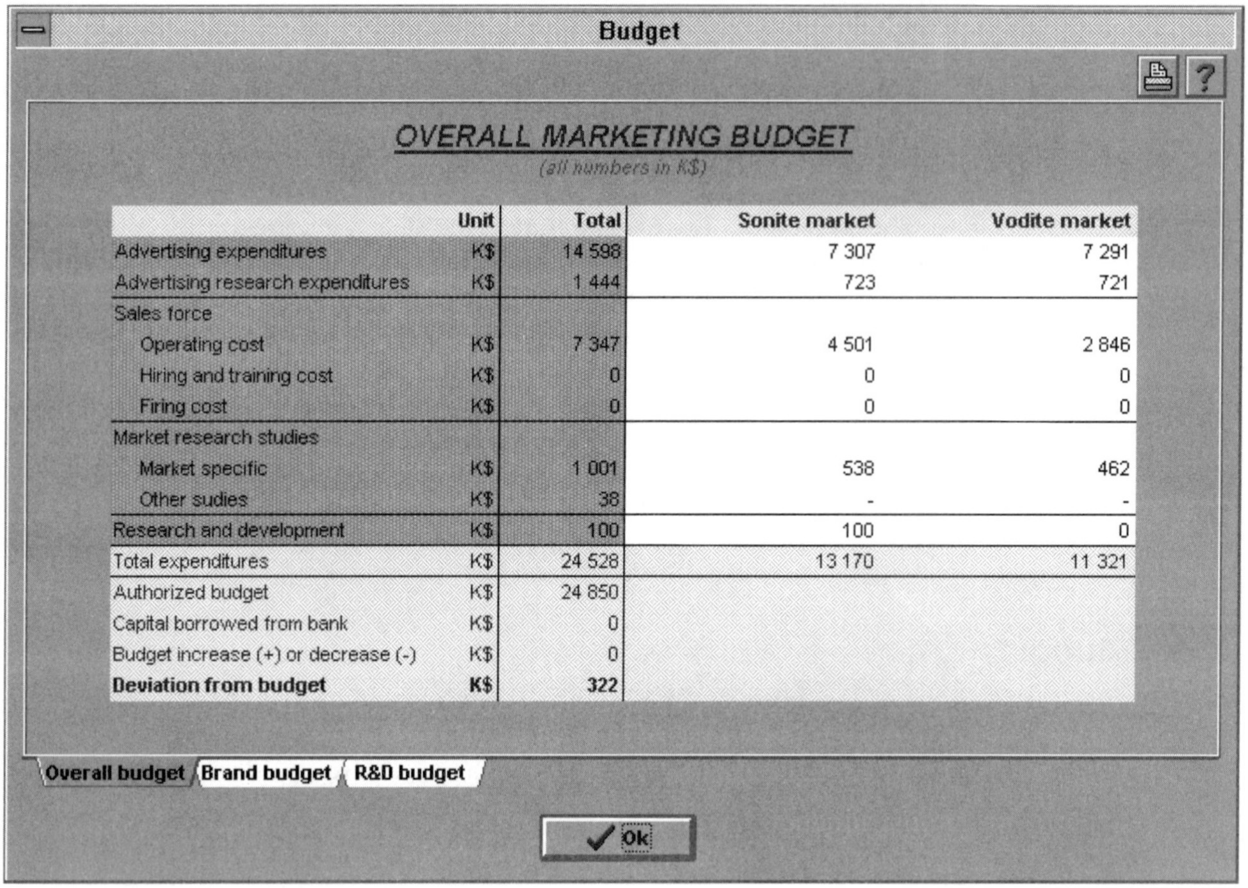

OVERALL MARKETING BUDGET
(all numbers in K$)

	Unit	Total	Sonite market	Vodite market
Advertising expenditures	K$	14 598	7 307	7 291
Advertising research expenditures	K$	1 444	723	721
Sales force				
Operating cost	K$	7 347	4 501	2 846
Hiring and training cost	K$	0	0	0
Firing cost	K$	0	0	0
Market research studies				
Market specific	K$	1 001	538	462
Other sudies	K$	38	-	-
Research and development	K$	100	100	0
Total expenditures	K$	24 528	13 170	11 321
Authorized budget	K$	24 850		
Capital borrowed from bank	K$	0		
Budget increase (+) or decrease (-)	K$	0		
Deviation from budget	**K$**	322		

Overall budget / Brand budget / R&D budget

✓ Ok

The budget items are presented on the **Overall budget** screen by market (Sonite and Vodite), as shown in Figure 4.14. The total expenditures are compared to the budget allocated to the firm, and a warning message appears if the budget is exceeded—in which case you should reduce your expenditures. Under some circumstances specified by your instructor, you may obtain a modification in your budget or a bank loan, as explained in the next section.

The **Brand budget** screen presents the allocation, by brand, for advertising and sales force expenditures. An example is given in Figure 4.15.

The **R&D budget** screen lists the R&D projects requested for the next period with the budget assigned to each (Figure 4.16).

Changes in Available Financial Resources

The financial resources available to a team can be changed through either a bank loan or a budget modification. Both of these changes have to be approved by your instructor. For this purpose, click on the **Interface** module to quit the **Decisions** module. The two options to obtain more resources are listed under the **Finances** sub-menu.

Figure 4.15   Brand Budget Section of Budget

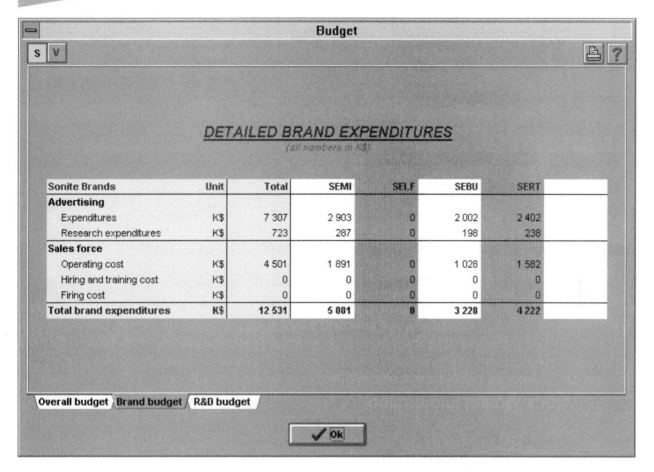

Firms can take bank loans to develop strategies that require greater budgets than they currently have but that are judged by the instructor to have good potential. You can enter the conditions of a new loan with the **New Loan** option and see the implications in the repayments to be made over the next few years by clicking the **Loan Schedule** option. Figure 4.17 shows the information required to specify the terms of a loan: the amount, the duration of the loan in number of periods, and the annual interest rate of the loan. The schedule, shown in Figure 4.18, assumes constant annuities over the loan period. Interest charges from a loan are automatically imputed to the team on the income statement. Capital borrowed does not have to be repaid, as normally repayment would appear on a statement of cash flow, which this simulation does not have. Note that the loan must be validated by the instructor—a space for the "Director's signature" appears in the New Loan Dialog Box.

Corporate budgets may change (**Change in budget** option) when corporate management is convinced that the budget allotted to a team should be modified to take into account unanticipated events or opportunities. Budget increases can be granted to a team if it demonstrates that its budget is

Figure 4.16   R&D Budget Section of Budget

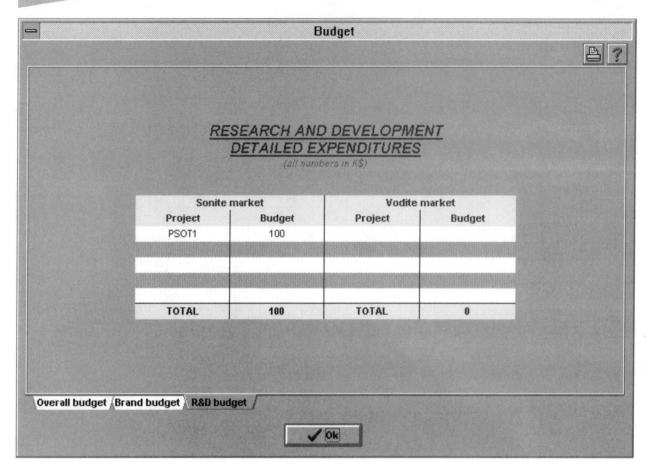

sub-optimal or for other reasons arising during the simulation. Budget cuts may be performed in exceptional circumstances. Although each team should use these options so that the real budget is reflected in its decision forms, pro forma analyses, and reports generated by the software, they will be considered effective only after they have been validated by the instructor (Figure 4.19).

Tabs appear at the bottom of the module window to allow you to move easily from one **Finances** option to another.

Summary

The **Summary** button in the **Decisions** module main window gives you access to five tables that provide a detailed description of all the decisions. You can view each of these tables by clicking on the corresponding tab at the bottom of the screen. The five tables are (1) **Brand management,** (2) **Sales force,** (3) **R&D projects,** (4) **Market studies,** and (5) **Loan and Budget.** The decisions can be either viewed on screen (as described below) or printed using the print icon, but they cannot be changed directly from the screen. To make

Figure 4.17 New Loan Dialog Box

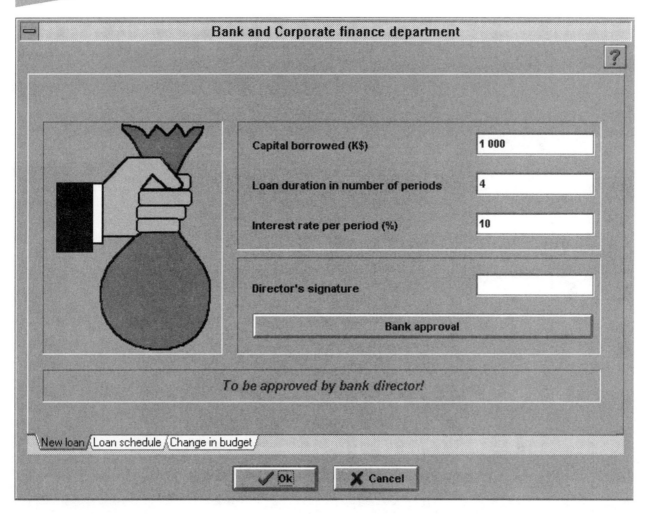

changes to the decisions, click on **OK** at the bottom of the screen and choose the section of the **Decisions** module where changes are desired.

An example of the "Brand management" table is shown in Figure 4.20. It recapitulates all the decisions about specific brands: the product portfolio in terms of the brands to be marketed, the prototype product on which each brand is based, the production level planned for next period, and the inventory sold to the trading company. It also shows the recommended retail price and the advertising decisions, including the perceptual objectives.

The "Sales force management" table summarizes the number of salespeople per channel of distribution and the recommended allocation of effort to each brand (see Figure 4.21 for an example).

Figure 4.22 shows the projects that the R&D department has been requested to research during the next period.

The market research studies are marked "Yes" to indicate that the study has been ordered or "No" otherwise (see Figure 4.23).

Figure 4.18   Loan Schedule Example

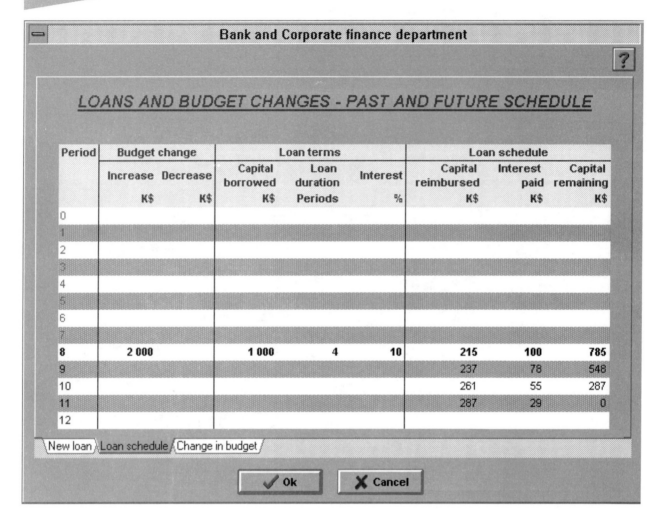

Period	Budget change		Loan terms			Loan schedule		
	Increase K\$	Decrease K\$	Capital borrowed K\$	Loan duration Periods	Interest %	Capital reimbursed K\$	Interest paid K\$	Capital remaining K\$
0								
1								
2								
3								
4								
5								
6								
7								
8	2 000		1 000	4	10	215	100	785
9						237	78	548
10						261	55	287
11						287	29	0
12								

New loan \ Loan schedule / Change in budget /

✓ Ok   ✗ Cancel

Finally, Figure 4.24 shows the screen summarizing the budget changes and loans that may have been agreed on with the instructor.

Errors and Warnings

Errors indicate corrections that should be made because of inconsistent decisions. Warnings draw attention to possible problems detected by the software and indicate that you need to check the entry carefully to make sure it is correct. Indeed, the software has been designed to catch errors of this nature. Some actions are clearly incompatible with the current status of a firm's operation, in which case the software for entering the team decisions will not accept the input. In other cases, however, only a warning message will appear in the **Warnings** window. Figure 4.25 shows examples of error and warning messages.

You are advised not to ignore these messages, even if they are only warnings, and to take appropriate action wherever desirable and possible. For instance, if you have exceeded the assigned budget, you will receive a warning

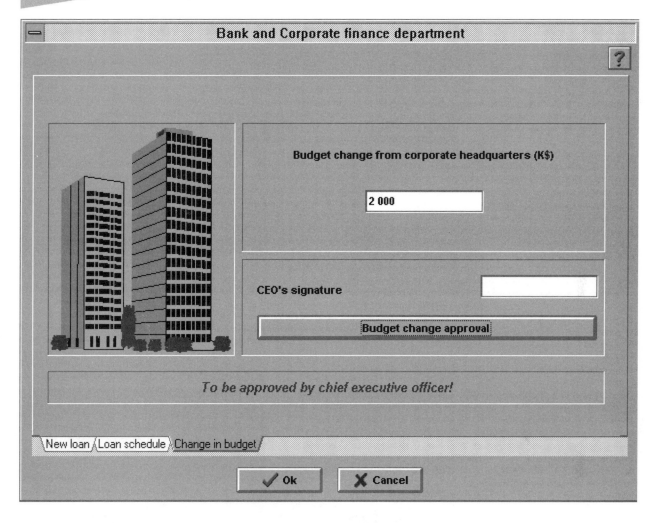

Figure 4.19 Budget Change Dialog Box

to avoid arbitrary cuts in marketing expenditures.* If the price of a given brand is increased to such a level that market response is very unfavorable, you will get a warning that downward adjustments will be automatically performed.

THE COMPANY REPORT

The **Company Report** has six sections (which are discussed in turn): **Company Results, Brand Results, Research and Development, Cumulative**

---

*In such a case, advertising expenditures are cut first. If this is insufficient to maintain the expenditures within the budget, sales force expenditures are cut next, then R&D project budgets are cut, and finally marketing research studies are deleted one by one until the expenses are within the budget limit.

Figure 4.20 Brand Management Section of Summary

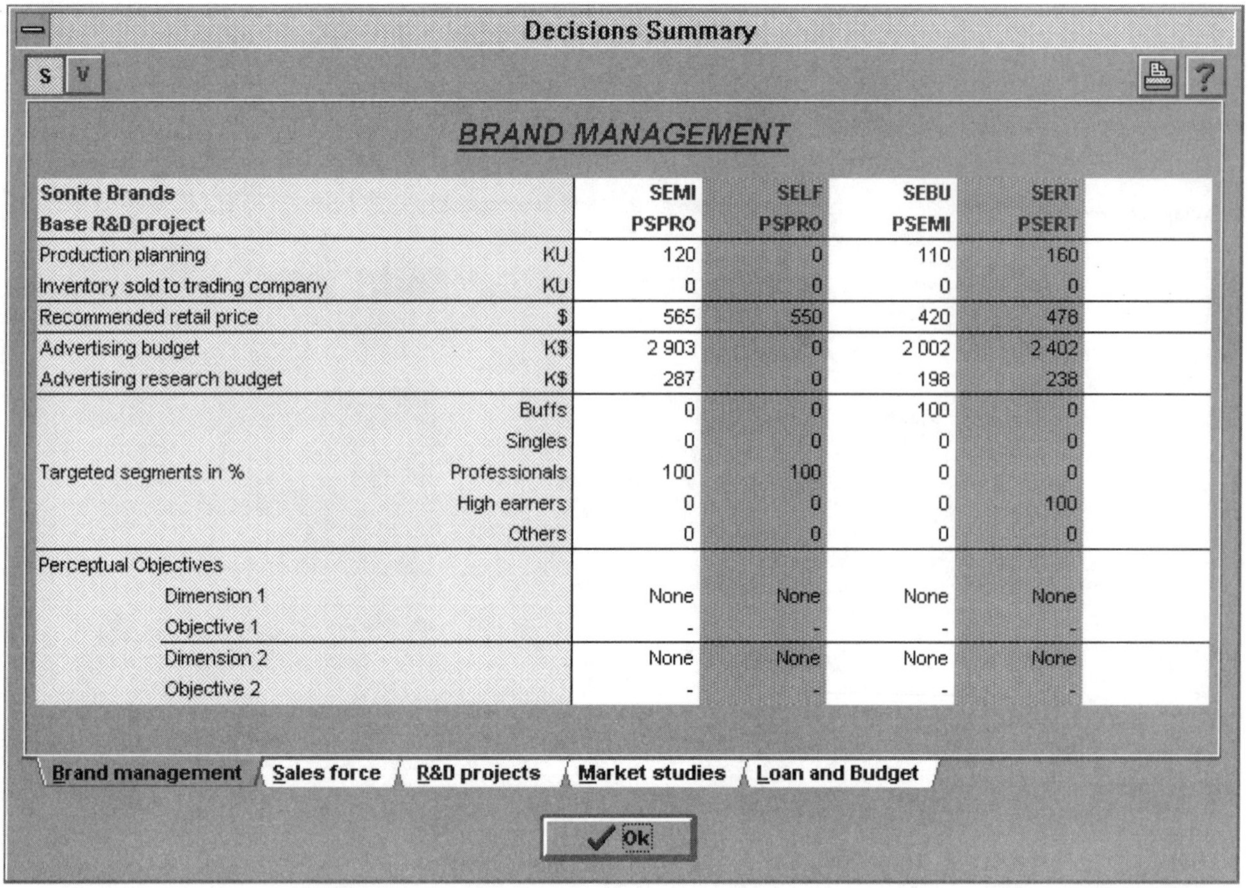

Sonite Brands		SEMI	SELF	SEBU	SERT
Base R&D project		PSPRO	PSPRO	PSEMI	PSERT
Production planning	KU	120	0	110	160
Inventory sold to trading company	KU	0	0	0	0
Recommended retail price	$	565	550	420	478
Advertising budget	K$	2 903	0	2 002	2 402
Advertising research budget	K$	287	0	198	238
Targeted segments in %	Buffs	0	0	100	0
	Singles	0	0	0	0
	Professionals	100	100	0	0
	High earners	0	0	0	100
	Others	0	0	0	0
Perceptual Objectives					
Dimension 1		None	None	None	None
Objective 1		-	-	-	-
Dimension 2		None	None	None	None
Objective 2		-	-	-	-

Results, Messages, and **Past Decisions.** Figures 4.26 through 4.38 present the sections of a sample Company Report. The sample is shown for illustrative purposes only, so do not use the displayed figures in making your decisions. The data in these figures have nothing to do with your run of MARKSTRAT.

Use the hands icon in the tools menu to move forward or backward through the multiple screens of the report. You can also access these screens directly, using the **Report** window menu items.

Company Results

The **Company Results** section shows the performance of the firm during the simulated period. First the "Company scorecard" provides an overall picture of the firm's performance. Then a table gives a more detailed description of the performance of the firm by market (Sonite and Vodite). Changes in budgets and information on current and past loans are given in the **Loan schedule** option.

Company Scorecard. The "Company scorecard" is a general summary of the firm's overall performance. It includes a comparison with the previous

Figure 4.21   Sales Force Section of Summary

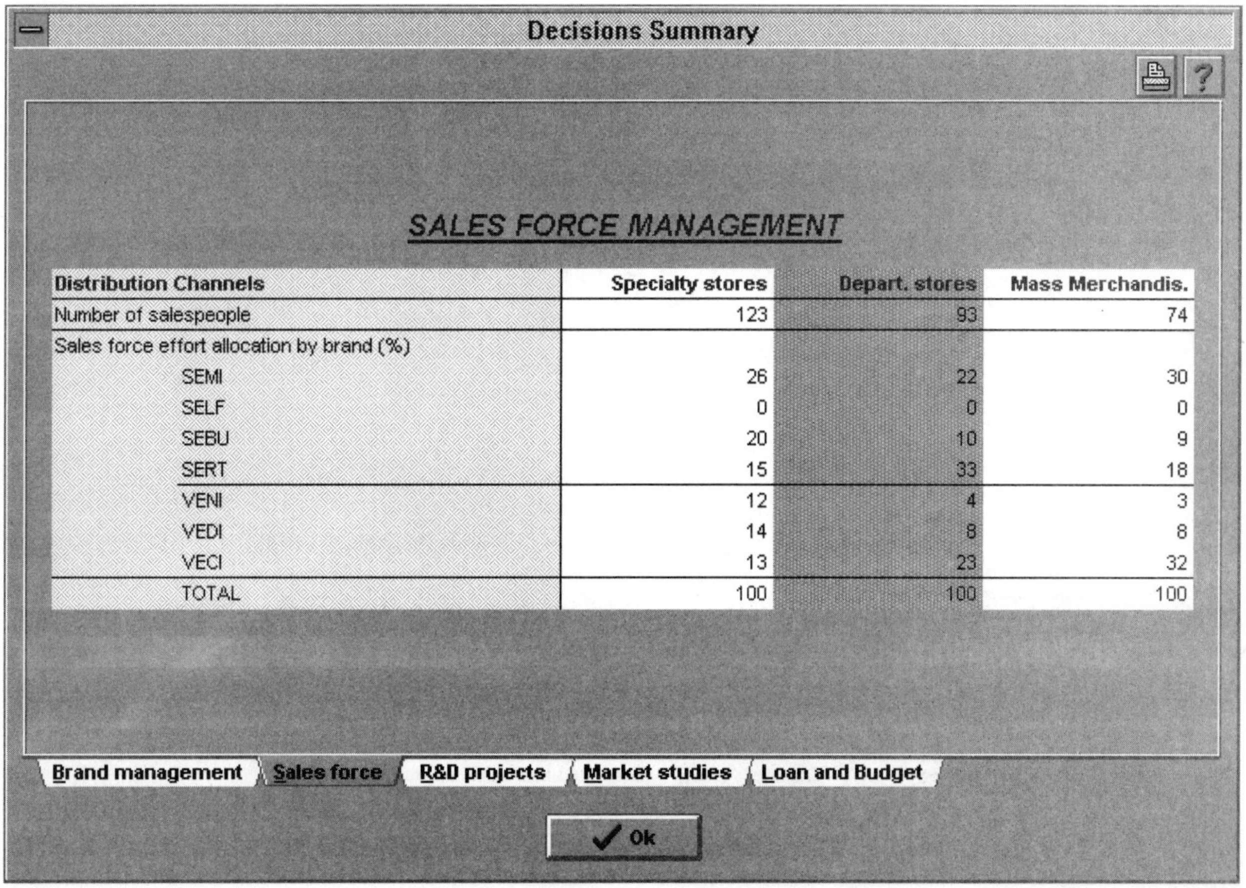

Decisions Summary

SALES FORCE MANAGEMENT

Distribution Channels	Specialty stores	Depart. stores	Mass Merchandis.
Number of salespeople	123	93	74
Sales force effort allocation by brand (%)			
SEMI	26	22	30
SELF	0	0	0
SEBU	20	10	9
SERT	15	33	18
VENI	12	4	3
VEDI	14	8	8
VECI	13	23	32
TOTAL	100	100	100

Brand management   Sales force   R&D projects   Market studies   Loan and Budget

✓ Ok

year's results and presents the firm's evolution since Period 0. An example appears in Figure 4.26.

Four overall measures of performance are reported: market share, retail sales, contribution, and shareholder value.

The stock price index is based on multiple measures of the performance of the firm in its industry. The return on investment is the ratio of the net contribution to the expenditures (marketing, market research, and research and development).

Company Performance. An example of company performance, by market, is given in Figure 4.27.

The sales data contain information on units sold, average retail price, average selling price, and revenues. The sales are reported in units for each market separately. The total number of units sold across markets is also reported, but interpret this figure carefully as it may include very different products; use it only as a general measure of the activity level of the firm. The "Average retail price" corresponds to the average prices paid by consumers, depending on the channels used by the brand, for all the firm's brands on the market. The "Average selling price" used in the computation of revenues also depends on the way brand sales are split among the three distribution

Figure 4.22 R&D Projects Section of Summary

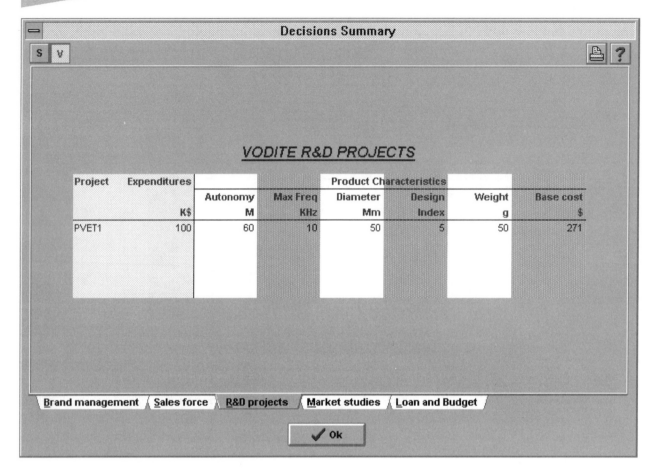

channels, since channel margins are different. Like the total number of units sold by the firm, the average retail and selling prices across markets are aggregate measures of two markets that are very different. As such, these numbers should be interpreted cautiously. "Revenues" are simply the sales in MMUs generated by each market and globally by the firm.

The "Contribution before marketing" is computed before including the marketing expenses for media advertising, advertising research, and sales force. It is based on revenues minus the cost of goods sold, inventory costs, and losses due to the disposal of inventory. The unit transfer cost is the price that the marketing department was charged for the units sold. Units produced but not sold are not charged to the marketing department. The marketing department is charged, though, for inventory holding costs, because it is responsible for the forecasts used for production volumes. The inventory is valued at transfer costs on a first in, first out basis, and its holding costs are computed as a percentage of its value, according to the rate given in the Newsletter. Inventory disposed of is written off at a cost of 20% of its transfer cost. These costs appear on the "Inventory disposal loss" line. Reminder: when a brand's physical characteristics are modified, the same charges apply for the inventory of the old product that is sold to the trading company. This

Figure 4.23 Market Research Studies Section of Summary

Decisions Summary

MARKET RESEARCH STUDIES

Study	Market covered by study		
	All markets	**Sonite**	**Vodite**
Industry benchmarking	Yes	-	-
Consumer survey	-	Yes	Yes
Consumer panel	-	Yes	Yes
Distribution panel	-	Yes	Yes
Semantic scales	-	Yes	Yes
Multidimensional scaling	-	Yes	Yes
Market forecast	-	Yes	Yes
Competitive advertising	-	Yes	Yes
Competitive sales force	-	Yes	Yes
Advertising experiment	-	Yes	Yes
Sales force experiment	-	Yes	Yes
Conjoint analysis	-	Yes	Yes

Brand management / Sales force / R&D projects / **Market studies** / Loan and Budget

✓ Ok

inventory disposal loss is *not* part of the expenses charged to the current period budget.

The total marketing expenses for advertising and sales force are then subtracted from the contribution before marketing to give the "Contribution after marketing."

The remaining expenses for market research studies and for R&D for each market are then subtracted, together with possible interest paid and exceptional cost, to give the net contribution (if there is any exceptional profit, it will be added). Note that for the market research studies costs the "Total" column includes the cost of the benchmarking study, which is not assigned to a specific market. (Therefore, the sum of the market research studies for the two markets does not necessarily equal the "Total" amount.)

The budget available for the next period is shown at the bottom of the **Company Performance** section. The corporate office guarantees your team a budget based on your performance using the simple rule of 40% of the net contribution generated in the previous period. However, a minimum budget level allows each team to sustain marketing activities even when the net marketing contribution is low or negative. There is also a maximum budget level, reflecting the reallocation of resources through the corporation as a whole.

Figure 4.24   Loan and Budget Section of Summary

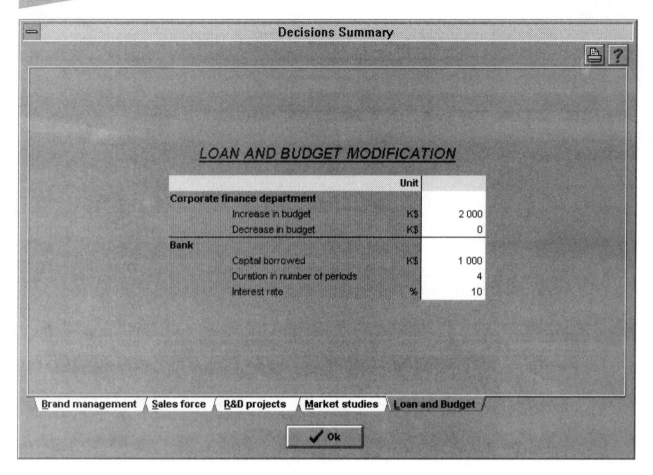

The corporate office may authorize changes in this budget in some circumstances, but a budget change requires specific arguments justifying a deviation from the normal budget allocation rule. The advertising, sales force, market research, and R&D expenditures for the next period should fit within this budget.

Loan Schedule. The **Loan Schedule** option gives information about changes in budgets and, more specifically, the details of all loans carried by the firm. Each loan is described with the terms of the loan (capital borrowed, loan duration, and interest charged), as in Figure 4.18. The status of the loan in each period is shown with the capital reimbursed, the interest paid, and the capital remaining. Information on past periods is dimmed. This corresponds to the information described earlier in this chapter under "Changes in Available Financial Resources."

Brand Results

For each of the company's brands, a detailed analysis of profitability is provided in the "Contribution by brand" table. Market share and distribution coverage information is provided in a separate window.

Figure 4.25   Example of Error and Warning Messages

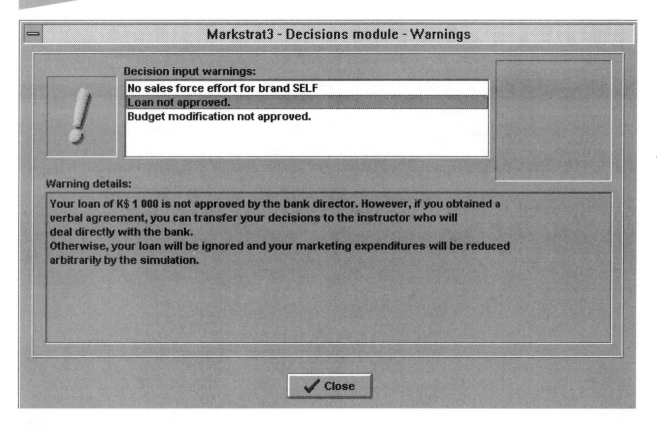

Figure 4.26   Company Scorecard

COMPANY SCORECARD

	Unit	Annual results			Evolution since P0	
		Period 6	Period 7	%change	Ratio P7/P0	Average growth
Market share						
Total	%$	26.5%	28.2%	+6.4%	× 1.17	+2.2%
Sonite market	%$	19.9%	23.5%	+18.1%	× 0.97	-0.4%
Vodite market	%$	38.8%	33.8%	-12.9%	-	-
Retail sales						
Total	K$	251 700	319 047	+26.8%	× 4.53	+24.1%
Sonite market	K$	123 753	144 616	+16.9%	× 2.05	+10.8%
Vodite market	K$	127 947	174 430	+36.3%	-	-
Contribution						
Before marketing	K$	80 195	108 968	+35.9%	× 6.13	+29.6%
After marketing	K$	67 974	85 736	+26.1%	× 6.83	+31.6%
Net	K$	63 245	84 618	+33.8%	× 6.87	+31.7%
Cumulative net	K$	238 424	323 042	+35.5%	× 26.24	+59.5%
Shareholder value						
Stock price index	Base 1000	2 097	2 459	+17.3%	× 2.46	+13.7%
Current return on investment	Ratio	3.73	3.47	-6.9%	× 1.54	+6.4%
Cumulative return on investment	Ratio	3.08	3.18	+3.0%	× 1.41	+5.1%

COMPANY PERFORMANCE				
	Unit	Total	Sonite market	Vodite market
Sales				
Units sold	U	525 247	298 326	226 921
Average retail price	$	607	485	769
Average selling price	$	398	314	507
Revenues	K$	208 844	93 803	115 041
Production				
Units produced	U	621 464	319 864	301 600
Cost of goods sold	K$	-96 150	-42 816	-53 333
Inventory holding cost	K$	-2 729	-1 073	-1 656
Inventory disposal loss	K$	-996	-996	0
Contribution before marketing	K$	108 967	48 916	60 051
Marketing				
Advertising expenditures	K$	-14 406	-7 211	-7 194
Advertising research expenditures	K$	-1 424	-713	-711
Sales force	K$	-7 400	-4 533	-2 866
Contribution after marketing	K$	85 736	36 458	49 277
Other expenses				
Market research studies	K$	-1 018	-527	-453
Research and development	K$	-100	-100	0
Interest paid	K$	0		
Exceptional cost or profit	K$	0		
Net contribution	K$	84 618		
Next period budget	K$	24 850		

Contribution by Brand. Figure 4.28 is an example of the information given for each brand. The information in the table follows the information described in the **Company Performance** section, but the data are not aggregated by market; instead, the data are presented by brand.

The only information in this table that is not in the "Company performance" table is the current unit base cost of a brand. This might differ from the average unit base cost if inventories were left at the end of the previous period. The average unit base cost is computed on a first in, first out basis.

Market Shares and Distribution Coverage. The market share of each brand in the market is computed on the basis of units sold as well as the retail price value, as shown in Figure 4.29. The percentage of retail outlets carrying the brand in each channel is given along with the total number of outlets available in each channel.

Research and Development Results

All the R&D projects that the firm has pursued in the current and past periods are listed, by product, in the **Research and Development Results** section. (Figure 4.30 is a "Sonite R&D projects" table.) These projects include those that already existed in the firm at the beginning of the simulation (PSEMI and PSELF in the example). For each R&D project, the following information is given:

Figure 4.28 ▶ Contribution by Brand

CONTRIBUTION BY BRAND
(SONITE BRANDS)

Sonite Brands Base R&D project	Unit	Total	SEMI PSPRO	SELF PSPRO	SEBU PSEMI	SERT PSERT	
Sales							
Units sold	U	298 326	103 864	888	86 730	106 844	
Average retail price	$	485	553	536	417	473	
Average selling price	$	314	358	346	260	316	
Revenues	K$	93 801	37 183	307	22 549	33 762	
Production							
Units produced	U	319 864	103 864	0	88 000	128 000	
Current unit transfer cost	$	-	171	171	103	145	
Average unit transfer cost	$	144	171	211	103	149	
Cost of goods sold	K$	-42 815	-17 760	-187	-8 933	-15 935	
Units in inventory	U	80 729	0	26 677	1 270	52 782	
Inventory holding cost	K$	-1 072	0	-450	-10	-612	
Inventory disposal loss	K$	-996	-996	0	0	0	
Contribution before marketing	K$	48 916	18 425	-330	13 606	17 215	
Marketing							
Advertising expenditures	K$	-7 209	-2 864	0	-1 975	-2 370	
Advertising research expenditures	K$	-712	-283	0	-195	-234	
Sales force	K$	-4 532	-1 904	0	-1 035	-1 593	
Contribution after marketing	K$	36 458	13 372	-330	10 400	13 016	

- Name.
- Physical characteristics: the specifications of each project on all five physical characteristics.
- Base cost: the average unit cost at which the product can be manufactured next period, with a first batch of 100,000 units, and the minimum cost at which the product could realistically be produced if the project were to be pursued.
- Cumulative expenditures: the total expenditures made on each project up to its completion or up to the current period.
- Budget required next period for completion: the budget necessary to complete the project. If the project has been successfully completed and

Figure 4.29 ▶ Market Shares and Distribution Coverage

MARKET SHARES AND DISTRIBUTION COVERAGE
(SONITE BRANDS)

Sonite Brands	Unit	Total	SEMI	SELF	SEBU	SERT	
Market shares	%U	15.2%	5.3%	0.0%	4.4%	5.5%	
	%$	23.5%	9.3%	0.1%	5.9%	8.2%	
Distribution coverage in %							
Specialty stores (27 273 outlets)	%		52.0%	0.0%	51.1%	44.6%	
Department stores (6 638 outlets)	%		41.7%	0.0%	25.9%	50.4%	
Mass Merchandisers (12 603 outlets)	%		28.0%	0.0%	13.2%	22.1%	

Figure 4.30   R&D Results

	Physical Characteristics					Base Cost $		Allocated Budget K$	
Name	Weight (Kg)	Design (Index)	Volume (Dm3)	Max Freq (KHz)	Power (W)	Current	Minimum realistic	Cumulative	Req. for completion
PSEMI	13	7	40	40	75	197	174	1 500	Available
PSELF	15	4	40	45	90	248	184	2 000	Available
PSEL1	15	4	40	45	90	196	184	500	Available
PSERT	13	7	50	30	55	198	139	940	Available
PSPRO	14	5	50	40	80	197	170	1 250	Available
PSSIN	15	5	65	30	60	181	133	1 000	Available
PSMO3	12	7	70	28	58	169	137	950	Available
PSOT3	14	5	70	15	35	111	89	1 150	Available
PSE77	15	5	77	20	30	85	85	100	730
PSOT1	15	7	60	30	35	110	110	100	580

is therefore available to introduce or modify brands, the availability of the prototype is indicated.

Some of the facts mentioned above concerning communication from the R&D department about additional investment required and minimum realistic unit cost are further explained in Chapter 7.

The information in this first R&D table concerns all the Sonite projects ever requested of the R&D department. It is also possible to view, in a separate window, only projects currently available or only ongoing (not yet completed) projects.

Cumulative Results

Cumulative results obtained by the company since the beginning of Period 0 are presented in two tables: "Cumulative brand results" (Figure 4.31) and "Cumulative company performance" (Figure 4.32). The cumulative market results (the "Cumulative company performance" table) aggregate the brand results for the Sonite and Vodite markets separately. For brands available at the start of the simulation, the cumulative results include the results of Period 0. No R&D projects are in progress and no market research studies are available in Period 0.

Messages

Some error and warning messages are given in the **Decisions** module. If your team does not make any change to its decisions, corrective action will be taken and a message in **Company Report** will inform you of such action. For example, if you have exceeded the assigned budget, the arbitrary cuts in marketing expenditures that need to be implemented to make the decisions fit within the budget will be listed. Messages also indicate cases where obsolete inventories of deleted or modified brands had to be disposed of, resulting in a cost to the firm. Each message is explained in this manual in the chapter

Figure 4.31 Cumulative Brand Results

CUMULATIVE BRAND RESULTS

Brand	Results since period	Sales			Production		Marketing		Contrib. after mktg.
		Units sold	Retail sales	Revenues	Cost of goods sold	Inventory costs	Advertising	Sales force	
		KU	K$	K$	K$	K$	K$	K$	K$
SEMI	0	1 057	496 102	319 302	127 897	1 742	14 142	7 725	167 796
SELF	0	173	92 247	58 599	35 886	4 383	6 612	3 551	8 167
SEBU	2	437	170 905	105 949	45 272	161	7 399	4 084	49 033
SERT	4	292	136 217	91 484	48 545	1 007	7 310	4 030	30 592
VENI	3	102	138 503	86 461	57 971	5 039	6 151	2 565	14 736
VEDI	4	113	110 473	69 934	38 327	2 344	5 501	2 054	21 707
VECI	4	292	213 858	144 528	79 363	3 622	6 570	3 525	51 448
Total Sonite		1 958	895 471	575 334	257 600	7 293	35 463	19 390	255 588
Total Vodite		508	462 834	300 923	175 661	11 004	18 223	8 143	87 891
Total all markets		**2 466**	**1 358 305**	**876 257**	**433 261**	**18 297**	**53 687**	**27 533**	**343 479**

corresponding to the specific issue. Note that many of these messages appear only if a team fails to consider the warning messages provided by the software for entering the decisions. Messages sent by the instructor to all firms or to a specific firm may also be given in this section. Examples are shown in Figure 4.33.

Figure 4.32 Cumulative Company Performance

CUMULATIVE COMPANY PERFORMANCE

	Unit	Total	Sonite market	Vodite market
Sales				
Units sold	KU	2 466	1 958	508
Retail sales	K$	1 358 305	895 471	462 834
Revenues	K$	876 257	575 334	300 923
Production				
Cost of goods sold	K$	-433 261	-257 600	-175 661
Inventory holding and disposal cost	K$	-18 297	-7 293	-11 004
Marketing				
Total advertising expenditures	K$	-53 687	-35 463	-18 223
Sales force expenditures	K$	-27 533	-19 390	-8 143
Contribution after marketing	K$	**343 479**	**255 588**	**87 891**
Other expenses				
Market research studies	K$	-5 808	-3 450	-2 152
Research and development	K$	-14 630	-5 990	-8 640
Interest paid	K$	0		
Exceptional cost or profit	K$	0		
Net contribution	K$	**323 042**		

Figure 4.33   Example of Messages in Company Report

INSTRUCTOR AND SIMULATION MESSAGES

Messages
Your budget limit of K$ 24 350 was overspent by K$ 211.
Your marketing expenditures were arbitrarily reduced as follows:
* advertising expenditures reduced by K$ 211 across all brands,
* R&D expenditures reduced by K$ 0 across all projects.
The physical characteristics of brand SEMI were modified this period. The obsolete
inventory (49355 units) was sold to a trading company at 80.0 % of transfer cost.
The difference was charged as an inventory disposal loss of K$997.

Past Decisions

This section recapitulates decisions made by your firm in previous periods. Its purpose is only to provide you with a record of the data that were actually used by the simulation. The period number is chosen in the selection menu. This **Past Decisions** section corresponds exactly to the decisions summary of the **Decisions** module, presented earlier. So that you can follow the complete Company Report, the decisions for the current period are shown in Figures 4.34 through 4.38. You can see how the team has managed its brands, its sales force, and its R&D; which market research studies it has bought for the Sonite and Vodite markets; and, finally, any loans and changes in budget authorized by the MARKSTRAT instructor.

NEWSLETTER

The **Newsletter** module provides information that would normally be known to the industry because it is public information or information that is easy to get without significant cost. This includes stock market information about competing firms and general key performance indicators. It also includes economic variables that may have an impact on the MARKSTRAT markets. The Newsletter gives the cost of market research studies that can be ordered for the next period.

Stock Market Information

Stock Price Indices. Stock prices are given for all the firms competing in the MARKSTRAT markets (Figure 4.39). The prices are indexed on a base of 1000 for each firm in Period 0. As indicated earlier, this stock price index is an overall measure of the performance of the MARKSTRAT firms. The market capitalization of each firm is also provided. The net contribution of each firm is given both for the current period and cumulatively since Period 0.

Figure 4.34 Example of Past Decisions (Brand Management) in Company Report

BRAND MANAGEMENT

Sonite Brands Base R&D project		SEMI PSPRO	SELF PSPRO	SEBU PSEMI	SERT PSERT	
Production planning	KU	120	0	110	160	
Inventory sold to trading company	KU	0	0	0	0	
Recommended retail price	$	565	550	420	478	
Advertising budget	K$	2 865	0	1 976	2 371	
Advertising research budget	K$	283	0	195	234	
	Buffs	0	0	100	0	
	Singles	0	0	0	0	
Targeted segments in %	Professionals	100	100	0	0	
	High earners	0	0	0	100	
	Others	0	0	0	0	
Perceptual Objectives						
Dimension 1		Convenience	None	Performance	Performance	
Objective 1	[1,7] or [-20,+20]	-4.0	-	11.0	1.0	
Dimension 2		Performance	None	Convenience	Convenience	
Objective 2	[1,7] or [-20,+20]	13.0	-	5.0	5.0	

Key Performance Indicators. The key performance measures described earlier for the "Company scorecard" (market share, retail sales, firm contribution, shareholder value) are summarized for each competing firm. They are presented for the current period as percentage changes from the previous year and relative to the values in Period 0.

Figure 4.35 Example of Past Decisions (Sales Force Management) in Company Report

SALES FORCE MANAGEMENT

Distribution Channels	Specialty stores	Depart. stores	Mass Merchandis.
Number of salespeople	123	93	74
Sales force effort allocation by brand (%)			
SEMI	26	22	30
SELF	0	0	0
SEBU	20	10	9
SERT	15	33	18
VENI	12	4	3
VEDI	14	8	8
VECI	13	23	32
TOTAL	100	100	100

Figure 4.36   Example of Past Decisions (R&D Projects) in Company Report

SONITE R&D PROJECTS

| Project | Expenditures | | Product Characteristics | | | | |
| | | Weight | Design | Volume | Max Freq | Power | Base cost |
	K$	Kg	Index	Dm3	KHz	W	$
PSOT1	100	15	7	60	30	35	10

Economic Information

The Newsletter gives economic information in two sections. The first section concerns economic variables, and the second gives market research costs for the next period.

Economic Variables. You will find GNP growth rate and inflation rate for the current period, as well as the corresponding forecasted values for the next period, in the "Economic variables" section of the Newsletter (see Figure 4.40). The inflation rate especially affects the costs of the MARKSTRAT firms, and it may also influence the markets. The new inventory and sales force costs are also given.

Figure 4.37   Example of Past Decisions (Market Research Studies) in Company Report

MARKET RESEARCH STUDIES

| Study | Market covered by study | | |
	All markets	Sonite	Vodite
Industry benchmarking	Yes	-	-
Consumer survey	-	Yes	Yes
Consumer panel	-	Yes	Yes
Distribution panel	-	Yes	Yes
Semantic scales	-	Yes	Yes
Multidimensional scaling	-	Yes	Yes
Market forecast	-	Yes	Yes
Competitive advertising	-	Yes	Yes
Competitive sales force	-	Yes	Yes
Advertising experiment	-	Yes	Yes
Sales force experiment	-	Yes	Yes
Conjoint analysis	-	Yes	Yes

Figure 4.38 Example of Past Decisions (Loan and Budget) in Company Report

LOAN AND BUDGET MODIFICATION

	Unit	
Corporate finance department		
Increase in budget	K$	0
Decrease in budget	K$	0
Bank		
Capital borrowed	K$	0
Duration in number of periods		
Interest rate	%	

Costs of Market Research Studies. The costs that the firm needs to incur to acquire market research information during the next period are indicated for all the market research studies available (Figure 4.41). Note that this information will be provided at the end of the period and will cover the situation at the end of the period.

Market Information

The Newsletter summarizes the specifications of all the brands that were marketed during the period and sales information about these brands.

Brand Characteristics and Price. A list of all the brands marketed during the period in each of the Sonite and Vodite markets is given, along with the physical specifications of each of these brands (Figure 4.42). The recommended retail price is listed, and the average base cost for a first batch of 100,000 units is estimated. If new brands have been introduced in the market during the simulated period or if existing brands have been modified, this

Figure 4.39 Stock Market Section of Newsletter

STOCK MARKET

Firm	Stock price index base 1000	Market capitalization K$	Net contribution (K$)	
			Period 7	Cumulative
O	4 143	896 066	132 531	516 148
E	2 459	612 865	84 618	323 042
U	1 537	509 295	57 997	259 490
I	1 261	239 982	13 347	104 142
A	585	100 974	11 723	49 560

Figure 4.40   Economic Variables Section of Newsletter

ECONOMIC VARIABLES

	Unit	Actual value Period 7	Forecast value Period 8	%change
GNP growth rates	%	2.0%	2.0%	+0.0%
Inflation rate	%	2.0%	2.0%	+0.0%
Production				
Inventory holding cost per annum	% transf. cost	8.0%	8.0%	+0.0%
Loss incurred for inventory disposal	% transf. cost	20.0%	20.0%	+0.0%
Sales force				
Salesperson operating cost	$	24 839	25 336	+2.0%
Salesperson hiring and training cost	$	3 726	3 800	+2.0%
Salesperson firing cost	$	6 210	6 334	+2.0%

information is given. The brands are listed by firm so that the breadth of each firm's product line can be easily recognized.

Sales and Market Share. For the Sonite and Vodite markets, the following information for each brand on the market is provided: unit sales, market share based on units, retail sales in MMUs ($), and market share based on value (Figure 4.43).

Figure 4.41   Costs of Market Research Studies

COST OF MARKET RESEARCH STUDIES NEXT PERIOD
(all numbers in K$)

Study	Market covered by study		
	All markets	Sonite	Vodite
Industry benchmarking	39		
Consumer survey		78	52
Consumer panel		130	91
Distribution panel		78	65
Semantic scales		13	13
Multidimensional scaling		46	46
Market forecast		26	26
Competitive advertising		39	39
Competitive sales force		20	20
Advertising experiment		33	33
Sales force experiment		46	46
Conjoint analysis		46	46
Total market	39	555	477
Total if all studies ordered	1 071		

Figure 4.42   Characteristics of Marketed Brands

CHARACTERISTICS OF MARKETED SONITE BRANDS

Firm	Brand	New or modified	Weight (Kg)	Design (Index)	Volume (Dm3)	Max Freq (KHz)	Power (W)	Base cost ($)	Retail price ($)
A	SAMA	No	17	6	92	23	32	105	204
	SALT	No	17	7	75	35	65	176	279
	SAND	No	14	4	50	40	85	198	514
E	SEMI	Modified	14	5	50	40	80	197	565
	SELF	No	14	5	50	40	80	197	550
	SEBU	No	13	7	40	40	75	197	420
	SERT	No	13	7	50	30	55	198	478
I	SIBI	Modified	19	8	60	36	66	187	271
	SIPE	Cost impr.	20	7	70	15	30	91	203
	SICK	Modified	19	8	60	36	66	187	290
O	SOLD	No	14	7	38	30	55	165	460
	SONO	No	14	5	50	40	77	192	545
	SODU	No	16	7	75	34	54	142	267
	SODE	No	15	7	40	38	77	205	417
U	SUSI	No	17	6	88	23	30	94	220
	SULI	No	14	5	50	40	77	190	540
	SUBF	New	17	4	65	35	70	146	325

Figure 4.43   Sales and Market Share by Brand

INFORMATION ON SONITE MARKET - SALES AND MARKET SHARES

Firm	Brand	Volume sold				Retail sales			
		Period 6 U	Period 7 U	Change %	Share %U	Period 6 K$	Period 7 K$	Change %	Share %$
A	SAMA	196 209	277 258	+41.3%	14.1%	37 476	54 065	+44.3%	8.8%
	SALT	71 862	138	-99.8%	0.0%	19 043	37	-99.8%	0.0%
	SAND	22 833	370	-98.4%	0.0%	11 531	185	-98.4%	0.0%
E	SEMI	57 950	103 864	+79.2%	5.3%	31 351	57 437	+83.2%	9.3%
	SELF	36 435	888	-97.6%	0.0%	19 711	476	-97.6%	0.1%
	SEBU	82 760	86 730	+4.8%	4.4%	34 594	36 166	+4.5%	5.9%
	SERT	80 374	106 844	+32.9%	5.5%	38 097	50 537	+32.7%	8.2%
I	SIBI	287 851	400 129	+39.0%	20.4%	84 340	106 034	+25.7%	17.2%
	SIPE	55 200	114 000	+106.5%	5.8%	13 027	21 888	+68.0%	3.6%
	SICK	42 695	20 151	-52.8%	1.0%	12 125	5 723	-52.8%	0.9%
O	SOLD	153 393	132 000	-13.9%	6.7%	74 549	60 060	-19.4%	9.8%
	SONO	76 522	83 766	+9.5%	4.3%	40 557	44 815	+10.5%	7.3%
	SODU	203 922	186 078	-8.8%	9.5%	53 224	48 566	-8.8%	7.9%
	SODE	29 650	42 886	+44.6%	2.2%	12 305	17 798	+44.6%	2.9%
U	SUSI	317 606	319 098	+0.5%	16.3%	67 968	66 691	-1.9%	10.8%
	SULI	133 038	83 524	-37.2%	4.3%	70 776	44 351	-37.3%	7.2%
	SUBF	0	2 143	-	0.1%	0	679	-	0.1%
Total Sonite market		1 848 300	1 959 867	+6.0%	100.0%	620 674	615 510	-0.8%	100.0%

In summary, this chapter has discussed the critical operations in MARKSTRAT. Assimilating the information contained in this chapter is critical to starting a MARKSTRAT simulation with a good base. It will allow you to concentrate on strategic marketing issues without needing to refer constantly to operational definitions and basic procedures that are necessary but that can also be peculiar to any industry or business.

CHAPTER 4 SUMMARY

Decisions

- Brand portfolio
  - New brand introduction
  - Brand modification
  - Brand withdrawal
- Production
- Price
- Advertising
  - Advertising budget
  - Advertising research budget
  - Targeted segments
  - Perceptual objectives
- Sales force and distribution
  - Sales force size by channel
  - Sales force effort by brand
- Market research studies
- Research and development
  - Ongoing projects
  - On-line query
  - New projects
  - Reintroducing suspended projects
- Budget
- Changes in available financial resources
  - Bank loans
  - Budget changes
- Summary
- Errors and warnings

Company Report

- Company results
  - Company scorecard
  - Company performance
    Units sold
    Average retail price (recommended price to be paid by consumers)
    Average selling price (retail price – distributor's margin)
    Revenues (units sold × average selling price)
    Production level in units
    Cost of goods sold (units sold × unit base cost)

Inventory holding cost (inventory units × unit transfer cost × holding cost as a percentage of transfer cost)

Inventory disposal loss

Contribution before marketing (revenues – cost of goods sold – inventory holding cost – inventory disposal loss)

Advertising expenditures

Advertising research

Sales force (total annual expenditures)

Contribution after marketing (contribution before marketing – advertising – sales force)

Market research (total costs of all the studies purchased)

R&D (total annual expenditures for all R&D projects)

Interest paid

Exceptional cost or profit

Net contribution (contribution after marketing – R&D – exceptional cost [or + exceptional profit])

Budget (increases with net contribution within minimum and maximum levels)

- Brand results
  - Contribution by brand
  - Market shares and distribution coverage
    Market share based on units of each brand
    Number of distributors by channel for each brand
- R&D
  - Project name
  - State of completion of project
  - Physical characteristics
  - Cumulative expenditures
  - Additional investment required
  - Minimum realistic base unit cost
- Cumulative results
  - Brand information
    Total units sold
    Cumulative retail sales
    Cumulative revenues
    Cumulative cost of goods sold
    Cumulative inventory costs
    Cumulative advertising and sales force expenditures
    Cumulative marketing contribution after marketing
  - Total cumulative market research expenditures
  - Total cumulative R&D expenditures
  - Total cumulative interest paid
  - Total cumulative exceptional cost or profit
  - Total cumulative net contribution
- Messages
- Past decisions

Newsletter

- Stock market information
  - Stock price indices
  - Key company performance indicators
- Economic information
  - Economic variables
    GNP growth rate during the current period
    GNP growth rate estimated for the following period
    Inflation rate during the current period
    Inflation rate estimated for the following period
    Inventory holding cost per annum as a percentage of transfer cost
    Cost of a salesperson for the following period
    Cost of firing a salesperson for the following period
    Cost of training a new salesperson for the following period
  - Costs of market research studies: Cost of each market research study for the following period
- Market information
  - Characteristics of marketed brands: Names, characteristics, and retail price of brands marketed in the current period
  - Sales and market share: For each market (Sonite and Vodite), sales, market share (based on units and on value), and retail price of each brand

5

Marketing Planning

As explained in the previous chapter, MARKSTRAT3 teams have to make decisions on a variety of dimensions, including brand portfolio, production, pricing, communication, sales force, distribution, market research, and research and development. In the process of making these decisions, your team will rely on three sources of information that have been described in the last two chapters: past market research studies, newsletters, and company reports. The decisions made by your firm will then have an impact on the market, its results, and those of your competitors. This will be reflected in future market research studies, newsletters, and company reports.

The multitude of decisions made by a firm in a given period have to be coherent at three levels: the budget level, the planning level, and the strategic level. At the budget level, the sum of the expenditures incurred by the management team must be within the limits of the authorized amount. If it is not, then either decisions must be changed to reduce expenditures or the team must negotiate for authorization of a higher amount or for a bank loan. In the MARKSTRAT3 software, the budget section within the **Decisions** module helps teams recapitulate their expenditures and check that they have not exceeded the authorized limit.

At the strategic level, decisions should be united by some forceful guidelines and provide for a balanced development of the firm in the medium and long term. The decisions should represent only the implementation of strategies. You should formulate strategies first and then translate these into decisions. It is, however, easier to deal first with individual tactical decisions on advertising or distribution than with a brand strategy or with the overall marketing strategy of the firm. This process of building from the tactical to the strategic corresponds to the normal evolution of a marketing career. This is the approach adopted here; the more strategic marketing issues will be considered in greater depth in the second part of the MARKSTRAT3 manual, Chapters 6 to 10. As you become more familiar with the operational aspects of the MARKSTRAT environment, however, remember that the strategic perspective has to lead the decisions and not the other way around.

Between the budget and strategic levels, the intermediate test of the coherence of decisions is the marketing plan. In practice, the marketing plan typically covers a time horizon of from one to five years. Given the powerful competitive dynamics in the MARKSTRAT environment, to minimize data entry, and to give more emphasis to the qualitative aspects of strategy, the time horizon in the MARKSTRAT3 software has been limited to one year. The changes brought over time by competing firms to the MARKSTRAT markets are such that beyond one year the emphasis should be placed more on strategic objectives and moves than on detailed planning.

The **Marketing Plan** sub-module of the MARKSTRAT3 software provides a projection of firms' results for the next period, based on the decisions made for that period. When you access the **Marketing Plan** sub-module by clicking on the corresponding button, six distinct components appear on the tabs at the bottom of the screen: **Segment sizes, Brand shares, Brand sales, Distribution mix, Brand contribution,** and **Company performance** (see Figure 5.1). Each component is accessed by clicking on the corresponding tab. The first four correspond to three types of estimates that have to be made as inputs to the plan. The last two represent a "simulation of the simulation" based on both the decisions and the estimates.

Figure 5.1   Estimated Segment Sizes

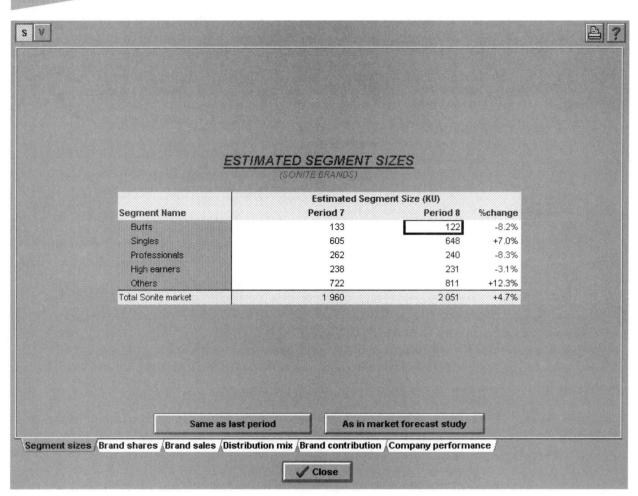

SEGMENT SIZES

The first estimates you will provide as inputs to the marketing plan concern the size (in thousands of units) of each segment. The table at the center of the corresponding screen presents a reminder of the size of each segment in the last period. The estimates for the evolution of the segments' sizes next period should be entered in one of the two columns on the right, in thousands of units or in percentage change. You can shift from the Sonite screen to the Vodite screen by selecting the corresponding button in the top left-hand corner.

Alternative automatic estimating approaches are offered by two buttons: "Same as last period" (assuming no change since the previous period) and "As in market forecast study" (using the market forecast projections from market research). The second alternative is available only if you have bought the corresponding study. If you have not, that button will be in grey.

The default values of the estimates when you first enter this screen are the same as the last period's segment sizes—that is, 0% change for each segment. These default values or the other automatic approach based on market forecast gives a basis from which individual adjustments can be made, either in thousands of units or in percentage change.

BRAND SALES OR BRAND SHARE ESTIMATES BY SEGMENT

One of the most important aspects of marketing planning is anticipating the market response to a specific set of decisions or actions. Anticipated market reactions must be entered for each brand in each segment. You can specify these either in terms of brand shares or brand sales by selecting the appropriate tab at the bottom of the screen (see Figure 5.2). The numbers for the previous period are displayed for each brand in each segment as well as for the total market. An estimate for the next period can be entered either as a target or as a change from the previous period.

Assuming that you first select brand share inputs, one easy way to start is to use the same market shares as in the previous period. Estimates can then be modified for each brand/segment combination, either as expected market shares or as expected changes in market share points. Whenever you modify any of the estimates in one mode of entry, the number for the other mode of entry (i.e., in "Change," if the expected market share is modified) is automatically updated. The total market share estimates for the market as a whole are also updated, in the right-hand column. Simultaneously, the estimates of the corresponding brand unit sales in each segment are calculated based on the segment sizes previously defined and the market share inputs. These numbers will be displayed when you select the **Brand sales** tab at the bottom of the screen (see Figure 5.3). The estimates of brand sales can then be updated as targets or as changes from the previous period in the same way as the brand shares estimates were.

The approach described above consists of (1) starting with brand share estimates, (2) displaying the expected brand sales resulting from the segment

Figure 5.2 Estimated Brand Shares by Segment

ESTIMATED BRAND SHARES BY SEGMENT
(SONITE BRANDS)

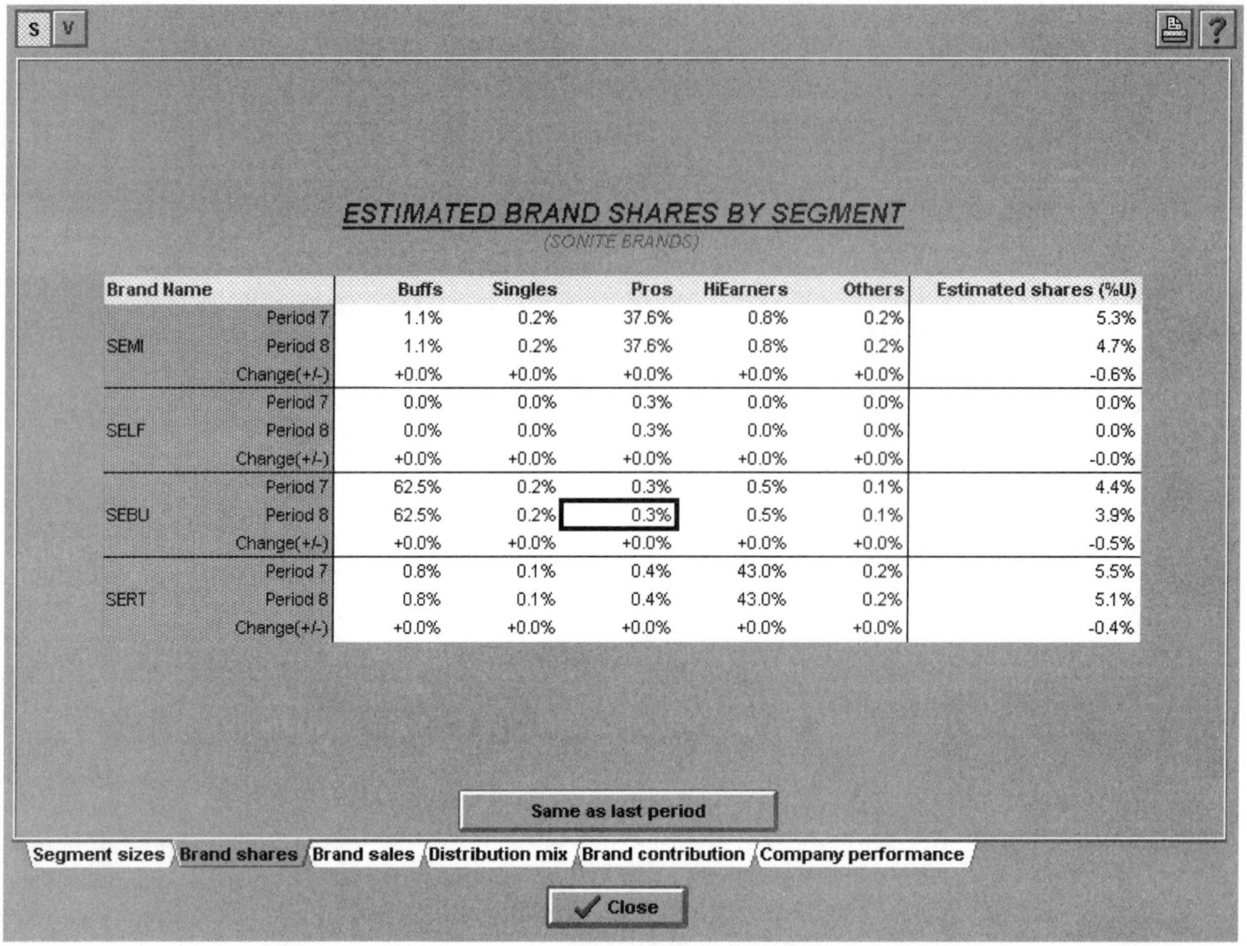

Brand Name		Buffs	Singles	Pros	HiEarners	Others	Estimated shares (%U)
	Period 7	1.1%	0.2%	37.6%	0.8%	0.2%	5.3%
SEMI	Period 8	1.1%	0.2%	37.6%	0.8%	0.2%	4.7%
	Change(+/-)	+0.0%	+0.0%	+0.0%	+0.0%	+0.0%	-0.6%
	Period 7	0.0%	0.0%	0.3%	0.0%	0.0%	0.0%
SELF	Period 8	0.0%	0.0%	0.3%	0.0%	0.0%	0.0%
	Change(+/-)	+0.0%	+0.0%	+0.0%	+0.0%	+0.0%	-0.0%
	Period 7	62.5%	0.2%	0.3%	0.5%	0.1%	4.4%
SEBU	Period 8	62.5%	0.2%	0.3%	0.5%	0.1%	3.9%
	Change(+/-)	+0.0%	+0.0%	+0.0%	+0.0%	+0.0%	-0.5%
	Period 7	0.8%	0.1%	0.4%	43.0%	0.2%	5.5%
SERT	Period 8	0.8%	0.1%	0.4%	43.0%	0.2%	5.1%
	Change(+/-)	+0.0%	+0.0%	+0.0%	+0.0%	+0.0%	-0.4%

Same as last period

Segment sizes / Brand shares / Brand sales / Distribution mix / Brand contribution / Company performance

✓ Close

size and market share estimates, and (3) updating selected brand sales estimates. This is probably the most logical process, but it is also possible to directly set estimates of expected brand sales. In this case, brand share estimates are calculated on the basis of the brand sales and the segment sizes.

DISTRIBUTION MIX

The price received by a firm for a product is equal to the retail price minus the distributor's margin. As the distributor's margin varies across channels, the average selling price of a brand will depend on the mix of its sales across the channels. Calculating the financial contribution of a brand thus requires an estimate of its distribution mix (see Figure 5.4).

By selecting the appropriate button at the bottom of the screen, you can set the distribution-mix estimates to the same values as in the last period or have them calculated automatically based on the shopping habits study. The second alternative is available only if you bought this market research study

Figure 5.3   Estimated Brand Sales by Segment

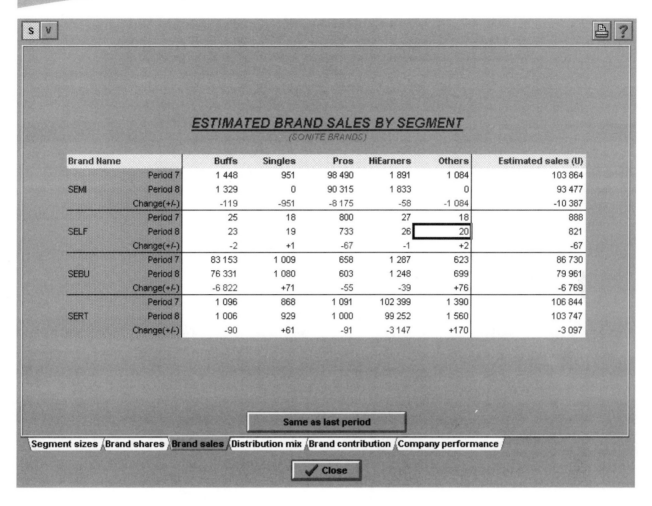

ESTIMATED BRAND SALES BY SEGMENT
(SONITE BRANDS)

Brand Name		Buffs	Singles	Pros	HiEarners	Others	Estimated sales (U)
	Period 7	1 448	951	98 490	1 891	1 084	103 864
SEMI	Period 8	1 329	0	90 315	1 833	0	93 477
	Change(+/-)	-119	-951	-8 175	-58	-1 084	-10 387
	Period 7	25	18	800	27	18	888
SELF	Period 8	23	19	733	26	20	821
	Change(+/-)	-2	+1	-67	-1	+2	-67
	Period 7	83 153	1 009	658	1 287	623	86 730
SEBU	Period 8	76 331	1 080	603	1 248	699	79 961
	Change(+/-)	-6 822	+71	-55	-39	+76	-6 769
	Period 7	1 096	868	1 091	102 399	1 390	106 844
SERT	Period 8	1 006	929	1 000	99 252	1 560	103 747
	Change(+/-)	-90	+61	-91	-3 147	+170	-3 097

Same as last period

Segment sizes / Brand shares / Brand sales / Distribution mix / Brand contribution / Company performance

✓ Close

in the current period. In this case, the software uses the brand sales projections entered in the previous steps of the marketing plan. For each brand, the purchases of each segment are split by channel, based on the shopping habits data. The sales of a brand in a given channel are obtained by adding up sales to all segments.

The distribution-mix estimates can also be entered or updated manually, one by one. Be particularly careful to ensure that the vertical sum of the percentages is 100. The average distribution margin corresponding to a given mix is displayed in the bottom line and is updated any time a change is made in the table.

PROJECTIONS

On the basis of the decisions and the estimates for segment sizes, brand shares, brand sales, and the distribution mix, the marketing planning software can make financial projections for the next period. You can see these

Figure 5.4   Estimated Distribution Mix

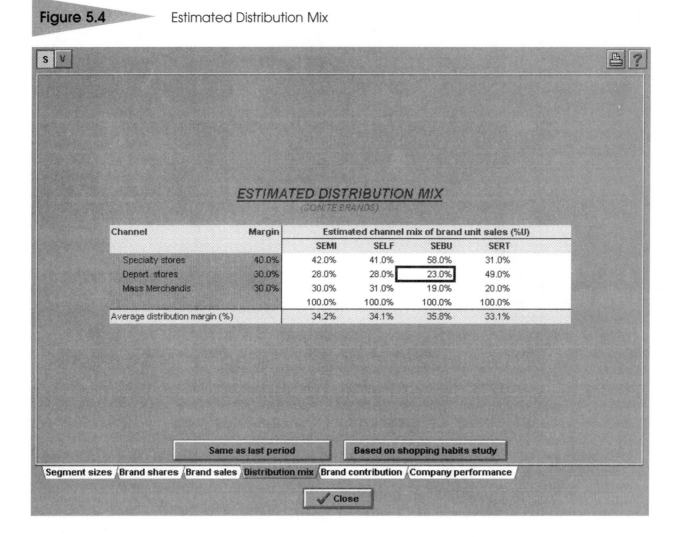

projections by selecting the **Brand contribution** and **Company performance** tabs at the bottom of the screen.

When you click on either of these tabs, the software makes a number of consistency checks. When you try to access the financial projections, an **Errors and Warnings** screen may be displayed if there is a problem—for example, if you forgot to enter some estimates, if the distribution mix for a brand does not add up to 100%, or if the sales forecast for a brand exceeds the available volume (equal to the starting inventory plus the production plan). Such errors and warnings will require corrections in either the marketing plan estimates or the decisions. In the first case, just select the appropriate tab and make the desired adjustments before returning to the financial projections. In the second case, go to the **Decisions** module by clicking on **Close** at the bottom of the screen, make any needed changes to the decisions, and return to the **Marketing Plan** sub-module. The previous estimates entered in this marketing plan section have been saved and will be available the next time you enter the **Marketing Plan** sub-module.

99

If all consistency checks are passed, selecting the **Brand contribution** tab gives access to a pro forma statement of brand contribution (see Figure 5.5). From the top line of the statement, "Units sold," to the bottom line, "Contribution after marketing," the software uses decisions to produce a simulation of the brand contribution statement in the same format as the Company Report. For instance, the average selling price is obtained from the retail price decision and the average distribution margin calculated from the distribution-mix estimates. Similarly, the inventory level is calculated on the basis of the previous inventory (from the prior period results) plus the production plan (a decision) minus the sales estimates, enabling upward or downward adjustments allowed in the manufacturing process.

You can get a pro forma statement of company performance by selecting the corresponding tab (see Figure 5.6). This is a simulation of the page of the same name in the Company Report. From the "Units sold" line to the "Contribution after marketing" line, the table provides information available in the brand contribution pro forma statement, aggregated for Sonites and

Figure 5.5   Pro Forma Statement—Contribution by Brand

PROFORMA STATEMENT - CONTRIBUTION BY BRAND
(SONITE BRANDS)

Sonite Brands Base R&D project	Unit	Total	SEMI PSPRO	SELF PSPRO	SEBU PSEMI	SERT PSERT	
Sales							
Units sold	U	278 003	93 476	820	79 961	103 746	
Average retail price	$	479	548	533	412	468	
Average selling price	$	315	360	350	264	313	
Revenues	K$	87 519	33 651	287	21 109	32 472	
Production							
Units produced	U	312 000	96 000	0	88 000	128 000	
Current unit transfer cost	$	-	157	157	104	138	
Average unit transfer cost	$	137	157	215	104	143	
Cost of goods sold	K$	-38 012	-14 675	-176	-8 317	-14 844	
Units in inventory	U	114 726	2 524	25 857	9 309	77 036	
Inventory holding cost	K$	-1 402	-31	-444	-77	-850	
Inventory disposal loss	K$	0	0	0	0	0	
Contribution before marketing	K$	48 101	18 943	-334	12 715	16 777	
Marketing							
Advertising expenditures	K$	-7 306	-2 902	0	-2 002	-2 402	
Advertising research expenditures	K$	-722	-287	0	-198	-237	
Sales force	K$	-4 500	-1 891	0	-1 027	-1 582	
Contribution after marketing	K$	35 569	13 862	-334	9 487	12 554	

Segment sizes / Brand shares / Brand sales / Distribution mix / **Brand contribution** / Company performance

✓ Close

Figure 5.6   Pro Forma Statement—Company Performance

PROFORMA STATEMENT - COMPANY PERFORMANCE

	Unit	Total	Sonite market	Vodite market
Sales				
Units sold	U	499 005	278 003	221 002
Average retail price	$	603	479	759
Average selling price	$	398	315	503
Revenues	K$	198 601	87 520	111 081
Production				
Units produced	U	613 264	312 000	301 264
Cost of goods sold	K$	-86 990	-38 014	-48 976
Inventory holding cost	K$	-4 179	-1 404	-2 774
Inventory disposal loss	K$	0	0	0
Contribution before marketing	K$	107 432	48 102	59 330
Marketing				
Advertising expenditures	K$	-14 598	-7 307	-7 290
Advertising research expenditures	K$	-1 443	-722	-721
Sales force	K$	-7 347	-4 501	-2 846
Contribution after marketing	K$	84 043	35 571	48 471
Other expenses				
Market research studies	K$	-1 038	-538	-462
Research and development	K$	-830	-830	0
Interest paid	K$	-100		
Exceptional cost or profit	K$	0		
Net contribution	K$	82 074		
Next period budget	K$	25 350		

Segment sizes / Brand shares / Brand sales / Distribution mix / Brand contribution / Company performance

✓ Close

Vodites as well as in total. Other expenses are deducted to provide the net contribution. Finally, a budget for the next period is estimated on the basis of these expected financial results.

THE PLANNING PROCESS

The MARKSTRAT3 **Marketing Plan** sub-module is a useful tool for checking the consistency of decisions made by your firm and anticipating their possible financial consequences. It does not guarantee, however, that the projected results will be achieved. The actual brand contribution and company performance statements for the next period may be quite different from the pro forma projections obtained from the plan. Many facets of the environment might change unexpectedly, including consumer needs and competitive actions. Other aspects more under your control may not have been acknowledged properly or may have been overlooked. For instance, the distribution-mix estimates may not take into account the fact that the deployment of the firm's sales force no longer corresponds to the new shopping trends or the share estimates for a given brand may not anticipate negative consumer reactions to the price increase. It could also be that the cut in the advertising budget does not have a negative impact on sales, and, as a result, the brand does better than expected and is sold out.

The process of planning in MARKSTRAT3 brings discipline to marketing thinking, action, and learning in at least three important ways: first, by imposing a focus on the tangible results of decisions at the brand level; second, by making it easy to check the validity of the overall financial results; and third, by providing support for a postmortem analysis.

Concerning the first point, the **Marketing Plan** sub-module helps teams focus on the three key elements of market evolution (segment sizes), brand performance (in shares or volume), and distribution coverage. Having to submit estimates for these components of the plan should induce your team to discuss and reflect on the variables affecting them. By modifying the estimates, your team can relatively conveniently perform sensitivity analyses to better understand how these components affect the brand contribution. Moreover, if the resulting projected brand contribution is significantly higher or lower than expected, questions can be asked about the validity of certain decisions. For instance, an "abnormally" high projected contribution for a given brand may lead you to check whether the share estimate is compatible with the competitive positioning, the retail price, and the advertising support of the brand. It is easy to switch between the **Marketing Plan** sub-module and the other components of the **Decisions** module in order to adjust either the decisions or the estimates and to reach a situation that has the confidence of the firm's management.

The marketing planning section of the MARKSTRAT3 software also allows you to conveniently check the expected overall financial performance of the firm. Within your firm's portfolio, you may decide to invest heavily in a new brand and to accept a substantially negative contribution for that brand as long as other products are generating enough funds to reach some desired financial objectives. This financial interdependence among brands is sometimes difficult to grasp, but it is easy to investigate and analyze with the **Marketing Plan** sub-module.

Finally, an important role of the marketing plan is to provide a tangible basis for learning over time. The **Brand contribution** and **Company performance** statements in the **Marketing Plan** appear in the same format as in the Company Report. This allows for an easy comparison between the anticipated projections and the actual results when they are obtained. A systematic analysis of the variance between the two documents will help you learn about both the market mechanisms and the planning process. In the long term, this learning dimension is probably the most important contribution of the marketing planning process.

CHAPTER 5 SUMMARY

The Marketing Plan

- From the tactical to the strategic
  - The marketing budget
  -- The marketing plan
  - The strategy statement
- The two parts of the marketing plan
  - Making estimates: segment sizes, brand shares, brand sales, and distribution mix
  - Making financial projections: brand contribution and company performance
- Segment sizes
  - Same as last period
  - Based on market forecast
  - Specific adjustments
- Brand shares
  - Same as last period
  - Specific adjustments: market share targets or changes in market share points
- Brand sales
  - Same as last period
  - Based on segment sizes and market shares
  - Specific adjustments: sales targets of changes in sales levels
- Distribution mix
  - Same as last period
  - Based on shopping habits
  - Specific adjustments
- Projections
  - Errors and warnings
  - Correction of decisions or estimates
  - Contribution by brand
  - Company performance
- The planning process
  - Focusing on tangible brand results
  - Checking the overall financial validity
  - Learning through postmortem analysis

6

Market Segmentation and Positioning

Each MARKSTRAT company starts with two Sonite brands in Period 0. During the course of the simulation, companies may introduce new Sonite or Vodite brands and reposition or withdraw existing ones. The positioning and repositioning of brands with respect to the specific needs of various consumer segments is a major aspect of the companies' marketing strategies.

The strategic issues concerning market segmentation and product positioning can be summarized in three questions, which will be discussed in turn:

1. Where do we want to be positioned?
2. How do we design the product appropriate for this positioning?
3. As the environment changes, how can we reposition our existing brands?

The purpose of this chapter is to provide a framework and some methodologies to help make these decisions. The proposed approaches rest on the notions of brand perceptions and consumer preferences. Therefore, we will first discuss how perceptions and preferences are assessed and the basic strategically relevant inferences that can be made from a perceptual map.

ASSESSING PERCEPTIONS AND PREFERENCES

One basis for analyzing the positioning of each competitive brand is the perceptual map obtained in the multidimensional scaling study (see Figure 6.1). The example in Figure 6.1 is presented for explanatory purposes only and should not be used during the simulation, as it does not correspond to actual conditions. The study provides a two-dimensional map, which, for the purpose of illustration, is considered to be a configuration found statistically satisfactory. The interpretation of the two dimensions shown is not reported here, although it will be in the actual study (the dimensionality of the map may also be different in the actual study). This interpretation is typically based on attribute assessment, such as from the semantic scales study. Each axis or dimension is arbitrarily scaled from –20 to +20.

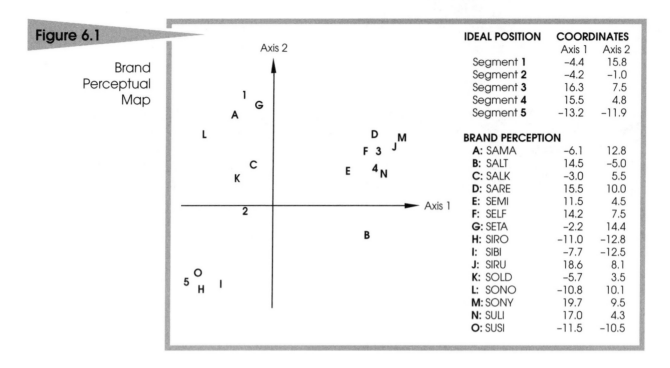

Figure 6.1

Brand
Perceptual
Map

IDEAL POSITION	COORDINATES	
	Axis 1	Axis 2
Segment **1**	–4.4	15.8
Segment **2**	–4.2	–1.0
Segment **3**	16.3	7.5
Segment **4**	15.5	4.8
Segment **5**	–13.2	–11.9

BRAND PERCEPTION		
A: SAMA	–6.1	12.8
B: SALT	14.5	–5.0
C: SALK	–3.0	5.5
D: SARE	15.5	10.0
E: SEMI	11.5	4.5
F: SELF	14.2	7.5
G: SETA	–2.2	14.4
H: SIRO	–11.0	–12.8
I: SIBI	–7.7	–12.5
J: SIRU	18.6	8.1
K: SOLD	–5.7	3.5
L: SONO	–10.8	10.1
M: SONY	19.7	9.5
N: SULI	17.0	4.3
O: SUSI	–11.5	–10.5

In the actual maps in MARKSTRAT, there are text labels to represent perceptions and ideal points. However, for the example in Figure 6.1, the numbers 1, 2, 3, 4, and 5 on the graph represent the positioning of the ideal points for the five segments. For instance, most consumers from segment 3 would globally prefer a brand with coordinates at 16.3 on axis 1 and 7.5 on axis 2 of the perceptual map. Note that this point represents only the average ideal or preference of individuals in this segment. In fact, each consumer has a different preference. This results in a distribution of ideal points around the mean preference. But the preferences within a segment are similar enough for the ideal point to well represent the overall global preference of the segment.

The letters on the graph in Figure 6.1 correspond to the positioning of the competitive brands on the market at the time of the study, as indicated in the lower right side of the figure. No significant difference was observed among the perceptions of the brands by the various market segments. This means that although the segments prefer different ideal products, they perceive existing brands in a similar way. Thus, only one map for all segments is needed, rather than a separate map for each segment.

This map graphically summarizes much information about the relative perceptions of the various brands. As a first step, it indicates the relative competition that may be expected among the different brands. The prime competitors for brand SEMI (E) are expected to be, in decreasing order of importance, brands SELF (F), SULI (N), SARE (D), SIRU (J), and SONY (M). These brands are indeed perceived by consumers as being positioned close to each other. The decreasing order of importance is determined by the straight-line distance between SEMI and the positions of other brands. On the other hand, little competition should be expected between brands SEMI (E) and SIRO (H), which are positioned far apart and should accordingly satisfy different needs. Cannibalization may occur if a firm's brands are positioned too close together, as, for instance, in the case of SIRO (H) and SIBI (I), which are both marketed by Firm I. One can infer the relative preferences of a segment for different brands from the distance between the segment's ideal point and the positions of the brands. In our example, SIRO (H), SIBI (I), and SUSI (O) are principal competitors for segment 5. SETA (G) is in a privileged situation with segment 1, and there are no brands positioned close to segment 2's ideal point.

The semantic scale ratings provided in the corresponding market research study also give perceptual and preference information for Sonites. The semantic scale results are less accurate than those obtained through perceptual mapping because of the cruder methodology used, but they are substantially less expensive to purchase. A brand map can be constructed from these data as well. For Vodites, only the semantic scale ratings are available until a sufficient number of brands are available for a multidimensional scaling study to be carried out.

To obtain the values on the semantic scales, the set of relevant attributes is determined a priori, contrary to MDS (multidimensional scaling) methodology. The scale (1 to 7) has fewer points as well, so the precision of the ratings is not as high. In particular, when perceptions of the degree to which a given brand possesses an attribute are related to the actual value of the brand on a physical characteristic, the reduced range might prohibit the discovery of complex nonlinear relationships. However, the ease of gathering data on semantic scales enables the use of a large sample size, which results in very reliable values of the semantic scales.

OPTIMAL BRAND POSITION

Key objectives of segmentation and positioning strategies are (1) to anticipate the needs of consumers, (2) to target attractive market segments, and (3) to position brands for segment dominance. These objectives can be reached by the choice of an appropriate segmentation and positioning strategy that recognizes the attractiveness of various market segments (in terms of profit potential and potential for long-term dominating positions) and the synergies among businesses or segments.

The issues of synergies among segments and risks associated with uncertainties will be discussed in detail in Chapter 10, on allocation of resources. This section concentrates on major questions leading to the positioning that would be appropriate for a given brand. From a strategic standpoint, one possibility is to position the product so as to best satisfy the needs of one specific segment. The other possibility is to position the brand so as to reach several segments and conceivably achieve greater economies of scale and greater experience through larger volume, leading to lower costs.

This second positioning strategy is illustrated in Figure 6.2. Brand SELT is shown equidistant from the ideal points of segments 1 and 2. In general, this strategy is not appropriate for the long term, as this position is difficult to defend. A competitor might decide to specialize in one segment and better satisfy its specific needs. This would leave you in the difficult position of

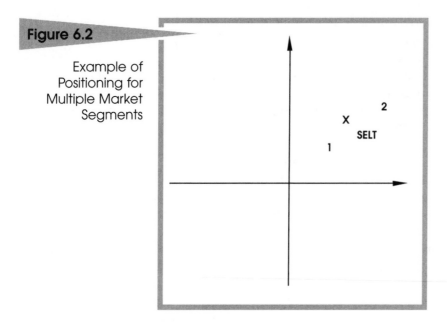

Figure 6.2

Example of
Positioning for
Multiple Market
Segments

being "stuck in the middle." However, there are conditions that could make this strategy feasible. These issues will be discussed in greater detail in Chapter 9, on competitive strategies. Briefly, this positioning strategy might be appropriate if the segments were too small for a single-segment dominance position to be profitable or if the brand "stuck in the middle" could establish barriers to entry—through large advertising expenditures, for example.

The exact position to search for depends on expectations of future needs for the segment or segments involved and on the demand for the brand in a given position. Once the "optimal position" has been found, the issue of finding the physical product attributes that correspond best to that positioning will be considered. Then the repositioning alternative will be discussed.

To determine the best position for a brand, the marketing strategist must analyze the dynamics of demand preference to anticipate the needs and preferences of the relevant segments. The demand by each of the segments should be forecasted as well as the market share for the brand in question, given its position and given the expected positions of competitive brands. Costs must then be evaluated to derive the profitability of different positioning strategies. The optimal brand position question can, therefore, be analyzed in a three-step process:

1. Prediction of ideal points
2. Forecasting of brand demand, which involves
   a. forecasting of segment demand
   b. forecasting of brand market share
3. Forecasting of brand transfer cost

Prediction of Ideal Points

Ideal points, or preferences, reflect the needs of the consumers within a given segment. These needs gradually change as the consumers' values and behavior evolve over time. Typically, these changes are due to changes in the environment, which does not change drastically from one period to the next. Therefore, changes in preferences are due for the most part to multiperiod environmental trends that are not necessarily external to the industry and that can be significantly influenced by the actions of the competitors in the industry.

Marketing decisions of the firms in the industry affect the evolution of a segment. They affect the size of the segment, the importance of the dimensions characterizing the brands in the consumers' perceptual space, and consumers' preferences in terms of the degree to which they would like a product to possess given attributes. One type of analysis appropriate for evaluating trends is tracking the evolution of the ideal points over time. The market research studies concerned with the semantic scales and the multidimensional study provide a map that tracks this ideal point evolution (see Figures 3.11 and 3.16 in Chapter 3). If the patterns over time are stable enough and if the information provided by the market research is reliable enough, it is possible to predict the position of an ideal point as a function of time. In Figure 6.3, for example, the preference for the dimension represented on the graph is decreasing over time (the dimension could be either from the multidimensional scaling study or from the semantic scales). The trend line can be drawn on the graph, or a regression equation can be estimated to predict the position several periods ahead. This analysis is performed automatically when one chooses **Ideal value trend—regression analysis** (see Figure 6.4) in the **Product design** menu of the **Analysis** module of MARKSTRAT. Either "semantic scales" or "multidimensional scaling" can be used. For the segment selected, the simple regression results of the ideal values over time are reported with the forecasted values for the following two periods for each of the dimensions.

Figure 6.3

Evolution of Ideal Points over Time

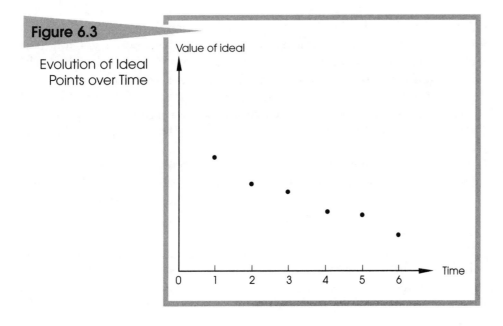

Figure 6.4   Ideal Value Trend—Regression Analysis

SEMANTIC SCALES - IDEAL VALUE EVOLUTION - BUFFS						
Period	Weight	Design	Volume	Max Freq	Power	Price
0	3.12	5.35	1.79	6.04	6.39	4.03
1	2.99	5.20	1.80	6.07	6.40	4.00
2	2.88	5.04	1.80	6.09	6.42	3.98
3	2.76	4.89	1.81	6.12	6.43	3.96
4	2.67	4.73	1.82	6.15	6.44	3.93
5	2.57	4.57	1.83	6.18	6.45	3.91
6	2.47	4.40	1.84	6.20	6.46	3.88
7	2.37	4.24	1.85	6.23	6.47	3.86
Parameters of linear regression						
Slope	-0.11	-0.16	0.01	0.03	0.01	-0.02
Intercept	3.10	5.36	1.79	6.04	6.39	4.03
R^2	0.9982	0.9998	1.0000	1.0000	1.0000	0.9991
Expected ideal values (based on linear regression)						
Period 8	2.25	4.09	1.86	6.26	6.49	3.83
Period 9	2.14	3.93	1.87	6.28	6.50	3.81

Forecasting Brand Demand

As indicated above, forecasting brand demand involves forecasting the size of each segment served by the brand, as well as forecasting the market share of the brand in each segment, given a certain positioning. Then the expected sales of the brand can be computed.

Forecasting Segment Sales. There are several alternative methods of forecasting demand for a given segment. The simplest method is a trend analysis. However, this implies that the environment will evolve in a consistent manner. Although trends are important, a saturation level might be reached when enough potential customers have purchased the product. This would suggest the use of a diffusion model that takes saturation into account. Although the trend probably represents the major environmental forces affecting demand, the decisions of the firm also have a significant impact, as indicated earlier. So a third possibility is to analyze the relationship between competitive actions and segment demand.

Figure 6.5 represents the evolution of sales in a segment over six periods. The trend line can be used to forecast demand in Periods 7 and 8. But because the trend is not necessarily a linear function of time, the curve that best fits past points might give a better forecast than a straight line. A curve is also shown in Figure 6.5.

This curve indicates a decline in the growth rate of the segment. This could be due to the potential market's becoming saturated. More complex diffusion models can sometimes be used to represent such an evolution. The sales (in units) in a given period can be regressed on (1) the cumulative sales

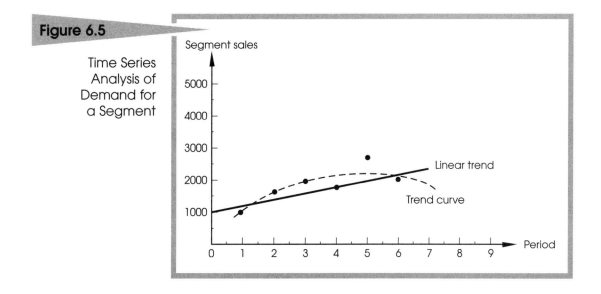

Figure 6.5

Time Series Analysis of Demand for a Segment

up to the previous period and (2) the square of the cumulative sales up to the previous period, using time series observations. The estimated coefficients can then be used for prediction purposes, since for each period the cumulative previous sales are known.

Instead of using the diffusion model approach, we could observe that the deviations from the trend curve in Periods 4 and 5 are due to a decrease in advertising expenditures for this segment in Period 4, followed by an increase in Period 5. It is then possible to add advertising expenditures for the brands competing in this segment as an independent variable in a regression, in addition to a trend factor.

Any of these methods (and possibly some combination) can be used to forecast the sales of the market segments.

Forecasting Market Share. Market share in the long term should be equivalent to purchase intentions, as the product should be available through appropriate distribution to those consumers who wish to buy it. Purchase intentions are determined by two main factors: brand awareness and brand positioning. Although it is difficult to assess the exact relationships, as a first step you could use information given in the consumer survey market research for the current position of the brand with the current awareness level. These will be accurate if brand awareness and brand positioning, the factors determining purchase intentions, are stable.

If changes in positioning can be anticipated, particularly for the firm's own brands, the impact of these changes should be assessed, as they will affect purchase intentions. In particular, if other brands are expected to be positioned close to the brand for which the forecast is being made, cannibalization is likely to occur. The degree of cannibalization in terms of purchase intentions would, therefore, need to be assessed.

Expected Brand Demand. Expected brand sales can now be computed by adding the brand sales of each segment. Table 6.1 provides an example of the

Table 6.1

Computing
Expected
Brand Sales

Segment	Segment Expected Size (in units)	Expected Purchase Intent of Brand SAND	Expected Brand Sales
1	133	0.350	18
2	916	0.035	32
3	333	0.028	9
4	1111	0.429	477
5	1521	0.005	8
		Total Expected Brand Sales:	544

computations involved. The sales level of the brand originating from a given segment is the product of the segment's expected size and the expected purchase intentions for the brand within that segment. The total expected brand sales level is the sum of the brand sales over the relevant segments.

Forecasting Brand Transfer Cost

To compute the expected profitability of a brand position, the costs of reaching that position need to be assessed, as well as the cost advantages due to increased sales obtained from a better position. The evaluation of the costs of reaching a given position must take into account R&D, advertising, and sales force expenditures, as discussed in Chapter 5. At this point, we will concentrate on the impact of production volume on unit transfer costs.

As indicated earlier, the base cost given for an R&D project prototype is the average cost for the first production batch of 100,000 units. This base cost, which serves as the transfer cost from the production to the marketing department, follows the gains in productivity obtained through production experience as per a contractual internal agreement between the two departments.

The Experience Curve. The origin of the experience curve is the learning curve. The learning curve resulted from the observation that productivity of repeated human labor tasks increases as the number of times the task is performed increases. Thus, the learning effect generally follows a specific pattern: every time the number of times the task is performed doubles, productivity increases by a constant percentage. This finding indicates decreasing returns to task repetition.

The Boston Consulting Group (BCG) observed similar patterns of cost reduction across a broad range of industries every time cumulative production of a product doubled. The phenomenon that BCG observed is more general than the learning curve, as it goes beyond labor costs. In fact, the "experience effect" can result from a variety of sources in addition to labor productivity—for example, substitution of cheaper or more efficient raw materials or components, production standardization, improved efficiency of production equipment, or new production processes.

Another source of cost reduction is the introduction, resulting from research and development programs, of new products that are more efficient. In MARKSTRAT, this last source is separated from the other sources of cost reduction listed above. Indeed, the above set of sources of experience effects is beyond the management of the marketing department. Although cost reductions from any of these sources do not occur automatically, in MARKSTRAT the production departments have the motivation to achieve these cost reductions. As for cost reductions due to development of new (more efficient) products, it is the responsibility of the marketing department to make such requests, as the marketing department controls the R&D budget. The experience curve in MARKSTRAT, therefore, is referred to as the *experience effect,* which is automatically generated by production management.

This cost reduction, which is distinct from the cost reduction obtained from research and development, is very regular in MARKSTRAT and applies to any new product design being produced. So for a given product design, every time cumulative production doubles, transfer costs from the production department to the marketing department fall by a constant percentage. The curve can be represented as in Figure 6.6. If several brands are based on the same product design (i.e., the same project), the experience effect is calculated on the cumulative production for all these brands. In other words, the brands manufactured with the same project have shared experience effects.

In this example, there is an 85% experience curve, meaning that every time cumulative production doubles, unit transfer cost decreases by 15%. A property of this constant rate of decrease in cost is that when the experience curve is plotted on log-log paper, as in Figure 6.7, it appears as a straight line. The units on the horizontal and vertical axes are now the logarithm of cumulative production and the logarithm of unit transfer cost, respectively. The

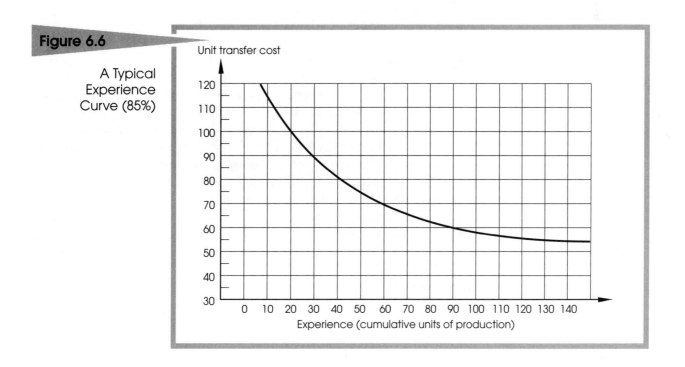

Figure 6.6

A Typical Experience Curve (85%)

Figure 6.7

The Experience
Curve with
Transformed Axes

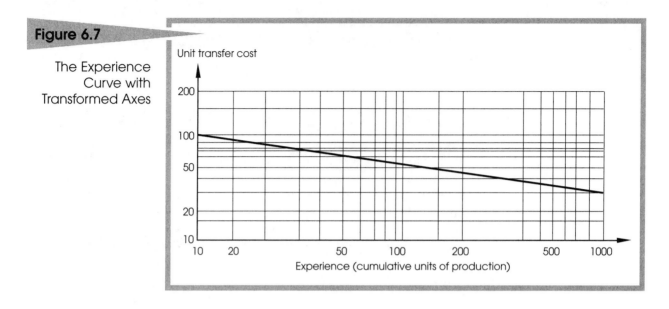

advantage of this property becomes evident in estimating the experience rate and forecasting future transfer costs.

The effect of experience on transfer cost can easily be estimated by changing the production level and evaluating the impact of the transfer cost indicated in the "Brand contribution" table of the **Marketing Plan** sub-module, described in Chapter 5.

However, to understand the principle, the following six-step procedure may be useful. Although this method is based on only two points, it has the advantage of being simple. You can easily extend it to multiple observations with the use of regression techniques.

Six-Step Forecasting Procedure. The process is as follows.

Step 1: The first step is to obtain the unit transfer cost at an early period, with the corresponding cumulative production of units at that time. The unit transfer cost is easily read from the **Company Report** in the **Brand Results** section. The cumulative production at that time is the cumulative sales shown in the **Cumulative Results** section of the report for the same period. To this should be added the inventory of the brand at the end of the period.

Step 2: The procedure in step 1 is followed for a later period. For that period, both the cumulative production and the new transfer cost should be obtained.

Step 3: The unit transfer cost needs to be adjusted for inflation so that the monetary value corresponds to that in the period of reference used in step 1. The inflation rates that should be used to adjust cost are given in the Newsletter.

Step 4: The experience curve, as discussed above, becomes a straight line when drawn on log-log paper. Therefore, the two points should be plotted on log-log paper, with cumulative volume on the horizontal axis and cost on the vertical axis. Then the line between the two points can be drawn.

Step 5: The cost for a new cumulative volume can be obtained by drawing a vertical line from the value of the new cumulative volume on the horizontal axis up to the curve. A horizontal line can then be drawn from the intersection point to the vertical axis to derive the new cost.

Step 6: The actual base cost is arrived at by adjusting the cost obtained in step 5 for inflation occurring between the period used as the base in step 1 and the period for which the projection is being made. Expected inflation rates need to be used for future periods.

Example of Transfer Cost Forecasting. An example of this procedure follows.

Step 1. In the relevant section of the company's report in Period 3, the cumulative sales at the end of Period 3 of brand SARA are 396,000 units. This is also the amount of cumulative production if there is no inventory. The current unit transfer cost is $155.

Step 2. At the end of the next period, Period 4, cumulative sales of SARA are 796,000 units. There is, in addition, an inventory of 44,000 units for this same brand. Cumulative production of SARA at the end of Period 4 is thus 840,000 units. The transfer cost for Period 4 was $144.

Step 3. The inflation rate during Period 4, found in the Newsletter, was 11%. Therefore, adjusted for inflation, the cost in Period 3 monetary units is $129.73 (that is, $144/1.11).

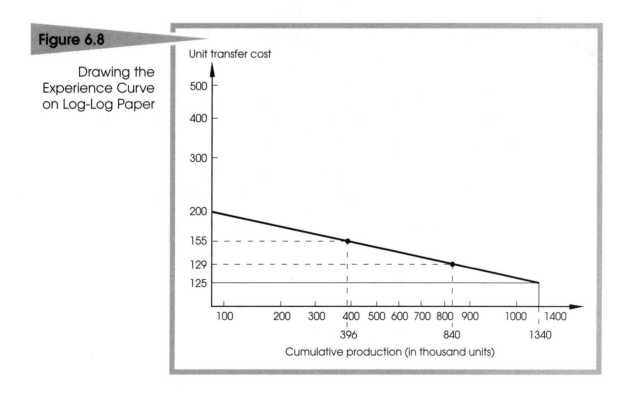

Figure 6.8

Drawing the Experience Curve on Log-Log Paper

Step 4. With the two points obtained in steps 1 and 3, the experience curve can be drawn on log-log paper, as illustrated in Figure 6.8.

Step 5. Assuming that the requested production for the next period is 500,000 units, the cumulative production for Period 5 will be 1,340,000 units (840,000 units plus the Period 5 production of 500,000 units). The cost corresponding to that level of cumulative production can be indexed from the graph in Figure 6.8. A vertical line starting on the horizontal axis at a cumulative production level of 1,340,000 units is drawn until it reaches the experience curve line. Then a horizontal line is drawn to the left until it reaches the vertical axis. The cost can be read at this point on the vertical axis in Figure 6.8—it is $125.

Step 6. The final step consists of adjusting the cost for inflation in Period 4 (11%) and expected inflation in Period 5, which is indicated in the Newsletter. Assuming this expected inflation rate is 13%, the final cost expected for Period 5 is $125 \times 1.11 \times 1.13 = 156.8.

Matching Product Attribute with Position

So far, the choice of the desirable position to attain has been driven by the size of demand of the segments and cost trends. In this section, the objective is to find the physical characteristics of the product that correspond to such a desirable position in the perceptual space. Therefore, at this point, the management team knows the coordinates at which the product should be positioned, either from the multidimensional scaling study or from the semantic scales study.

In the semantic scales study, the brands are evaluated by consumers on scales measuring their perception of the characteristics of the product. In the multidimensional scaling study, a dimension is interpreted using attributes of the product that correlate most highly with the dimension. In both cases, it is possible to relate the perceptual dimension, or scale, to an actual physical characteristic of the product (one of the five characteristics) and to price. Consequently, in order to find the physical characteristic levels that correspond to a given perception, the strategic analyst must investigate the relationship between the actual physical attribute of a product or brand and the consumers' perceptions of that attribute.

A simple way to summarize the information that a team possesses about that relationship is to plot the perceptions versus the actual characteristics. Figure 6.9 illustrates such a plot. The horizontal axis corresponds to perceptions about the prices of the various brands, and the vertical axis shows the actual recommended retail prices. Each brand has a data point that can give information about this relationship. Consumers' perceptual distortions are due to the natural psycho-physical property of a given physical attribute, to past experience with existing products, and to advertising effects.

In the MARKSTRAT market, although consumers may not know the precise value of a brand on a physical characteristic, they cannot be duped, and plots of the type described above (as in Figure 6.9) should describe the nature of perceptions relatively well. The relationship can be summarized, as in Figure 6.9, by drawing the curve that fits the data. A straight line can be used as a first approximation. In Figure 6.9, the deviations around the line are relatively

Figure 6.9

Relationship
between Perceived
Price and Actual
Price (Semantic
Scale Data)

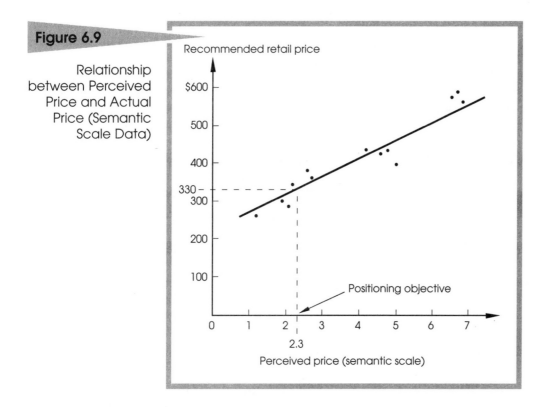

small, indicating that the relationship can be summarized relatively well by a straight line. The line corresponding to the best fit to the data can be found by regressing actual price on perceived price. Then, by projecting the positioning objective on the line, the actual physical value for the corresponding characteristic can be found easily. In Figure 6.9, the retail price corresponding to a perception of 2.3 on the semantic scale is found to be approximately $330.

This analysis is performed automatically in the **Product Design** menu of the **Analysis** module of MARKSTRAT. One of the options available in the menu is the **Estimation of ideal characteristics—regression analysis.** Another option is **Estimation of ideal characteristics—graph.** The first option displays the results of the regression analysis discussed above for each of the semantic scales (Figure 6.10). It also shows the estimated value of the physical characteristic of the product that matches the current ideal value on the perceived scale. The second option provides a graphical display of this analysis (see Figure 6.11), just as discussed above with reference to Figure 6.9. Therefore, the semantic scales study not only provides perceptual data, as discussed in Chapter 3, but also enables an analysis of the correspondence between the current evaluation of what consumers in one segment prefer and the actual product characteristics that would satisfy those needs.

These regression results can be used to estimate the position of a new or modified brand. This analysis is done when you click on the **Estimation of perceptions for new or modified brands** option in the **Product design** menu of the **Analysis** module. When the physical characteristics and price of a brand are entered, the estimated values of the perceptions are reported on the semantic scales (Figure 6.12).

Figure 6.10   Estimation of Ideal Characteristics—Regression Analysis

SEMANTIC SCALES - ESTIMATE OF IDEAL CHARACTERISTICS

	Weight (Kg)	Design (Index)	Volume (Dm3)	Max Freq (KHz)	Power (W)	Price ($)
Linear equation						
Slope (m)	1.58	1.03	12.28	8.38	15.63	72.23
Intercept (b)	8.46	2.47	9.43	-5.78	-10.48	53.69
R²	0.8405	0.7878	0.7006	0.9654	0.9634	0.9582
Estimated ideal characteristics						
Buffs	12	7	32	46	91	332
Singles	17	7	83	36	65	377
Pros	16	8	72	34	25	368
HiEarners	17	7	73	38	33	480
Others	19	4	85	13	72	298

The same regressions can be used to identify the combination of characteristics required to achieve a targeted brand position on the perceptual map. The **Estimation of characteristics for brand positioning** option computes estimated values of the physical characteristics of the product for desired perceived positions. For example, Figure 6.13 shows that the weight of SEXY, 15 kg, is perceived to be 4.00 on the corresponding semantic scale. If the firm were to attempt to reposition the brand to be perceived as a 3 on that scale

Figure 6.11   Estimation of Ideal Characteristics—Graph

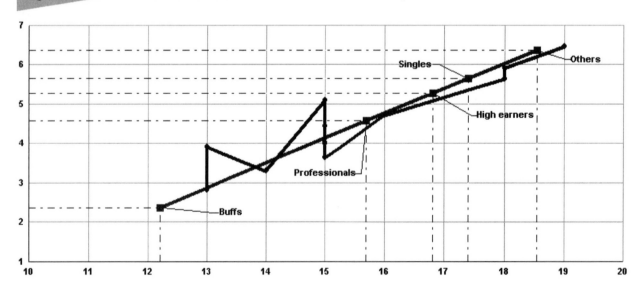

SEMANTIC SCALES - ESTIMATE OF IDEAL WEIGHT
Percentage of variation explained = 84%.
Segments not shown on the graph are outside the feasibility range.
See additional explanations in quick help.

Figure 6.12   Estimation of Perceptions (Semantic Scales) for New or Modified Brands

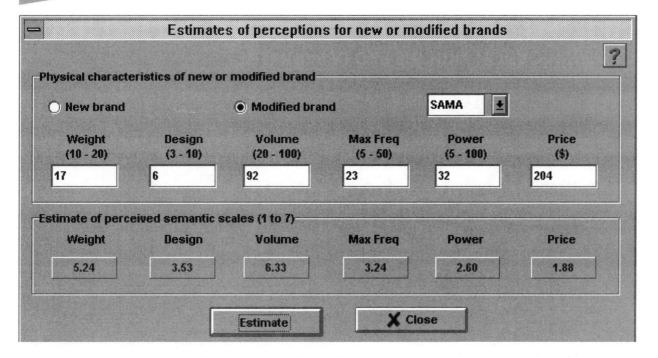

(the target), using the information from the regression (Figure 6.13), a weight of 13 kg would be required.

Figure 6.14 provides the same information as Figure 6.11. However, the scale from the multidimensional study is used on the vertical axis. As indicated earlier in this chapter, these scales are more precise, as they provide a continuous scale from –20 to +20 instead of the seven-point scale used with the semantic scales. The direct consequence of this greater range and scale refinement is that the information about the relationship between perceptions and actual characteristics may be more precise. In particular, if the relationship is not linear, as in the illustration discussed above, the MDS scale should provide better information. However, sampling errors should not be ignored (this study is based on a sample of only 200 consumers), as they could hide more complex relationships. The curve that best fits the data should be used.

Although the information provided by the multidimensional scaling study might be more valid, the complexity of the scales forming the dimensions in the perceptual space may complicate assessing the degree to which a physical characteristic contributes to a certain perception, or vice versa. In fact, although the attributes chosen in the semantic scales have a close correspondence with the physical characteristics of the products, it is difficult to determine a priori which characteristic of the product should be used for the horizontal axis on Figure 6.14. The graphical representation of the relationships may help determine which characteristics of the product are related to the perceptual dimensions. This graphical analysis can be easily performed using the **Estimation of ideal characteristics—graph** option in the **Product design** menu of the **Analysis** module.

Figure 6.13   Estimation of Characteristics for Brand Positioning (Semantic Scales)

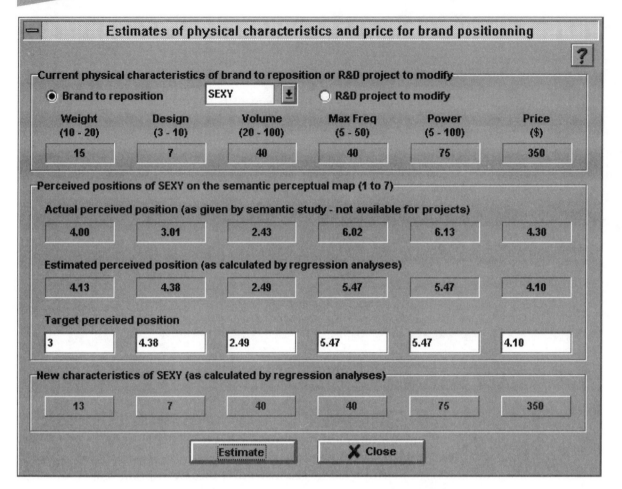

This analysis, however, considers each characteristic one by one. It could be that a perceptual dimension is constructed from multiple cues associated with the product characteristics, in which case it might be useful to perform a multivariate regression, as is offered by the **Multiple regression analysis** option in the **Product Design** menu of the **Analysis** module. Perceptions on a specified dimension of the MDS solution are regressed on the physical characteristics of the products, including the brands' prices (Figure 6.15). The coefficients represent the influence of each characteristic on perception of the brand.

With such a regression model, perceptions on the map can be estimated for a new brand or a brand in which the physical characteristics have been modified. This analysis is done by clicking on the **Estimation of perceptions for new or modified brands** option in the **Product Design** menu under the **Analysis** module. When the physical characteristics and price of a brand are entered, the estimated values of the perceptions are reported on the MDS scales. For example, in Figure 6.16, changing the volume of SAMA to 92 dm^3 modifies the brand perceptions, especially on the convenience dimension.

Figure 6.14 Relationship between Characteristics and Perceptions (MDS Scale)

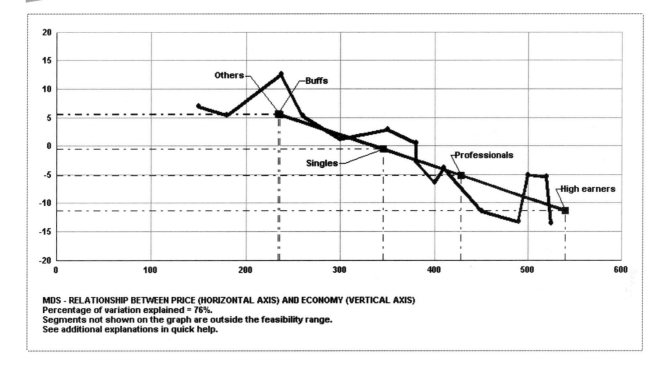

MDS - RELATIONSHIP BETWEEN PRICE (HORIZONTAL AXIS) AND ECONOMY (VERTICAL AXIS)
Percentage of variation explained = 76%.
Segments not shown on the graph are outside the feasibility range.
See additional explanations in quick help.

This multiple regression can also be used to search for the characteristics necessary to reposition a product at a given location on the MDS perceptual map. The **Estimation of characteristics for brand repositioning** option searches for a combination of physical characteristics that will lead to a given

Figure 6.15 Multiple Regression Analysis

MDS - REGRESSION ANALYSIS - ECONOMY

	Physical characteristics						Constant
	Weight (Kg)	Design (Index)	Volume (Dm3)	Max Freq (KHz)	Power (W)	Price ($)	
Equation of best-fit line							
Coefficients	0.9766	-0.8167	-0.0206	0.5187	-0.1909	-0.0786	13.9610
Regression statistics							
Std. error for the coefficients	0.2513	0.3549	0.0443	0.1768	0.0886	0.0056	6.7192
Observed t value	3.8857	-2.3009	-0.4656	2.9343	-2.1546	-14.0288	
Significance level	< 0.01	< 0.05	> 0.10	< 0.01	< 0.05	< 0.01	
R^2	0.9961						
Adjusted R^2	0.9938						
Std. error for the Y estimate	0.9149						
Degrees of freedom	Regression: 10		Numerator: 6		Denominator: 10		
Observed F value	426.46						
Regression sum of squares	2 141.58						
Residual sum of squares	8.37						

Figure 6.16 ▸ Estimation of Perceptions (MDS Scale) for New or Modified Brands

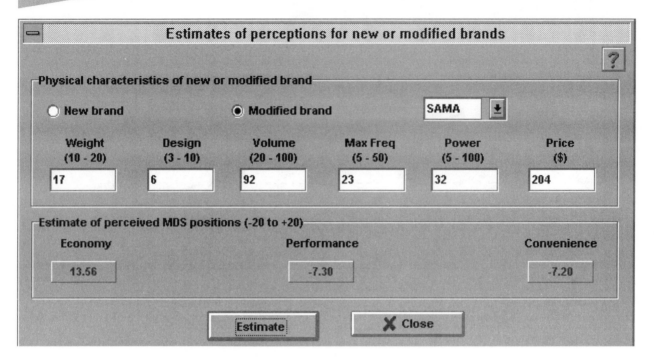

perception of the product on the MDS perceptual map. For example, if a value of 8 is targeted on the economy dimension (less economical than the current product), the optimization suggests a change of price from $204 to $275 (see Figure 6.17).

In this option window, choose the brand to be repositioned. Its characteristics and its perceptions on the MDS dimensions are displayed. Enter the values of the new target position on each of the perceptual dimensions, and check the boxes corresponding to physical characteristics of the product that you are willing to modify. Click the **Optimize** button (you may also choose one of the three speed levels, keeping in mind that the slower the search, the more accurate the solution may be). The solution will appear as the optimized characteristics values. There may be multiple solutions to this problem; the solution shown is the one closest to the current product specification.

These analyses assumed that there were sufficient data available, especially around the region corresponding to the perceptual objectives. If there is no brand in the market (as is the case before the first entry in the Vodite market), the only information available concerns some perceptual measure of an ideal product. It is very difficult, however, to restate these perceptions as a physical characteristic; with a completely new product, consumers might not even comprehend the physical attributes because of their lack of reference.

These difficulties, typical of completely new products, are probably best resolved by test marketing the product. A pioneer who does not need fast market penetration because of the lack of competitive threat might develop one or several products, produced in small quantities, in order to learn how

Figure 6.17   Estimation of Characteristics for Brand Repositioning

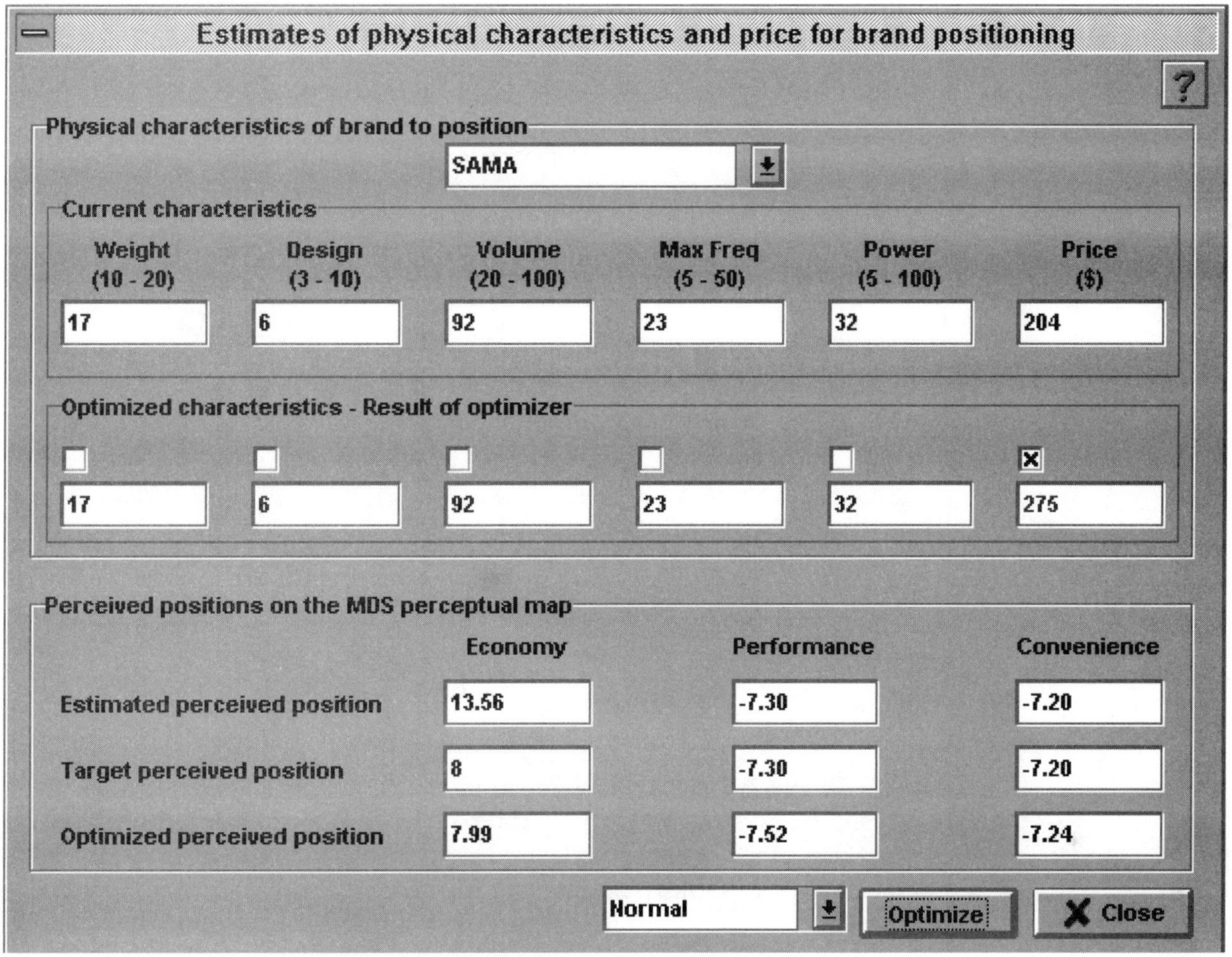

they are perceived in the market. This approach, however, provides that same information to competitors!

When few data points are available, it may be preferable simply to determine the range of physical characteristics from the closest brands available in the market, without fitting the curve to the entire range of products. Figure 6.18 shows that, in terms of design, brands A and E are the closest brands on either side of where the new brand should be positioned. The closest brand on the design dimension is E, which has a perceived design of 4.5 on the semantic scale. Information available on the physical characteristics of brand E indicates that the actual design index of this product has a value of 6. This brand is perceived a little lower than where the new brand should be positioned. The closest brand higher than the objective is brand A, with a perceived design of 6 and an actual design index of 8. Consequently, the new brand should be between 6 and 8. If the distance between these two neighbors is not too large, a linear interpolation can be done between the two

Figure 6.18

Determination of
Physical Attribute
Range (from
Semantic Scales)

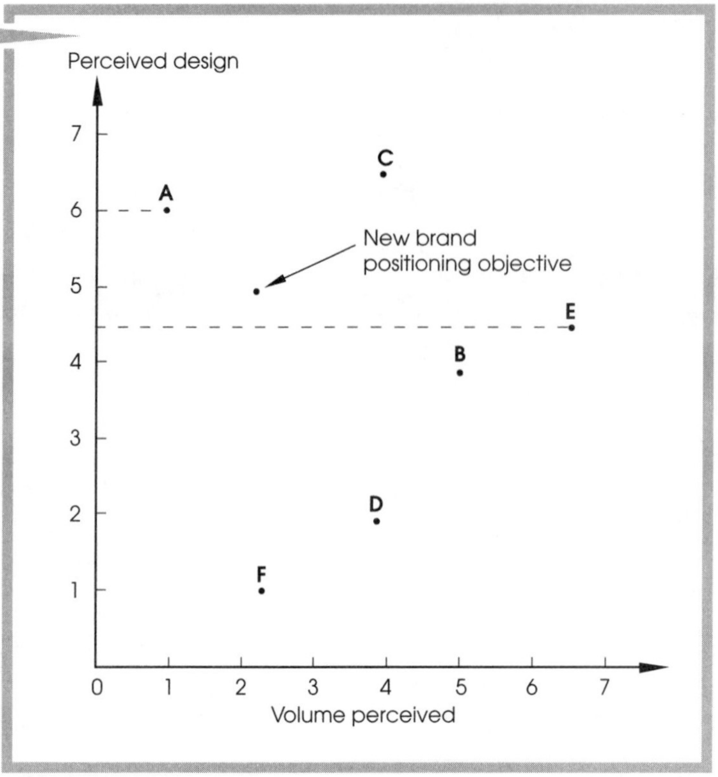

points. In the example discussed, the design index specification would be
$6 + (8 - 6)(5 - 4.5)/(6 - 4.5) = 6.7$, rounded to 7.

In summary, several methods can be used to specify the physical characteristics of a product once the desired perceptions are known. The choice depends on the availability of data. All of these methods, although imperfect, offer approximations that should become more accurate as more data become available.

REPOSITIONING STRATEGIES

Once a brand has been sold in the market, consumers have a certain idea about the brand, which is represented by its position in a perceptual space. Over time, demand and competitive dynamics affect the optimal positioning of a brand. In MARKSTRAT, brands may be repositioned to adapt to new environmental conditions.

Repositioning can be achieved by advertising or by research and development. Using advertising to reposition a product requires four types of decisions (see Figure 6.19):

1. Selecting the target segment(s).
2. Specifying perceptual objectives for the brand. For instance, if you want to reposition SEMI (E) closer to the ideal point of the Professionals segment in Figure 6.1, you can specify a communication on MDS scales by checking that option: use Economy for Dimension 1 and Per-

Figure 6.19   Decisions for Repositioning a Brand through Advertising

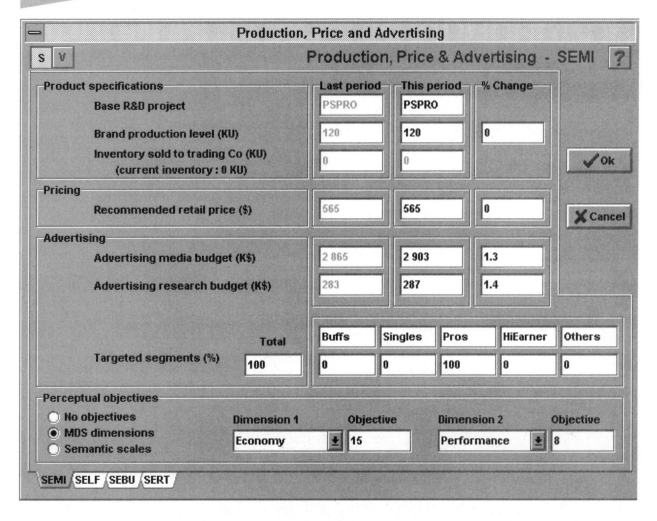

formance for Dimension 2 (a maximum of two perceptual dimensions can be used because beyond that level the message would be too complex to communicate effectively). Perceptual objectives of 15 on Economy and 8 on Performance can be entered in the corresponding boxes. These will serve as a guideline for the design of appropriate advertising platforms and copy.

3. Allocating an advertising media budget for the brand (e.g., $3000 K). The higher this budget, the further you can expect to be able to move the position of the brand.

4. Allocating an advertising research budget (e.g., $300 K). This is necessary for copy testing and effective media selection. The higher the advertising research budget, the more accurate you can expect the repositioning to be in terms of reaching the perceptual objectives.

It should be noted that simply indicating the targeted segment (100% of the budget to the High Earners) is insufficient to reposition a brand. Target selection affects only the media vehicles selected to communicate the message; it does not affect the message itself. These decisions are entered in the **Production, Price & Advertising** section of the **Decisions** module.

As discussed in Chapter 4, a brand might not need to be repositioned on both dimensions. Indeed, if the perceptions on one dimension correspond to what consumers want, there is no reason to use advertising to change that perceptual value. Instead, changes in perceptions should be concentrated on only one dimension, and the advertising copy should be designed so that the other dimension remains unaffected. The **None** option in the list for Dimension 2 should then be selected.

If the brand's position is satisfactory on both axes, the advertising objective is purely to improve brand awareness with persuasive arguments that reinforce the current perceptions held by consumers. In that case, to indicate to the advertising agency that the advertising should not change current perceptions, the corresponding **No objectives** option should be checked.

The mass communication budget should reflect the communication objectives. If the product is modified with new physical characteristics, a larger budget may be necessary. Similarly, advertising a complex message involving two dimensions requires greater repetition and, therefore, a larger budget. Also, the amount of advertising research to be devoted to such communication objectives should be higher (for example, 10% versus 5% of total advertising budget) because more copy testing is needed to ensure that the message is correctly grasped and to generate the highest quality creative work possible. This budget will be used to improve the efficiency of the repositioning, as well as the efficiency of each MMU ($) spent on media space and time.

The ability of advertising to reposition brands is limited, however, by the actual physical characteristics of a product; advertising can shift consumers' perceptions of these characteristics within only a certain range. At some point, it becomes more profitable to reposition a brand by changing its physical characteristics rather than by advertising alone. This requires the successful completion of an R&D project, which results in a product with the desired new characteristics.

Issues concerning the development of new products will be discussed in the next chapter. However, it is important to point out that the decision as to whether to reposition through an advertising strategy or through a new product development strategy depends on the extent to which repositioning is desired and is a function of the current level of brand awareness. A brand that consumers are extremely familiar with will be difficult, if not impossible, to reposition. It also depends, of course, on the ability of the firm to complete R&D projects in which the physical characteristics of the products correspond to the market needs.

As described above, the perceptual map is an important tool for the design of positioning and repositioning strategies. It may, however, lead to inadequate decisions if other factors are not taken into account. It is important to note that brands have different awareness levels. A brand may be positioned close to a segment's ideal point but draw few purchases from consumers if it is unknown. In addition, it can be expected that the higher the awareness level of a brand, the more difficult it will be to reposition it because consumers are knowledgeable about the brand. The five segments represent different volumes of potential sales and are at different stages of their development. Their needs evolve over time and so, too, do their ideal points. Although the multidimensional scaling analysis reproduces brand similarities and preferences satisfactorily, as expressed by a sample of individuals, it is certainly incomplete; other dimensions may enter into consumers' perceptions.

It is obviously possible to change the perceptions of a brand through a product change. The appropriate advertising program must also be designed in order to let consumers know of the changes in the physical characteristics of the brand. These repositioning issues in the context of a product modification are discussed in the next chapter, concerned with research and development of new products.

CHAPTER 6 SUMMARY

Assessing Perceptions and Preferences

- Consumers' perceptions of products affect their purchasing decisions.
- Competition is more intense between products that are perceived by consumers to be similar.
- Consumers have a higher preference for brands that they perceive to be closer to their ideal combination of benefits (ideal point).

Optimal Brand Position

- Multisegment positioning strategy: attracting consumers from several segments
- Mono-segment positioning strategy: concentrating on a targeted segment
- Prediction of ideal points: anticipating the evolution of consumers' needs
- Forecasting brand demand: anticipating the growth of each market segment and the market share obtainable in each market segment
- Forecasting brand transfer cost: using the experience curve concept to project the evolution of unit transfer cost according to cumulative production

The Marketing and R&D Interface

This chapter discusses issues involved in implementing a marketing strategy as it relates to interaction with the R&D department. After you have assessed a situation and developed a marketing strategy that anticipates the needs of the market, the strategy must be implemented. One of the most important aspects of implementation is specifying the characteristics of the product that will be offered to consumers. Given the uncertainty about the evolution of the market, it is probable that you will need to develop a portfolio of products so as to be ready to implement contingency plans and strategies. Therefore, in this chapter the methods by which the marketing department and the R&D department communicate with each other are detailed. Then the relationship between the specific R&D strategy and the implementation of the marketing strategy is discussed.

Figure 7.1 summarizes the marketing-R&D interface. Marketing requests a project from the R&D department by specifying a project name, a budget, and the physical characteristics of the desired product. The Company Report for the following period will indicate whether or not the project has been successfully completed. If the desired product has not been found, the marketing department may ask R&D to continue the project. In this case, it will have to invest additional funds in the project, without changing its name or characteristics. Alternatively, the project may be dropped, in which case the investment already made is lost. Or, if one of the characteristics (except cost) of the desired product is changed, a new project with a different name must be launched—without benefit from the investment previously made. Only the cost characteristic of an ongoing project may be changed, particularly if inflation is to be taken into account.

If an R&D project has been completed successfully, the marketing department may use the newly developed product to modify an existing brand or to introduce a new one. The name of the project does not in any sense restrict the application of the new product. For instance, a new product developed through R&D project PSARO may be used to modify the existing brand SALT or to launch a new brand, SAFE. Alternatively, the firm may choose not to exploit the new product immediately, in which case it still

Figure 7.1

The Marketing-R&D
Interface

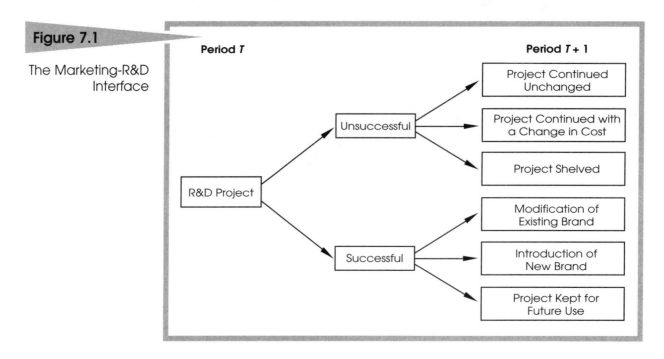

remains available for use in future years. The product is then always available at the cost at which it was completed, adjusted for inflation.

It is important to note that research and development is an activity that takes time. In some industries, several years are necessary to complete a project. In MARKSTRAT, there is a minimum of one period (and sometimes there are several periods) between the launching of an R&D project and its use in the marketplace. Thus, the marketing-R&D interface requires particularly careful planning.

COMMUNICATION WITH THE R&D DEPARTMENT

Project Code Names

An R&D department is composed of research teams working on specific projects that are identified by code names. (For example, Project Chicago at Microsoft gave birth to Windows 95.) These code names have nothing to do with the use of the completed project by the marketing department. The codes are used simply so that the marketing department can ask an R&D team for information about the progress of the corresponding R&D work over time. The marketing department chooses the code names. These names follow the conventions presented in Chapter 2: the first letter must be P to indicate that this is a project rather than an actual brand, the second letter is an S for a Sonite or a V for a Vodite, and the last three characters of the project code name are chosen by the team.

Once a project has been completed, the code name remains forever associated with the product resulting from the R&D project. So the project, with its associated product characteristics, is filed under that code name. No new project should use the same code name, as this would only create confusion.

The name of a completed project cannot be reused for a new project, even if the new one is only seeking a minor modification of the product. Each firm has two completed R&D projects at the beginning of the simulation. These two projects are the prototypes used to launch the two brands each firm has commercialized. For example, Firm I markets two brands, SIRO and SIBI. The R&D projects corresponding to these brands are, respectively, PSIRO and PSIBI. Therefore, no new R&D project can use these names, as the projects have been completed in the past and are registered in the files of the firm under these two code names.

A project is not necessarily completed by the R&D department within the year in which the marketing department requests it. In fact, the budget given to the R&D department is often insufficient. In this case, the project can be continued the next year until it is completed, or the marketing department may decide to abandon it. If the firm decides to continue the project, its specifications should not be changed (except possibly the unit cost) and the same code name should be used. Therefore, a project code name is associated with the search for a product with specific physical attributes defined by the values on the five physical characteristics.

If the marketing department realizes that one (or several) of the five characteristics requested is wrong for the market, a new project code needs to be issued. The budget invested in the abandoned project is a sunk cost that will not be used toward the completion of the new project. This situation is illustrated by the following example, for which the decisions are summarized in Table 7.1.

In Period 3, the marketing department requests project PSILK, with a budget of $1 million. This budget proves to be insufficient, and the R&D department asks for an additional $1.5 million to complete the project. In Period 4, the same project code, PSILK, is used with the same characteristics, and an additional $1.5 million is provided. The targeted unit cost is increased from $200 to $204 to take into account the 2% inflation in the last period. Eventually, the marketing department realizes that because of changes in preference in the market, a volume of 50 dm^3 is too high and 45 dm^3 is more appropriate. Thus, a new R&D project with a new code name, PSILI, is started. The money spent for PSILK in Period 3 is lost, since the project has been canceled.

Table 7.1

Continuation of an R&D Project

Project Name	Budget	Weight	Design	Volume	Max. Freq.	Power	Base Cost
Period 3 Request:							
PSILK	1000	15	8	50	10	50	200
PVIVA	3000	80	15	80	7	60	200
Period 4 Request:							
PSILK	1500	15	8	50	10	50	204
PSILI	2000	15	8	45	10	50	200
PVIVA	1000	80	15	80	7	60	350

On the other hand, if the five characteristics remained unchanged, but the cost needed to be adjusted to reflect more realistic expectations, the project code would still be valid, because the same R&D team would continue to work on the same product with the same specifications. Therefore, in the case of PVIVA in Table 7.1, for which the minimum realistic cost is $350, the cost is adjusted from $200 in the Period 3 request to $350 in the Period 4 request. The five physical characteristics remain unchanged, and the project code remains PVIVA.

Product Physical Characteristics Requests

The characteristics of the Sonite and Vodite products are described in Chapter 2. In particular, the feasible range for each characteristic is reported in Table 2.2 and is also summarized at the end of this chapter. A product specification may consist of any combination of these characteristics, as long as each is an integer number and remains within its respective range.

As illustrated in the previous chapter, you cannot assume that a higher level on a characteristic is better for consumers. Neither can you assume that it is easier (requires a lower budget) to "downgrade" a product on one characteristic than to "upgrade" a product. In other words, it is quite possible that it would take a $1 million budget to complete a project for a product with a power of 50 watts and $2 million to complete a project for a product with a power of 30 watts. The base cost of a product clearly depends on the characteristics of the product. However, the base cost also depends on the specific experience of a firm with similar products, which could be a source of advantage over competitors and a barrier to their entry in a given market.

The product characteristics to be requested for a given project follow directly from the analyses in Chapter 6.

Unit Cost Request

There are different strategies that the marketing department can use in interacting with the R&D department. One simple way to specify a cost in an R&D project is to start at the price that consumers are willing to pay for that product. Given an objective of returns or margins, the maximum cost possible to realize that objective can be computed. This might not be the lowest cost achievable, but it provides a level above which the strategy would not be attractive.

For example, if the market is not willing to pay more than $300 for the product, the following calculations are implied. The distributors' margins should be subtracted from the price to obtain revenues at the manufacturer's selling price. Given the distribution channels' expected shares for the product (for instance, 15%, 40%, and 45% for specialty stores, department stores, and mass merchandisers, respectively) and given that the three channels of distribution have margins of 40%, 30%, and 30%, respectively, the average distributor's margin is the weighted average of the three margin rates, where the weights are the channel shares, after correction for the expected retail price in each channel. Therefore, in this example, the average distribution margin is

$$(40\% \times 0.15) + (30\% \times 0.40) + (30\% \times 0.45 \times 0.90) = 30.15\%$$

(The 0.90 correction factor is because the mass merchandiser channel sells at 90% of the recommended retail price.) Consequently, the manufacturer's selling price is the retail price minus the margin, which is $90 (i.e., $300 × 0.3015), or a price of $210. If the objective of the firm for gross margins is 40%, the maximum cost that would satisfy this objective is $126 [i.e., 210 − (210 × 0.4)]. A request can then be made to the R&D department to research a product with such a cost. Once this project is complete, new projects can be started to modify the product and reduce cost.

An alternative method for determining the cost characteristic is doing many feasibility studies, as the R&D department will give the lowest cost that it is willing to guarantee. Indeed, the unit cost depends on the physical specification of the product, as indicated in Chapter 2. Because not all physical characteristics are equally important to consumers, a tradeoff must be found to achieve a cost that will provide appropriate margins for the firm. This is discussed in greater detail in the next section.

Budget

The last question that must be decided in a request for an R&D project is how much should be spent on the project. This is particularly important given the nature of the interaction with the R&D department. When it makes a project request, the marketing department determines the size of the investment to be made on a yearly basis. If the budget is insufficient, additional funds can be provided in subsequent years.

However, the R&D department operates, like the marketing department, as a profit center. Consequently, it makes profits by accepting more than it needs to complete a project if the marketing department is willing to pay this amount. This could happen if the marketing department were ignorant of the efficiency of the firm's R&D department. So it is important for the marketing department to develop a good understanding both of the cost structure of the products and of the efficiency of the R&D department. Again, this calls for requesting R&D product feasibility studies.

A request for a feasibility study is like that for any other product, except that the budget invested is relatively small. The minimum budget below which the R&D department does not guarantee information is $100,000 for both Sonite and Vodite products.

More generally, the budget required to complete a project depends on both the characteristics specified and the experience of the firm with similar products—in particular, the experience of the R&D department in completing similar projects in the past. Consequently, the transfer of know-how from accumulated R&D experience comes only from R&D projects that have been completed successfully in the past. The budget depends also on the unit cost requested. If a firm has already benefited from the experience curve, reducing the cost through R&D is less expensive for that firm than it is for a firm with fewer cumulative production units. In summary, it can be expected that the more similar a new project is to one that has been completed, the lower the budget required to complete it. Also, if a base cost can be lowered because of production experience, this will facilitate the completion of a project at a lower cost.

Of the characteristics specified in a given project, some are easier to deliver than others. It could be cheaper, for example, to improve volume than to improve weight. Therefore, the marketing department might have to trade off certain characteristic specifications, given the unit cost and the budget for the project.

As in any research enterprise, the completion of the project is subject to uncertainty. Although the performance of the R&D department is far from random, at a given budget there is always a probability of its not completing the project. The probability of completion increases with the R&D budget, however.

Given all these influencing factors, it is difficult to indicate a general order of magnitude for R&D budgets. However, as indicated in Chapter 2, industry experts estimate that an adequate budget in Period 1 for a Sonite project ranges from $100,000 to $1,000,000. This range would apply to products similar to those currently available in the market. For a Vodite project, it has been estimated that $2,000,000 is the minimum budget for expected completion. Again, the budget depends on the specification of characteristics.

R&D DEPARTMENT RESPONSES

The R&D department organizes its work by assigning projects to R&D teams. These teams work during the year on the many requests they receive from the entire firm, including divisions other than marketing. It takes a period of one year for any division to obtain a response from the R&D department. For the marketing department, the upshot of this is that it is critical to plan ahead. Otherwise, its efficiency suffers, as opportunities may be missed and costs may be higher.

The on-line query, discussed in Chapter 4, is a rapid method of communicating with the R&D department to obtain answers to questions that would, otherwise, take one period to answer. However, because an R&D team is assigned to work on the project during the whole period, the information it gets as a result of a full-fledged R&D study (including a feasibility study) is more accurate.

Assuming that the product has feasible characteristics—that is, features that fall within the range of feasible characteristics summarized in Table 2.2—the R&D department will respond to the marketing department in one of the following three ways.

Project Available Message

The R&D department indicates that a project has been successfully completed by noting in the R&D section of the Company Report that the product is available for production. An example is given in Figure 7.2. A completed project can be used in the following period or any future period, as discussed in the section on using completed R&D projects. In the example in Figure 7.2, projects PSEMI to PSOT3 are available, among others.

Figure 7.2 Example of R&D Section of Company Report—Period 6

SONITE R&D PROJECTS

Name	Physical Characteristics					Base Cost $		Allocated Budget K$	
	Weight (Kg)	Design (Index)	Volume (Dm3)	Max Freq (KHz)	Power (W)	Current	Minimum realistic	Cumulative	Req. for completion
PSEMI	13	7	40	40	75	197	174	1 500	Available
PSELF	15	4	40	45	90	248	184	2 000	Available
PSEL1	15	4	40	45	90	196	184	500	Available
PSERT	13	7	50	30	55	198	139	940	Available
PSPRO	14	5	50	40	80	197	170	1 250	Available
PSSIN	15	5	65	30	60	181	133	1 000	Available
PSMO3	12	7	70	28	58	169	137	950	Available
PSOT3	14	5	70	15	35	111	89	1 150	Available
PSE77	15	5	77	20	30	85	85	100	730
PSOT1	15	7	60	30	35	110	110	100	580

Insufficient Budget

As shown in Figure 7.2, project PSE77 calls for an additional budget of $730,000. The marketing team may decide to continue the project in the next period with the same five characteristics attached to the project code. However, the unit cost may be changed without changing the project name. In fact, given that there is a certain level of inflation in this MARKSTRAT environment, leaving the cost unchanged would, in effect, be equivalent to requesting a real cost lower than that of the previous period. The R&D department does not guarantee such a lower cost. Therefore, in order to keep the project request the same, the cost requested is automatically adjusted for inflation. The Newsletter indicates the expected inflation rate that is applied for the future period. The information provided by the R&D department on the unit costs at which all the products would be transferred is automatically updated based on this expected inflation rate.

This updating is illustrated in the R&D decision shown in Figure 7.3. Project PSE77 is continued in Period 7, with the additional budget of $730,000. The five characteristics remain unchanged from the project PSE77 requested in Period 6 (see Figure 7.2). However, the cost request, which had been $83 in Period 6, has been adjusted in Figure 7.2 by the R&D department for a 2% expected inflation rate next period. Therefore a cost of $85 is now requested to complete the project in Period 7 (see Figure 7.3).

Under these specified conditions of cost and additional budget, the R&D department guarantees that the project will be completed next period. Clearly, the additional funds could be perceived as a high price to pay for such a guarantee from the R&D department. Indeed, the marketing department might decide not to invest so much and, instead, risk completing the project with a particular probability that is subject to chance.

Figure 7.3   Decisions to Complete R&D Projects—Period 7

Project	Expenditures		Product Characteristics				
		Weight	Design	Volume	Max Freq	Power	Base cost
	K$	Kg	Index	Dm3	KHz	W	$
PSE77	730	15	5	77	20	30	85

Table heading: **SONITE R&D PROJECTS**

Unrealistic Cost

The last response possible from the R&D department is that the requested base cost is too low to be feasible, given the other characteristics, and that the requested cost has been adjusted to the minimum realistic cost. The R&D department then specifies the additional funds it needs to guarantee the completion of the project at this cost.

Note that in both cases—insufficient funds or unrealistic cost—the additional budget required to guarantee completion does not need to be invested in the next period. The guarantee applies to any future period, provided that the amounts (both *additional budget* and *cost*) are adjusted for inflation during the waiting period.

UTILIZATION OF COMPLETED R&D PROJECTS

Once an R&D project has been completed, the corresponding product is made available for production. The marketing department might choose not to use this availability in the next period—it might keep the product in reserve for future use. But if the team does decide to use the new product opportunity, it has two options. It can introduce the product in the market as a new brand, or it can reformulate an existing brand with the physical characteristics corresponding to the project.

Brand Introduction

A brand is introduced in the market by entering a brand name (one that has not been used in the past) in the **Brand portfolio** section of the **Decisions** module. This brand name is completely independent of the code used for the R&D project. The R&D project code, however, needs to be specified so that the production department knows the product specification. This is also indicated in the **Brand portfolio** section of the **Decisions** module, as described in Chapter 4.

In the example given in Figure 7.4, product SELA is being introduced in the market using the product with the specification corresponding to R&D project PSSIN. Given that the brand is just being introduced, expenditure on advertising is needed to develop consumers' awareness of the brand. However, in this case, brand SELA is being introduced with a small advertising budget and without perceptual objectives, probably to provide information to management on how the brand is perceived. If the positioning is satisfactory, greater investment in advertising will be made in the next period. If, however, the perceptions need adjustment, advertising can still be used to reposition the brand. In cases where a high advertising budget creates a high level of brand awareness, it becomes difficult to adjust perceptions through advertising. This example illustrates a safer but slower approach, which might be appropriate only if the level of competition is low.

Figure 7.4 Example of Brand Introduction

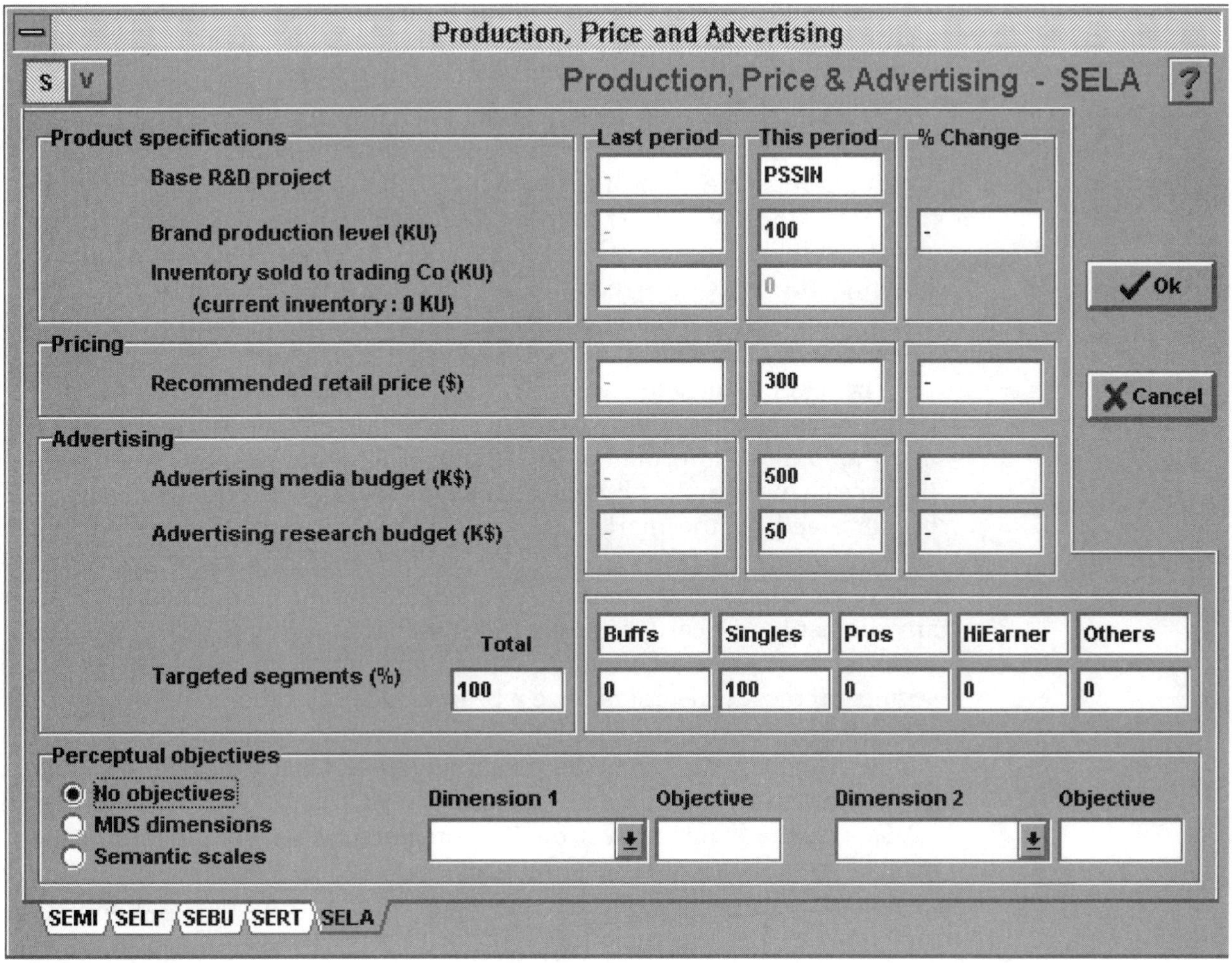

Brand Modification

In the brand portfolio decisions shown in Figure 7.5, brand SEMI, which is one of the original brands marketed by Firm E, is being modified using the physical characteristics corresponding to project PSOT3. Again, the code name of the R&D project does not place restrictions on what the project can be used for. The only difference between this procedure and a brand introduction (described above) is that brand SEMI was on the market before; therefore, the brand name is not new.

A brand modification decision has several consequences. First, the production department is now producing units of SEMI with the new product characteristics. The inventory of the obsolete products must be sold outside the MARKSTRAT world, as MARKSTRAT consumers would not accept an old version of the product. Obsolete inventories are sold to a trading company at a price equal to 80% of the transfer cost. As the units are still with the production department, which charges the marketing department when units are sold, the obsolete units must be purchased from the production department. Consequently, a loss of 20% of transfer cost is taken on the obsolete inventory. This loss will appear as a cost for inventory disposal in the Company Report for the next period, as discussed in Chapter 4.

As an illustration, suppose Firm E has an inventory of 56,118 units of brand SEMI at the end of Period 7. The transfer cost of SEMI at this time is $107 per unit. In the next period, Period 8, the brand is being modified with the specification of a new R&D project, PSOT3. Consequently, the inventory of 56,118 units evaluated at a transfer cost of $107 per unit will be sold to the trading company at 80% of that cost, or $4,803,700. The loss of $1,200,925 (i.e., 20% × 56,118 units × $107 transfer cost) will be shown as an inventory disposal loss in the Company Report of Firm E in Period 8. Note that there could be some differences between the loss reported and the computations, due to the rounding off of the unit transfer cost reported in the output, but these differences are minor.

The second consequence of a brand modification concerns consumers' perceptions. Both Sonites and Vodites are products that consumers buy after a fair amount of information processing. Therefore, when a brand is modified, the changes in the physical characteristics of the product will eventually be perceived by the market. The usual perceptual distortions and biases apply. However, a firm's ability to reposition the brand depends on awareness of the brand in the various segments. A brand with little awareness in any segment can clearly be easily repositioned anywhere on the map. On the other hand, it will be difficult to reposition a brand closer to the needs of a segment if most consumers have a prior belief about the brand that is different from the position implied by the new physical characteristics.

Because the brand name has not changed, however, the awareness levels for that brand in each segment are preserved. This may give brand modification a clear advantage over the introduction of a new brand, as a firm will need to spend less to establish the brand in its new position and, therefore, to gain market share. Advertising is ineffective in repositioning a brand with a high level of awareness, so modification of the physical characteristics of a well-established brand will usually be required (although not necessarily sufficient) to reposition it effectively.

Keeping a Product for Future Use

An R&D project that has just been completed does not have to be used immediately in the following period. In fact, a company planning ahead would have products available in advance. Also, given the uncertainties in demand and in competitors' strategies, a company should develop contingency plans and have products readily available to implement these plans. Once an R&D project has been completed, the company can put it in reserve and bring it to the market whenever it wants. The characteristics of the project remain unchanged, but the transfer cost, which is increased by inflation every period, will rise.

Multiple Brands with the Same Physical Characteristics

The completion of a project indicates that manufacturing has been found feasible and production can start. Decisions on the marketing side about how to market the product are an independent issue. Consequently, the same product can be marketed under different names. This might happen in competitive situations where multiple brands could pose a barrier to the entry of competitors with new brands. It could also happen when the same basic products would be distributed to different segments, which may be willing to pay different prices.

Figure 7.5   Example of Brand Modifications

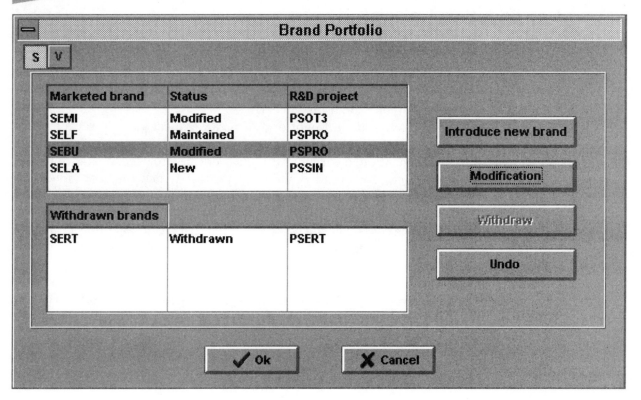

This situation is illustrated in Figure 7.5, where brands SELF and SEBU use the same R&D project, PSPRO, although the price charged for each can be different. Therefore, two brands with the same basic physical characteristics are available in the market. This is made possible by differentiating the brands through different packaging and differences in minor features of the product that are not perceived by consumers and are not essential. Hence, these differences are implicit and do not necessitate additional consideration in the MARKSTRAT simulation.

Although the brands need some degree of differentiation through these nonbasic characteristics, the two products are produced on the same production lines, and so they share production costs. In particular, each brand benefits fully, in terms of cost, from the experience that is gained from the cumulative production of both brands.

R&D STRATEGIES

Most R&D projects concern new products with a specific combination of physical characteristics that differ from those designed by the firm in the past. However, in this section, we discuss a different kind of R&D, designed not to modify physical characteristics of the product but to reduce the cost of production (transfer cost). Special issues in developing R&D strategy are also discussed. The role and procedures of R&D feasibility studies are described, as are the implications of the accumulation of know-how on the strategies of the R&D department over time. Finally, the issues involved and the procedures to follow in developing the R&D plan are discussed.

Cost Reduction Projects

Although the experience effect contributes to declining costs over time, experience alone is insufficient to maintain margins in competitive industries. Consequently, firms must turn to the R&D department to find new processes, substitute materials, and/or change the technology to reduce costs of production and, therefore, transfer cost.

The marketing department of a firm can request such projects from the R&D department. It just has to specify a project code that satisfies the requirements mentioned earlier in this chapter (the project code has nothing to do with the current brand or R&D project for which the cost is being reduced). The five physical characteristics of the project correspond to those of the existing product for which the cost is being reduced. Then the cost characteristic is the cost set as the objective of the cost reduction project. The marketing department does not indicate or get involved in suggestions about how to decrease cost. The R&D team in charge of this project seeks a way to lower cost without affecting the values of the five physical characteristics.* It first checks past projects and the brands currently marketed, so that it can use past completed projects with the same physical attributes and their current

---

*Of course, the five characteristics of a product can be changed to lower the cost as well.

costs as the base for improvement. The budget required to complete such a cost reduction project varies by firm and depends on the amount of R&D experience developed over time by each firm.

Apart from the funds to budget for that project, the only other decision the marketing department has to make is the cost to request. Of course, as for the other characteristics, requesting a very low cost enables the marketing department to get information from the R&D department for the next period about the minimum cost the R&D department is willing to guarantee. If the cost returned by the R&D department is higher than the cost of the first 100,000 units of the current product, this is a sign that the lowest cost possible has already been achieved.

However, this does not mean that the cost specified should be lower than the current cost. Clearly, if the cost of the first 100,000 units can be lower than the current cost, so much the better. It will certainly happen, though, that the cost the R&D department can provide is lower than the average cost for the first 100,000 units of the current product but higher than the current cost. This new project can, however, lead to a cost lower than that of the current product. This is because after the product modification, production starts a new experience curve. By the time the brand is known in the market, sales could be substantial and cumulative production could double extremely fast, possibly within the first year of production. Consequently, whereas the older product might have been in the part of the experience curve where gains in productivity were minimal (the flat portion of the curve), the new product starts on a new experience curve and therefore benefits from high levels of productivity gains.

Consider an example where the current product had an average base cost for the first 100,000 units of $170. Now, cumulative production has doubled and the current cost is $110. If the marketing department requested a new base cost of $70, the objective would be achieved. However, this would correspond to a drastic cost reduction, which might not be possible. A base cost of $120, although higher than the current cost of $110, can yield a cost that within a brief time will be lower than the current product cost. This is illustrated by Figure 7.6, which shows that this cost would occur at between 100,000 and 200,000 cumulative production units.

This example has just demonstrated that the cost in an R&D cost reduction project does not need to be lower than the current cost. But what cost should the marketing department actually request?

There are two ways to decide. The first, briefly mentioned earlier, is to specify a very low cost with a low budget (as a feasibility study) and wait for the R&D department to indicate the lowest cost it can achieve. This will be efficient when time is not important—that is, when planning for R&D is done well ahead of time. The R&D on-line query can also be used, but, as described earlier, the estimates will be overstated relative to the cost that a real feasibility study would give.

Although long-term planning clearly indicates good strategic management, responses to the marketplace often have to be very quick. A second approach can then be used. Part of the strategic plan consists of profitability objectives that require a certain level of margin. Given that the marketing department knows the price at which the brand can be sold, the distribution

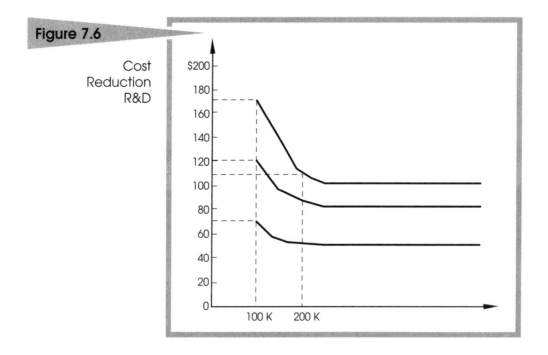

Figure 7.6

Cost Reduction R&D

margin of the distributor, and the required company margin, the maximum cost possible to enable that margin level can be computed. This will be the cost objective for the product. However, it is not yet the cost to be specified, as cost reduction will be achieved through experience.

Let us assume that the retail price needs to be $400 and that the average distribution margin for the product with the projected distribution in the various channels is 38%. The manufacturer's selling price is therefore $248 [i.e., $400(1 − 0.38)]. If the objective for the gross margin is 40%, the cost should be $148.80 [i.e., $248(1 − 0.4)]. However, it is expected that 400,000 units will be sold and therefore produced during the period. The cost of $148.80 is therefore the cost after benefiting from production experience.

Figure 7.7 shows the cost of $148.80 on the experience curve at the location corresponding to a level of cumulative production of 400,000 units. To find the cost for the first 100,000 units (the cost to specify in the R&D project), it is sufficient to move back along the experience curve to the level of cumulative production of 100,000 units. This cost is $200 in Figure 7.7. This example assumes that the experience curve rate has been estimated as discussed earlier.

Feasibility Studies

As already noted several times, it is particularly important to learn as much as possible about the feasibility of products and the funds necessary to complete research and development projects. Although they require time, since the information is not available before the end of the period during which they are requested, feasibility studies are part of the implementation of a long-term strategy. If the R&D program is established in good time, a more systematic approach can be used. A lack of strategy and planning indeed re-

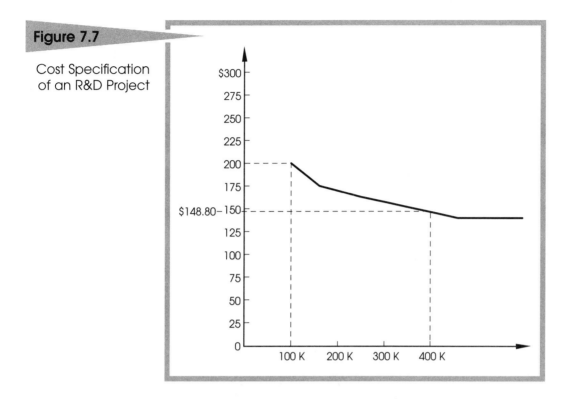

Figure 7.7

Cost Specification of an R&D Project

sults in unanticipated short-term reactions, in which case the R&D activity is not planned and the firm might not have the opportunity to request feasibility studies. Greater inefficiencies will result.

The product is obviously the most important marketing-mix variable in the implementation of a strategy, as without a product there can be no strategy at all. Therefore, R&D activity is crucial to the implementation of a marketing strategy. Feasibility studies can be ordered for a minimal budget of $100,000, for either the Sonite or the Vodite market. All opportunities for investigating R&D possibilities should be used, as they provide the information necessary to (1) complete a project efficiently, (2) investigate cost structure and physical characteristic combinations that will provide maximum margins, and (3) implement contingency plans rapidly.

Sequential R&D Projects

As indicated before, the R&D department does not start each project from scratch. In fact, its teams work by marginally improving upon products similar to others for which projects have been completed. This has a direct effect on the order in which projects should be undertaken. Instead of requesting R&D on similar projects in the same time period and moving to different product characteristics in the next period, it is more efficient to work sequentially and improve on existing products. In one period, R&D might be working on a product with a maximum frequency of 30 Hz and a volume of 60 dm³. Only after this project has been completed will the company search for a product with a high maximum frequency of 40 Hz, all other characteristics remaining unchanged.

Planning R&D Activities

Product policy, although not sufficient in itself, is the most critical aspect of the implementation of a strategy. It determines the businesses (products) in which the firm will compete. This in turn determines the allocation of resources to the various businesses. Consequently, R&D activities should be viewed as a means of arriving at a particular strategy. The strategy must, therefore, be well thought out before an R&D program is even begun, just as is the case for advertising or sales force expenditures. Given the critical role of R&D in the implementation of the marketing strategy and given the possibility of delays in completing projects, R&D activity needs to be carefully formulated for the entire period covered in the strategic plan. A three-step planning process can be useful:

Step 1: Define overall marketing strategy and contingency strategies.
Step 2: Define R&D objectives.
Step 3: Define the R&D program.

The content of each of these steps—particularly the last step of defining the R&D program—is discussed below.

Defining Overall Marketing Strategy and Contingency Strategies. As indicated above, this step is indispensable because no coherent R&D program can be elaborated without a knowledge of where the firm is going. Therefore, the strategy of the firm should be clearly stated in terms of the businesses in which the firm plans to compete and the particular positions that it wants in each market in the future. The timing is particularly important, as it takes a fair number of products to implement the strategy.

Contingency strategies should also be defined with the same concerns and the same degree of elaboration. Given that the firm would have to quickly implement these strategies if it were faced with environmental and competitive factors that had been considered less likely to occur, the basic ingredients, such as the product, should be ready so as to avoid any delay in implementation.

Defining R&D Objectives. Once the strategy and the contingency strategies have been developed, the objectives of R&D need to be set out. These concern the number of R&D projects to be started, corresponding to each business, and the priorities involved in these projects. The priorities should be established in terms of cost reduction projects versus development of products with new physical characteristics.

Defining the R&D Program. Now the positions corresponding to the businesses in which the firm wants to compete have been stated, and the general characteristics of the R&D program (R&D objectives) have been established over time. However, the R&D program is only defined after the actual physical characteristics of products to be developed have been detailed. Only then can the R&D budget be determined, since the physical characteristics determine the funds that must be invested to complete projects. Finally, the timing of R&D should cover the design of feasibility studies that will provide information to improve the efficiency of the R&D.

1. *Determine physical characteristics of products corresponding to positioning desired in the future.* It is assumed here that the position to be reached in the perceptual space is known. It should be emphasized, however, that given the time necessary to complete R&D projects and the long-term nature of strategy, these positions should not be based on current preferences but on expectations of where the product/brand will be positioned in the future. "The future" could very well refer to periods three, four, or five years from now. The exact characteristics of a product corresponding to a future position should therefore be specified. This specification can be made efficiently only if the relationship between actual product characteristics and the perceptions on the corresponding dimensions is known (as discussed in Chapter 5).

Such a relationship is illustrated in Figure 7.8. The horizontal axis shows the semantic scale value of design, and the actual ratings are indicated on the vertical axis. Given this relationship, the design index (physical attribute) perceived on the semantic scale as a 5 has a value of 6. This number is obtained by a vertical projection onto the line representing the relationship and then by a horizontal projection from that point to the vertical axis. Chapter 6 discussed this process in detail.

2. *Estimate funds (R&D budget) necessary to complete R&D projects.* One of the elements of the strategic plan is the financial considerations involving expected returns and investments necessary to achieve specified objectives. The investments in R&D represent a large part of the budget. Consequently, these funds have to be determined carefully. In particular, the proposed plan

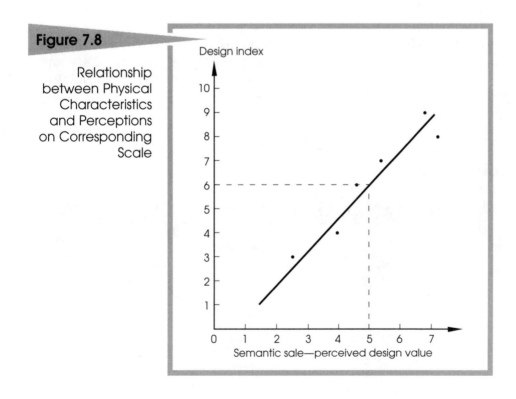

Figure 7.8

Relationship between Physical Characteristics and Perceptions on Corresponding Scale should establish the feasibility of a strategy in terms of providing over time the resources necessary to implement the strategy.

A prerequisite for judging the funds that will be necessary for R&D is knowledge of what type of research can be expected from the R&D department and with what budget. Therefore, it is critical to learn as much as possible about the effectiveness of the R&D department. This suggests intensive interaction between the marketing department and the R&D department. Communication is established through R&D project requests that take the form of feasibility studies.

3. *Request feasibility studies that will improve the efficiency of the R&D.* A feasibility study is basically identical to any R&D project request. The only difference is the size of the budget given to the R&D department to study the feasibility of the product. For a budget of $100,000, the R&D department gives feedback on the budget required to complete the project and minimum realistic costs. Any additional budget will be used toward the completion of the project.

However, given the uncertainties associated with such projects, it is more efficient to gather as much information as possible by requesting multiple feasibility studies than to spend more on one project that might have to be abandoned. Figure 7.9 presents four R&D projects and information about the budget required to complete a project at two levels of characteristic 3 (50 and 45) and at different costs. A low-cost feasibility study, PSURR, will probably provide the minimum realistic cost as well. However, to be sure you obtain the lowest base cost possible, check the box **Develop project at minimum base cost** in the **R&D Decisions** window, shown in Figure 7.10.

Although they will be less accurate, feasibility studies can be requested on-line through the R&D on-line query. For a project with the characteristics specified in the **Project Specifications** section of the R&D window, the on-line query provides an estimate of the minimum base cost and an estimate of the budget required to complete the project (see Figure 7.11). These estimates are guaranteed by the R&D department. However, because they result from preliminary research, the R&D department does not guarantee that the base cost and the budget will not be reduced.

Figure 7.9   Feasibility Studies

SONITE R&D PROJECTS

Project	Expenditures			Product Characteristics			
		Weight	Design	Volume	Max Freq	Power	Base cost
	K$	Kg	Index	Dm3	KHz	W	$
PSUVA	100	15	8	50	10	50	200
PSUMA	100	15	8	45	10	50	180
PSULL	100	15	8	50	10	50	150
PSURR	100	15	8	50	10	50	100

Figure 7.10 Specifying an R&D Project with Minimum Base Cost

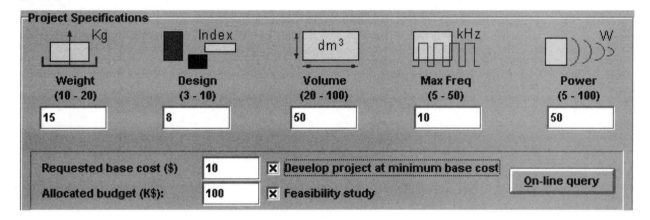

CONCLUSION

This chapter has discussed the key basic component of the implementation of a marketing strategy: the product design via research and development. The R&D projects that are requested by the marketing department do not deal with fundamental research, which would not be under the control of the marketing department. On the contrary, these projects are basic to the implementation of the firm's marketing strategy, as they concern production feasibility and processes for specific product features. The information in this chapter will help teams implement their strategies, as well as manage R&D over time.

Figure 7.11 R&D On-Line Query

R&D On-line Query	
Number of allowed on-line queries	5
Number of queries already made	2

Response from R&D to on-line query

Minimum base cost ($)	139
Requested base cost (adjusted to minimum value if too low) ($)	200
Budget required for completion at requested base cost (K$)	610

Query   ✓ Adjust decisions   Close

This chapter and Chapter 6 offer indispensable basic tools for developing and implementing a marketing strategy. Chapter 8 covers additional types of analyses that should improve the evaluation of alternative strategies and the efficiency of the implementation.

R&D Project Naming Conventions

- R&D project names consist of five letters.
  - The first letter is always P.
  - The second letter identifies the type of product that is being sought (S for Sonite and V for Vodite).
  - The last three characters may be freely chosen by a company, as long as all of its projects (current and past) have different names.
- The R&D project name bears no relationship to the commercialized brand name. Thus, PSUZZ may be used to improve existing brand SULI or to create a new brand, SUZI.
- An R&D project name should be structured as follows:

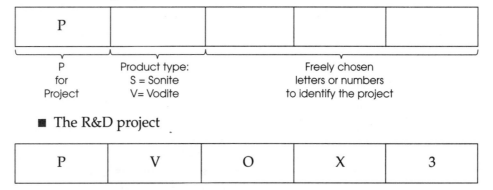

P				

| P for Project | Product type: S = Sonite V = Vodite | | Freely chosen letters or numbers to identify the project | |

- The R&D project

P	V	O	X	3

is a Vodite; the last three characters identify the project, and consequently the letter following the product type (O in this example) does not mean that this project is developed by Firm O.

Feasible Ranges of the Physical Characteristics

	Physical Characteristics	Feasible Range
Sonites	Weight (kg)	10–20
	Design (index)	3–10
	Volume (dm^3)	20–100
	Maximum frequency (1000 Hz)	5–50
	Power (W)	5–100
Vodites	Autonomy (m)	5–100
	Maximum frequency (1000 Hz)	5–20
	Diameter (mm)	10–100
	Design (index)	3–10
	Weight (g)	10–100

Key Rules of Communication with the R&D Department

- Communications with the R&D department are made through the R&D section of the **Decisions** module. Answers from the R&D department come in the R&D section of the Company Report. Therefore, the R&D department response time is a one-year period.
- The name of a project that has been completed cannot be reused for a new project, even if it is a cost reduction project. (Each team has two completed projects in Period 0: PSAMA, PSALT, PSEMI, PSELF, PSIRO, PSIBI, PSONO, PSOLD, PSUSI, PSULI.)
- Once a project has been started under a given name, the only modification of the uncompleted project that can be requested under the same project name is a change in the base unit cost.
- R&D citations of cost and budget required to ensure completion of a project requested during the period are adjusted for inflation. Note that if a project is not completed, the R&D department automatically changes the base unit cost for the next period to take inflation into account. Maintaining the same cost as in the previous period would correspond to making a request for a lower real cost. The R&D department could not guarantee the completion of such a requested project.
- Each product, whether marketed under an existing brand name (brand modification) or under a new brand name (introduction), starts a new experience curve upon introduction. Consequently, in the case of a product modification due to a cost reduction, cost goes down faster than it did before the modification. This fact needs to be taken into account in requesting the base unit cost of the new product. In particular, although a project with very low cost might be impossible to complete, a somewhat higher cost than the current cost could quickly result in a lower cost than could ever be realized without a new R&D project.
- If a product is modified and marketed under an existing brand name, consumers' perceptions of the new characteristics will depend on their degree of familiarity with the old characteristics of the brand.
- New products are different from existing products unless they share the five physical characteristics but at a different cost. Consequently, disposing of inventory results in an exceptional cost equal to 20% of transfer cost.

Planning R&D Activities

- Define overall marketing strategy and contingency strategies.
- Define R&D objectives.
- Define the R&D program by doing the following for each time period covered in the strategic plan:
  - Determining physical characteristics of products corresponding to positioning desired in the future
  - Estimating funds (R&D budget) necessary to complete R&D projects
  - Requesting feasibility studies for improving the efficiency of the R&D activity

8

Consumer Analysis

Consumers in the MARKSTRAT world, as in any market, behave in different ways that are not always easy to understand or predict. However, some patterns of behavior may emerge within market segments. The objectives of consumer analysis are to better understand how consumers end up buying a brand and to assess the impact that marketing activities have on their behavior. It is only with this knowledge that management can design marketing mix programs that will improve brand performance. Consumer analysis also provides a method for diagnosing a brand's position in a market.

In doing an analysis of consumers, one has to understand why and how consumers decide to buy within the product category and how they arrive at the decision to buy a particular brand. Because the products in MARKSTRAT are not items bought on impulse, a decision to buy follows a certain amount of thinking on the part of consumers. They process information acquired about the market and make purchasing decisions based in part on their conclusions. These patterns are representative of the way consumers think and behave, although they vary by individual. Therefore, the following discussion presents the general patterns found among consumers in the MARKSTRAT world and in no way suggests a rigid or complete consumer decision-making process. However, the analysis proposes a relevant method for assessing consumer behavior in MARKSTRAT, which considers the major behavioral phenomena.

CATEGORY PURCHASE DECISION

The products in MARKSTRAT are consumer durable goods, which consumers typically do not make decisions to buy while browsing in retail outlets. Instead, they gather some information about the available products and compare the data with their individual needs.

These needs are not the same for all consumers. Some individuals are very interested in the product category of electronic entertainment products. These people have a tendency to adopt innovations earlier. Others prefer to wait until the products have been tried and tested and then rely on information they get from the earlier adopters. Interest in a product category differs by consumer segment. It also changes over time within segments. Therefore, primary demand by segment evolves with the different stages of the product life cycle, as defined by the evolution of interest in the product category and interpersonal communication between consumers. These general trends are relatively strong in that they correspond to the long-term trends in the market. However, the strategies and the marketing-mix decisions of the firms also significantly determine whether consumers will purchase in the product category at a given point in time. In particular, advertising, the degree to which products satisfy the needs of consumers, and prices contribute to market expansion.

Consumers have to be willing and able to buy the product. Advertising gives them information about the product at the same time as it communicates specific messages about individual brands. This raises awareness of the product class in the MARKSTRAT population. Consequently, advertising has a primary demand effect in that it contributes to convincing consumers of their need for the product.

Consumers' decisions to purchase products depend on the products offered in the market. Although consumers may feel a certain need for the product, if the brands offered in the market are not satisfactory, they will not buy the product. Therefore, the size of the market depends on the extent to which the brands offered in the market satisfy the needs of the consumers in the MARKSTRAT population.

Willingness to buy a product is not enough; consumers must also be able to buy it. A major determinant of consumers' ability to buy a product is whether they can afford it. A large number of product categories compete for consumers' money. For a given product, consumers have a price level above which they are unwilling to buy. They compare this reservation price with the prices at which brands are available in the market in order to determine whether or not to buy the product.

These various factors explain why the segment growth curves and the absolute sales levels differ between runs of the simulation. Therefore, the product life cycle is partly determined by a process of information diffusion among consumers and by the firms' strategies and marketing-mix decisions.

BRAND CHOICE

Once a consumer decides that she or he wants to buy within the product category, a particular brand must be chosen. Brand choice is the result of a process in which the consumer first becomes aware of the brand and its features, then realizes that the brand best satisfies his or her needs, and finally purchases it from the retail outlet where he or she shops. This hierarchy of effects, where consumers follow the stages of awareness, preferences, and choice decision, is typical of high involvement products.

This hierarchy can be useful in assessing the state of a brand in consumers' minds. A brand high in awareness but low in preference has a low probability of being selected among the alternative choices. A brand with low awareness is also unlikely to be purchased, but for another reason. Consumers cannot buy a brand of which they are unaware. Therefore, brand awareness is a precondition for consumers to consider a brand. This awareness of a given brand does not need to be created before the individual goes to the store. In fact, retail personnel play a significant role in defining the set of brands considered by consumers. Therefore, consumers in the MARKSTRAT world are influenced by the pull effect of mass communication, as well as by the push effect of personal selling, although to different degrees, depending on the situation. In spite of this added complexity, it is useful to present the main decision-making process within the context of these three stages of awareness, preference formation, and choice decision. The three stages, with the main factors affecting them, are represented graphically in Figure 8.1. They are discussed in turn.

Brand Awareness

As indicated above, a necessary precondition for buying a given brand is awareness of the brand and of what it does—that is, of its attribute values. Awareness of a brand does not develop instantaneously. Although the presence of a brand in the distribution outlets may contribute to creating brand awareness in consumers' minds, awareness is mostly due to the mass communication program for the brand. Awareness, therefore, is a learning process, taking place over time through the effects of advertising. In addition, consumers who are not exposed to information about a brand tend to forget about it over time. Awareness of various brands competing in the market is measured through the consumer survey, which can be obtained in the market research studies.

This learning process is complex, and advertising effects are obviously not linear. Small levels of exposure may not be sufficient to be noticed by the

Figure 8.1

The Brand Choice
Decision Process

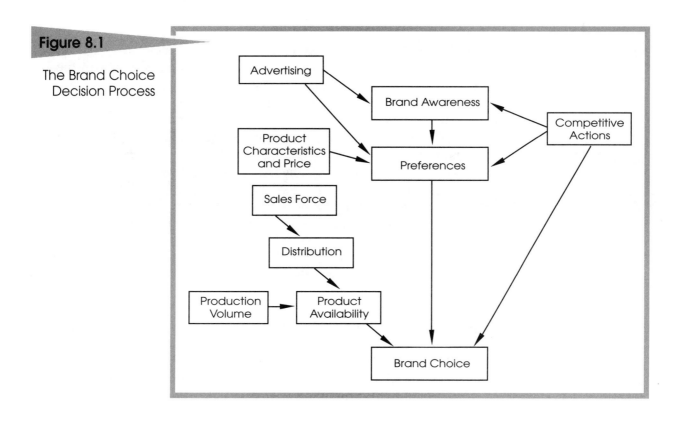

consumers. Indeed, in most cases where competitors send many messages to consumers, there is a threshold below which advertising effects are negligible. An important implication is that it would be wasteful to spend insignificant amounts on advertising. Economies of scale come into play. It can also be expected that, after a point, decreasing returns to scale occur, as a saturation level is reached. This saturation level may not reach 100% of a segment, however, as some individuals could remain uninterested in the products. In addition, the impact of a brand's advertising on its awareness is not independent of competitors' advertising, which negates some of the effects of the brand's advertising.

A strategic implication of the complexity of the impact of advertising on brand awareness over time is that it creates asymmetries across brands, with the possibility of establishing mobility barriers. This possibility is further reinforced by inertia in the market, especially as consumers do not completely forget a brand even in the absence of advertising.

Preference Formation

Once consumers are aware of a brand, the information they possess about it is processed and combined with their evaluation of their needs to form an attitude about the brand, which, compared with their attitudes toward other brands, leads to the formation of preferences. Because, by definition, needs are relatively similar within market segments, preferences tend to be analyzed by market segments as well. We will first define the concept of preferences and then discuss how these preferences change over time. Finally, we will compare the concept of preferences with the measures of purchase intentions obtained from the consumer survey provided in the market research studies.

The Concept of Preferences. Preferences are determined by consumers' perceptions of the various brands in relation to the ideal brand of the segment. The closer a brand is perceived to be to the ideal point in a multidimensional perceptual space, the more it tends to be preferred. Similarly, the further a brand is perceived to be from the ideal brand, the less it is preferred over other brands. Preferences are formed relative to perceptions and attitudes about all the brands competing in consumers' minds. Not every dimension, however, carries the same weight; everything else being equal, the more important dimensions have a larger impact on attitudes and preferences. Consequently, a brand that is closer to the ideal than a competitor's on a less important dimension but further away on an important dimension may be less preferred than the competitor's.

The ideal point of each segment indicates that there is an optimal level of each attribute desired by consumers. Consumers in MARKSTRAT may include perceived price as one of the attributes used to evaluate a brand. It is possible for some segments to believe that price has more than an economic component. In fact, price often connotes quality in a global sense, which is not represented directly by other attributes. As a consequence, a brand that is inexpensive is not necessarily preferred to a more expensive one. But a price higher than the ideal that the consumer is willing and expecting to pay may be detrimental to a brand vis-à-vis a brand situated at an equal distance from the ideal but with a lower price. This asymmetry may favor pricing below the ideal price, although other competitive factors and margins also come into play.

Preference Dynamics. Preferences are not static, as is suggested by the above discussion. In fact, the importance of the dimensions that consumers use to integrate the information they have about the brands in order to form preferences is not fixed.

The importance of each dimension used by consumers to represent their perceptions of the various brands depends on the set of brands available in the market at a given point in time. Although consumers prioritize the features they are looking for in a Sonite or a Vodite, the features of the available brands have a significant impact on their preferences. For example, if all the brands considered have the same level on the most important feature, that feature cannot be used as a discriminatory dimension to form consumer preferences. Although that feature is still an important component of attitude toward the brand, the other features become more important in determining which brands are preferred.

The ideal points are not stagnant over time. Therefore, even if perceptions of brands do not change, brand preferences will. What drives the ideal points? Needs do not change drastically from period to period; they are, as is typical in most markets, relatively stable over time. Nevertheless, what consumers look for in a product evolves. First, ideal products follow evolution in society, so economic and cultural factors have an impact on these needs. This societal evolution is slow and follows relatively stable trends. The ideal product is also influenced by all the products offered in the market—to a large extent, the ideal product is *defined* with reference to the products that are available in the market. The product specification as well as the communication programs of the successful brands affect the ideal product. A brand that is first to establish a strong position in the market may serve as a reference in the future, even if it also evolves.

In addition, preferences vary because of changes in perceptions brought about by the repositioning of a brand through advertising. The ability to reposition a brand is determined by the brand's existing position and its awareness level. It is harder for advertising to change the perceptions of a brand with high awareness than to change the perceptions of a brand with low awareness, even though physical characteristics of the brand may have been changed with a successful R&D project.

Furthermore, new entries in the market can alter the market share structure substantially from one period to another. This means that the preferences in MARKSTRAT are fluid and subject to many forces.

Preferences and Purchase Intentions. To develop preferences for a brand, as discussed above, the consumer must first be aware of the brand. Purchase intentions, which are obtained from the consumer survey of the market research study, represent the relative attractiveness of brands for a segment. Purchase intentions constitute a measure of the preferences within that segment, although purchase intentions are also affected by the awareness level of the brand. Therefore, the awareness level of a brand and its distance from the ideal point of a segment are the major determinants of the attractiveness of the brand and of the purchase intentions. These measures are extremely important, as they reveal what consumers would buy if the desired brand were available. Indeed, if we assume a new brand can achieve an awareness level comparable to that of existing brands, our ability to position the new brand close to the ideal point determines the extent of the market share for the new brand and the loss in share for existing brands, other things being equal. Also, positioning a brand better on the most important dimension will ensure a greater purchase intention. It is important to note that the measures of purchase intentions provided in the consumer survey study do not concern intentions to purchase during the next period. The study was carried out for the current period during which the actual sales have occurred. Consequently, these purchase intentions indicate the degree to which consumers would have bought the various brands if they had all been available. This point is further discussed below, when we consider actual brand choice.

In summary, positioning is a central part of marketing strategy. A perceptual map is an essential element of analysis used to understand consumers and competitive behavior in the MARKSTRAT world. Maps can be obtained from the semantic scales market research study or the multidimensional scaling study, as discussed in previous chapters.

Brand Choice

Consumers will normally choose to purchase their most favored brand, as represented by purchase intentions. However, the brand must be available on the market when the consumer goes shopping for it. Availability depends on the brand's being carried by the channels where the interested consumers shop and on retailers' not running out of stock.

Distribution Coverage. Consumers tend to shop in certain distribution channels according to their retailer preferences and habits (these are found in the consumer survey). They should be able to find their preferred brand in the retail outlets at which they shop. However, not all the retail outlets will carry this brand. The willingness of distributors to carry a brand is a function of several factors, such as the sales force, advertising levels, and the trends in the brand sales. Again, this function is not linear, and the interactions between marketing-mix variables explain why the marketing-mix strategy must be coordinated for maximum efficiency. However, typically, a successful brand that is well advertised and supported with a good sales force will be carried more broadly than a brand that is losing market share and has little communications support.

Brand Availability. For consumers to find the brand, the distribution channel must not be out of stock. So products should be available in quantities sufficient to satisfy the demand of consumers who prefer them. This assumes that the brand has been manufactured in adequate quantity. A consumer who cannot find the most favored brand may decide to wait until the next period to acquire it. However, a number of consumers may prefer to buy their second choice if it is available right away.

Distribution Push. Brands may be pushed to some extent by the distribution channels, through the support of the salespeople at the retail outlets, and by the manufacturers.

CONCLUSION

Brand choice is a key determinant of a brand's market share. Purchase intentions are, therefore, an essential element of market share. They are affected by a number of marketing variables. As indicated above, awareness is a strong determinant of behavioral intentions. Because advertising is the main source for building awareness in MARKSTRAT, it affects purchase intentions through the awareness level. However, the perceptions of each brand, which are determined by the physical characteristics of the brand, including price, are also affected by any advertising that aims to persuade or to reposition the brand. Therefore, market share is a function of the marketing-mix variables, as explained by this set of relationships.

Competitive actions in terms of marketing-mix variables are clearly represented through the purchase intentions variable, which is relative to all the brands in the market. Competition is also represented by the marketing variables themselves; share of voice, rather than an absolute budget measure, is often used to reflect advertising effort levels. Similarly, the pressure created by the sales force on distributors is relative, depending on the sales forces of all competitors. The marketing variables affect market share as described above, but firms' decisions also have an impact on primary demand, segment by segment. Therefore, the marketing-mix strategies of the firms determine not just market share but the market's evolution. The segment sales volumes and the brand market shares completely determine the sales of each brand. The gross profits of the brand follow, after costs are taken into account—costs that vary as a function of past cumulative sales because of the experience effect.

A good understanding of how consumers behave and how they react to the marketing-mix variables is useful in two areas of the strategic decision-making process. When evaluating a marketing plan, marketing strategists must evaluate the implications of each change in the marketing activities of their firm and those of competitors. In addition, when they finalize the allocation of resources to each brand and to each marketing-mix variable, the response of consumers to these decisions is an essential consideration.

This chapter has provided the basis for each team in MARKSTRAT to better understand the impact of the various marketing-mix variables. Although knowledge of these relationships is necessary to make "optimal" marketing-mix decisions, it is not sufficient to evaluate the marketing strategy of each firm. In particular, the relationships presented in Figure 8.1 provide little information about the portfolio decisions that the firm must make. This issue is discussed in Chapter 10. This chapter on consumer analysis has also pointed out the need to consider competitors' decisions, as they have an impact on consumer behavior. The next chapter elaborates on competitive analysis and strategies that are based not only on consumer analysis but also on competition.

The Main Stages of Consumer Decision Making

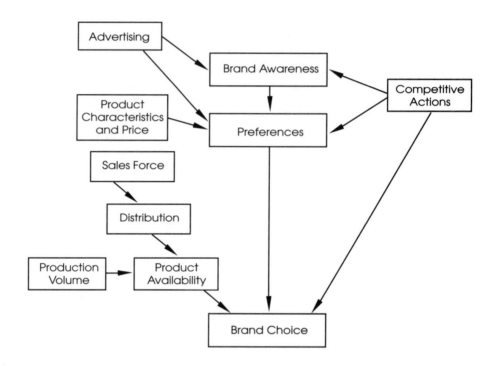

Competitive Strategies

The design of a marketing strategy is based in large part on the assessment of competition. Therefore, competitive analysis constitutes a basic preliminary investigation upon which the strategic plan rests. The first section of this chapter briefly covers the main elements of a competitive analysis. These elements affect the marketing strategy of a firm and should be considered in developing a strategic marketing plan in the MARKSTRAT simulation. The second section of the chapter discusses alternative competitive strategies open to the MARKSTRAT firms. The conditions under which each of these generic marketing strategies might be appropriate are also discussed. The last two sections deal with specific strategic issues that arise when a new brand is introduced in an existing or new market and when a firm's position is defended from attack by a new or existing competitor.

COMPETITIVE ANALYSIS

Industry and competitor analysis often follows an established checklist of conditions that affect the level of competition in an industry. Although such analysis has been the predominant perspective in strategy, its economic emphasis has restricted it mostly to understanding competitive structure. The marketing orientation of strategy leads to a consideration of additional factors that help address the fundamental questions guiding the marketing strategy of a firm:

1. Who are the firm's/brand's competitors?
2. How intense is the competition in a market?
3. How does competition affect market evolution and structure?
4. How do competitive actions affect the firm's marketing decisions?
5. How do firms achieve and maintain a competitive advantage?

Clearly, question 5 encompasses all aspects of a strategy and therefore is covered by all the chapters of this manual. The rules, principles, and generalizations that concern the design of a marketing strategy as discussed in the manual have for an objective a long-term, sustainable competitive advantage.

The answer to the first question is a precondition for answers to any of the others. This issue, related to the definition of market boundaries, will be discussed first. However, the emphasis of this section will be on assessing the intensity of competition in a market as it affects the choice of markets to compete in. The effects of competition on the market, and consequently on the firm's marketing decisions, will also be discussed.

Defining the Set of Relevant Competitors

Competitors are, potentially, the five firms in a MARKSTRAT industry. However, in terms of brands, the competition is usually within a market segment. So one issue is the definition of the brands competing in a market segment. The product/market analysis or methodologies used in marketing research can supply an important input here. However, the product/market analysis provides only a snapshot of a competitive situation at a point in time. When dealing with strategic planning, the long-term perspective forces the analyst to consider the factors that might change the competitive situation in the years ahead.

Marketing has offered the market product perspective, with such methodologies as the multidimensional scaling analysis provided in MARKSTRAT. The notion of strategic group or, more recently, industry segment offers a broader perspective. The firms in a strategic group face the same environment and compete with similar strategies. This typically implies that the firms in the same strategic group compete in the same market segment. However, this is not always the case. A firm could compete in a segment but with a different strategy than other firms in the segment; therefore, it would not belong to the same strategic group. Also, a firm might not compete in a given segment but might have a strategy generally similar to that of firms in the segment, which would make it a likely new entrant into that segment.

In Figure 9.1, brands A, B, and C compete in segment 1 and brand D satisfies the demand by itself in segment 2. Let us assume that the horizontal axis represents perceived price and the vertical axis represents a product quality dimension. In a typical analysis, the relevant market—and, therefore, competitors for segment 1—would be brands A, B, and C. The firm marketing brand D might not be part of the set of competitors. In fact, the firm marketing brand D produces a brand with the same level of quality as brands A, B, and C but charges a lower price, which could mean that brand D is produced at a lower cost. Consequently, that firm could enter segment 1 and enjoy higher margins, which in the long term would give it a competitive advantage. That threat of entry has to be considered, and, from a strategic standpoint, brand D should be part of the competitive analysis of the firms present in segment 1. Therefore, the strategic group notion gives a somewhat different perspective than the product market approach. The two approaches are, however, complementary. The notion of industry segment reflects this complementarity. The basic analysis of perceptions (competitive positions) and preferences (segmentation) provides the major quantitative assessment of competitive analysis at a given time. However, the more qualitative evaluations of industry structure and competitors' strategies allow a longer term view, which, for marketing strategy purposes, enables a better assessment of

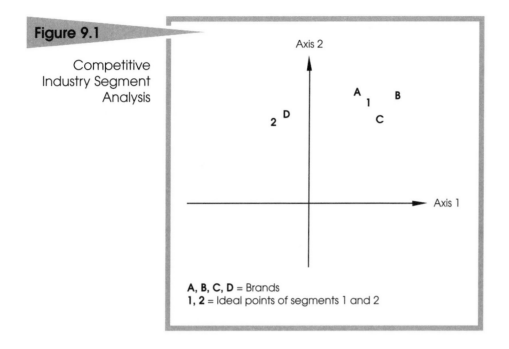

Figure 9.1

Competitive
Industry Segment
Analysis

A, B, C, D = Brands
1, 2 = Ideal points of segments 1 and 2

who the competitors really are. Therefore, the analysis of perceptions and preferences is crucial in competitive analysis but should be complemented by an industry type of analysis.

Assessing the Intensity of Competition

Structural Factors. In addition to direct competition between firms offering similar products, four structural forces generally influence the intensity with which firms compete in an industry: the degree of threat of entry, the power of suppliers, the power of customers or buyers, and the threat of substitutes. Two of these factors, the power of suppliers and the power of customers, are not relevant in MARKSTRAT, because each segment and market (Sonite and Vodite) faces the same supply characteristics and has the same marketing channels to individual consumers. Consequently, differences across markets or segments cannot be attributed to various degrees of suppliers' power or buyers' power. However, the threat of entry and the threat of substitutes are clearly important concerns for the marketing strategists in MARKSTRAT, since these threats are different in different markets or segments.

Each firm is distinct in terms of its past experience in different markets and segments. Consequently, the competitive advantages of the firms vary. Some firms are better able (e.g., at lower costs) to satisfy the needs of particular markets than their competitors. Consequently, it is easier for them to enter these markets. Apart from the number and size of competitors present in a given market segment, the various segments and markets have different levels of barriers to entry. This may be due to the nature of the needs to be satisfied, as indicated above. Or it may be because the existing competitors have been able to erect barriers to entry. The following are examples of entry barriers in the MARKSTRAT world.

■ The capital required to satisfy needs varies by market segment. This is particularly clear for an innovation about which many uncertainties exist—particularly in terms of predicting what consumers want. For example, there are risks associated with entering the Vodite market, and, consequently, the expected expenses to develop the "right" product might act as a barrier to entry. For firms that can afford to enter the market, this might provide a first mover's advantage. The extent of the barriers depends, of course, on the capital necessary to enter and maintain a position in that market. The key questions are (1) what level of investment is necessary to enter a market and maintain a position in it and (2) what capabilities, particularly in terms of R&D, are required?

■ The degree to which existing firms satisfy the needs of a market segment also acts as a barrier to entry. If existing competitors provide consumers with products that are perceived to correspond to their preferences, there is little room for a new entrant in this market. However, as is typical in the early stage of a product life cycle, if needs are difficult to assess and the offerings of the market do not correspond to what consumers want, the door is open to new entrants. Important marketing investments, especially in communications, make consumers better aware of the existence of a product and may persuade them of its superiority. In addition, important marketing investments make those of competitors less visible and less effective. Thus, marketing intensity also acts as a barrier to entry. The questions to ask here are (1) how well are the needs of the market segments served and (2) what level of marketing investment do existing competitors make in this market segment? For example, Figure 9.2 represents a competitive situation where the needs of segment 2 are very well satisfied by brand A, as brand A is positioned next to the ideal preference for that segment. Even though there are more brands directed at segment 1, it will be easier to enter segment 1 than segment 2 with a new brand, assuming similar marketing investments by the firms currently present in these segments.

■ The degree to which existing competitors control the distribution channels is also an indicator of the height of barriers to entry. If existing competitors extensively cover the key channels of distribution used by consumers in a market segment, it will be more costly to enter that segment. The distribution channel plays an important strategic role, for it has a considerable impact on the sales of a brand. This impact is typically of long-term duration. The relevant questions are (1) what are the crucial channels for the market segments and (2) what level of effort is expended by the sales forces of existing competitors in these channels?

■ Finally, an important barrier is economies of scale and cost declines through experience. Cost reductions that can be achieved in some market segments because of their size might not be possible in other market segments. It is critical to have low costs to generate profits greater than competitors' profits in order to reinvest and possibly create higher barriers to entry. Hence, competition in a market must be assessed in cost terms. The questions to ask are (1) what is the size of this market,

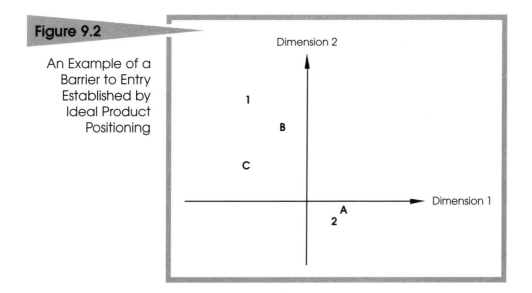

Figure 9.2

An Example of a
Barrier to Entry
Established by
Ideal Product
Positioning

now and in the future and (2) how fast can costs decline for the type of products in this market (through basic learning and through R&D)?

All these structural factors are certainly key to understanding competition in the MARKSTRAT environment. The questions that they raise help in developing a broader strategic perspective. However, these structural factors do not indicate how firms can be expected to behave in each market segment. Marketers are interested in evaluating what is happening and what will happen in an industry. Consequently, it is important for the design of a marketing strategy to also assess the *behavior* of competitors.

Competitive Behavior. Market researchers assessing the effectiveness of the marketing-mix variables have realized the importance of considering competition as part of the marketing system to be modeled. Indeed, if competitors in a market make their marketing-mix decisions as a function of what other firms are doing or are expected to do based on their past behavior, the level of resources invested in that market is likely to follow a cyclical pattern. This pattern can very easily be observed by considering the evolution of expenditures and prices in the market, separately for each competitor or at the aggregate industry level. In a very competitive market, advertising expenditures and sales force expenditures would increase over time. In a less competitive market, these marketing investments may have a tendency to decrease. This is illustrated in Figure 9.3, where advertising expenditures are plotted over time for two market segments. Segment 2 is shown to be more competitive than segment 5, because expenditures rise more steeply over time. The plot of sales force expenditures by channel also indicates that more competition occurs in channel 1 than in channel 2.

An essential part of competitive response concerns the product itself. Therefore, one would expect R&D expenditures also to increase in competitive markets. However, what often happens in highly competitive markets is that resources are diverted from long-term objectives—of which new

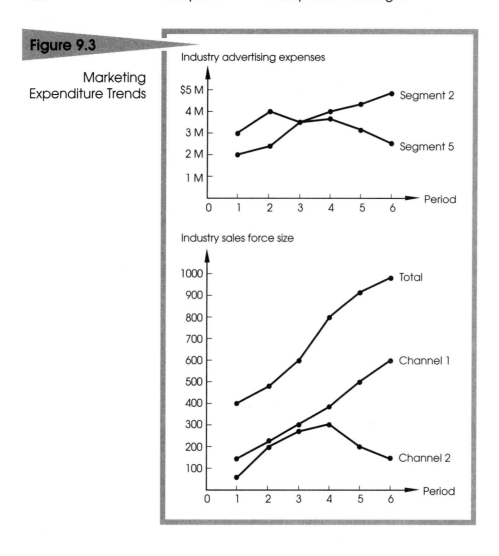

Figure 9.3

Marketing
Expenditure Trends

product development is a crucial part—to short-term reactions to and antici-
pation of competitive moves. This is due partly to the lack of a budget to
cover all fronts, short term and long term, and partly to an overemphasis on
defending short-term performance. Consequently, although expenditures on
existing products/brands might increase over time in intensely competitive
markets, R&D expenditures might not follow the same pattern. In fact, they
might increase at first, but, as competition becomes more and more intense
and resources are depleted, R&D expenditures might decrease.

Determining the pattern of reaction is essential to understanding the type
and extent of competition in a market and should therefore be part of the
competitive analysis task. Competitive reaction is taken into account specifically in a model of the firms' marketing decisions. Marketing-mix decisions
are expressed as a function of the current values of competitors' marketing
mixes and as a function of their past decisions. These functions allow the estimation of reaction elasticities. Reaction elasticity is the percentage change
in the value of a marketing-mix variable (say advertising) of a brand when
another brand changes the same or another marketing-mix variable by 1%.
Therefore, reaction elasticity represents the behavior of one brand in reaction

to another. These reactions are simple if one firm (a brand) reacts with the same marketing instrument it is reacting to—for example, it reacts to a competitor's advertising increase by increasing its own advertising expenditures. A reaction is complex if the firm reacts with a different marketing-mix variable—for example, it decreases price when the competitor increases advertising expenditures.

In general, a positive reaction shows active competitive behavior; the greater the reaction, the more competitive the pair of firms. Reaction elasticities can also be negative, indicating a lack of competition or even showing evidence of competition avoidance. For example, when one firm increases its advertising, the other pulls back. So there is a continuum of competitive reactivity, varying from competition avoidance to strong rivalry. Although these approaches have limitations (e.g., stability over time), they offer quantitative measures that are relatively easy to estimate using simple regression analysis on time series data about the marketing activities of each competitor. These data can be obtained in MARKSTRAT to assess the intensity of competition in each market segment. The competition of a market directly affects the attractiveness of this market, as a competitive market will require greater resource commitment. Consequently, the number of brands competing, the way the existing brands compete, and the degree to which new brands are likely to enter the market are important strategic factors to be analyzed when deciding whether to enter a market. It is also important to decide how to enter a market. The size of the initial commitment and the speed with which one would enter the market depend on these factors. For example, the decision to build awareness fast or, instead, to cautiously ensure an adequate positioning for the new brand is clearly dependent on these factors. In a highly competitive market, speed is required, because existing competitors would respond quickly to weakness of an entrant. If, on the other hand, the market is not very competitive, working slowly on brand positioning before awareness is too high would be recommended. The analysis of competition can provide crucial information on the competitive strategy to adopt. The long-term competitive advantage of one firm can be assessed only by understanding the competition. Industry structure, as well as the nature of competitive reactions and behavior, enables the marketing strategist to assess what the strengths and weaknesses of the various competitors, including his or her own firm, are. This assessment will determine the competitive strategy to adopt. However, several basic competitive strategies often compete. The next section of this chapter presents general, or "generic," bases of competitive advantage. The conditions under which each generic basis is appropriate for designing the marketing strategy are then discussed.

COMPETITIVE STRATEGIES

Competitive strategies are based on the objectives of developing and maintaining a long-term, sustainable competitive advantage. In this section, two generic bases of competitive advantage are discussed. The bases of competitive advantage that can be used are first defined. Then, the characteristics of the environment that determine which strategy is appropriate are discussed.

Basis of Competitive Advantage

A generic marketing strategy can be represented along two main dimensions: the scope of the targeted market and the basis of the competitive advantage. The scope of the targeted market corresponds directly to the segmentation strategy discussed in Chapter 6. The basic conclusion of that chapter was that each segment must be evaluated separately and, in most situations, each segment that the firm decides to serve should be reached with a differentiated strategy. Therefore, the segment should be the basic level of analysis. Because of mobility barriers between segments, however, a more global view is also necessary.

Two broad classes of competitive advantage have been identified in the strategy literature: cost advantage and product differentiation advantage. In a given segment, the firm must attain at least one of these competitive advantages to be effective in the long run. For that, the firm must have (1) an advantage over the competition (2) on an attribute that consumers will perceive as important. For example, an advantage over the competition in ability to manufacture a high-frequency product better (higher levels and/or at lower costs) is not a competitive advantage if consumers do not care about the attribute "frequency." Similarly, a cost advantage where the differential profits cannot be used to better satisfy demand (in quality or quantity) is not a competitive advantage. Therefore, if its costs are lower than its competitors' costs, a firm must be able to lower its price, if the market is price elastic, or spend the additional profits (on, for example, advertising), if and only if it pays to advertise. These bases of competitive advantage are considered in turn, and then the issue of when one may be more appropriate than the other is discussed.

Cost Leadership. Cost leadership can be achieved in MARKSTRAT through experience (the experience curve) and/or research and development. Because of the gains in costs due to the experience curve (which applies to transfer costs), a firm can achieve a cost lower than its competitors, everything else being equal. Although production levels can be inflated (relative to sales of the brand) in early periods of the brand introduction in order to lower costs, in the long term this strategy assumes market dominance in terms of market share. Otherwise, inventory holding costs would counter the gains obtained through higher levels of production. Market share is therefore an important objective for such a strategy. The basis for gaining share and the cost of attaining market dominance are discussed below. Briefly, however, market share can be gained by appealing to consumers' needs either for low prices or for a "better" product (i.e., perceived to be closer to their ideal preference) or for both.

Competitors, however, can challenge this cost leadership with cost gains achieved through R&D. Consequently, cost leadership cannot in general be attained solely from market dominance. Such a strategy requires an appropriate R&D program, as discussed in Chapter 7. It should be pointed out here that, from a competitive strategy standpoint, different firms have different positions with respect to their costs and the likelihood of success of their cost reduction R&D activities. This type of competitive advantage is not, however, predetermined by exogenous factors. Indeed, the nature and extent of past R&D activities of each firm is the most significant contributor to its ability to become a cost leader. Although some firms might have this advantage in the early periods of the simulation, their leadership or potential leadership can be challenged by other firms during the simulation.

Cost reduction through R&D can be achieved through projects that concentrate solely on costs of material and manufacturing processes but that keep the key characteristics of a product unchanged. Another means of cost reduction is through product redesign. Some physical product characteristics are more expensive to produce than others. Your team might be willing to lower the level of a physical attribute in return for a cost reduction, as long as this trade off affects consumer perceptions negligibly. Some characteristics do not appear important to consumers, so preferences would be practically unaffected. Therefore, the objective should be to design the product with the level of that product characteristic that provides the lowest cost. This approach must be considered, even though the strategy of the firm might not be based on cost leadership. In both cases, the R&D expenditures for reducing the cost of the product might not be justified.

Additional sources of cost advantages could be synergies with other products. In MARKSTRAT, because each product is marketed under a different brand name without umbrella branding or advertising, no synergy is achieved through advertising or firm image. If two brands share the same R&D project but are differentiated by their prices, they follow the same experience curve, as indicated in Chapter 7. Consequently, major cost synergies can be achieved. In addition, synergies do exist in terms of R&D and distribution. For R&D synergies, refer to Chapter 7. Distribution synergies arise because the sales force carries all the brands marketed during a period. Therefore, selling multiple brands demanded by consumers shopping in the same distribution outlets decreases the cost of selling these brands.

Production cost can be a very important factor in success in some competitive environments, in particular because lower costs provide better margins than competitors' margins; these can then be reinvested in marketing activities, which other firms do not have the resources to respond to. In general, but especially for the firm adopting a cost leadership strategy, it is crucial to investigate the three sources of cost reduction discussed above: experience curve effects, R&D cost reduction programs, and product synergies. Ignoring one of these sources can give competitors the opportunity to challenge this cost leadership. In addition, cost leadership does not mean that the product features can be worse than those of competitors. At the least, parity on the product itself might be required to implement a successful cost leadership strategy.

Product Differentiation. Product differentiation in MARKSTRAT concerns the decisions that enable the firm to position a brand at a given location in the consumers' perceptual map. These decisions are discussed in Chapter 6. Product differentiation can be attained through R&D or advertising. Product positioning and, therefore, product differentiation play central roles in MARKSTRAT. More specifically, each firm can evaluate the sensitivity of demand to the position of a product. Given the importance of having a correct position and given the difficulty of maintaining a position in a segment due to demand and competitive dynamics, the implementation of a product differentiation strategy can present a real challenge.

As indicated earlier, consumers in MARKSTRAT have preferences in terms of the product attributes they desire. The brand that is perceived as closest to the ideal of a consumer segment should have the highest market share, given that the consumers are aware of the brand and given that the brand is available in the proper distribution outlets. Consequently, it is essential that a brand be perceived as corresponding to consumers' preferences for a given segment, at least from a market share perspective. From a profitability point of view, a "perfect" position might not necessarily be worth the cost of achieving such a position. However, a brand that is not positioned close to an ideal point offers an opportunity to competitors to move in and establish a position in this segment. Therefore, a proper position is crucial for the product differentiation strategy as a basis of a sustainable competitive advantage.

It is not guaranteed, though, that such an advantage is sustainable in the long term. The ability to sustain a competitive advantage through positioning depends on multiple factors. One factor is the stability of consumer preferences. In some segments, for example, consumers' needs and preferences are changing only very slowly, if they are changing at all. Other segments keep up with the latest technologies and modify their product requirements over time. Another factor is the existence of barriers to entry or mobility barriers that prevent other brands from being repositioned so as to displace the current leader. Competitors might not have the technology and/or expertise to bring into the market a new brand that would be better positioned. For example, different companies have different abilities to complete R&D projects with specific characteristics. Some companies can develop products with high power with a reasonably low budget; others find it easier to have a better design. Even imitation can be harder on some characteristics than on others. If imitation is possible, other firms might have a cost disadvantage. Also, competitors might not be able to change the perception of their existing brands in a market because of the high level of awareness of these brands or because of the lack of funds needed to reposition a brand through advertising. Some of these barriers can be created or heightened by the segment leader.

Generally, it is difficult to sustain a differentiated advantage in MARK-STRAT, although it is not impossible. Competitors have relative advantages that they develop. However, they all have opportunities to compete in most segments. Consequently, the bases of competitive advantages are not determined once and for all. Indeed, a firm's ability to sustain an advantage depends on the decisions of its competitors over time and on its ability to plan for protecting its competitive advantages.

Choice of Basis of Competitive Advantage

An essential part of the marketing plan is to establish which of the two broadly defined bases of competitive advantage is appropriate and to design a consistent plan over time to sustain that advantage. This choice of a basis of competitive advantage depends on a number of factors related to the firm itself and to demand characteristics. However, these two bases of competitive advantage are not mutually exclusive. In many cases, they actually operate as complements, although this complementarity does not eliminate the need to choose one as the main basis of the initial strategy. A final element in making this strategic choice is the cost involved in maintaining the competitive advantage.

- *Firm characteristics.* Firm characteristics concern the relative ability of one firm to perform a particular function. For example, one MARKSTRAT firm might be able to improve a Sonite brand's power characteristic at a minor cost differential. Other firms might complete the same project with a cost substantially higher than the first firm's cost. Such abilities are fundamental to the choice of the basis of competitive advantage on which to develop a marketing strategy. Differential cost advantages exist not only for R&D, as discussed above, but also in terms of the firm's performance in positioning and repositioning its brands in the market and its efficiency in advertising and obtaining distributors for the brand. To choose the cost basis of competitive advantage, the firm must be able to maintain a dominant position in the market, as discussed earlier.

- *Price elasticity of demand.* Demand for a brand is said to be price elastic if it increases significantly when price is decreased. In this case, cost becomes a crucial element of competition, as any competitor with a lower cost can reduce its price and gain a substantial market share. Consequently, in price-elastic segments or markets, cost leadership will be a necessary requirement to maintain the brand's market share position. This might not be the only requirement, however.

- *Complementarity of bases of competitive advantage.* To sustain a cost advantage, whether or not demand is price elastic, a high market share is often required because of the gains in productivity due to experience. Market share is particularly important when each firm has exhausted the possibilities for reducing cost through technological progress. Therefore, when the market matures and R&D produces marginal cost-reducing innovations, the experience curve becomes the main source of competitive advantage on cost. An important question is how this market share dominance can be obtained. When the market is price elastic, cutting price will increase market share. Depending on the competitive situation, though, the impact may be only temporary. Indeed, it can be expected that competitors in the segment will react by cutting their prices as well, starting a price war. A product differentiation strategy can also achieve a gain in market share that will result in lower costs. This indirect way of obtaining lower costs might avoid direct confrontation with competitors. It might be harder for competitors to react on product attributes, or at least their reactions might take longer, since product differentiation through R&D or advertising can take longer to implement than a price cut. Consequently, product differentiation might, in some cases, be the best way to also achieve a cost advantage.

■ *Costs of achieving a competitive advantage.* The costs for R&D programs are a substantial part of the MARKSTRAT firms' budgets. All firms gather information about the feasibility of specific R&D projects and about the budgets required to complete them. It is also important to estimate the R&D budgets of other firms. In MARKSTRAT, different firms can complete the same R&D projects with different budget levels because of dissimilarities in their past R&D experience. This means that the cost of maintaining a position in a market segment is different for different competitors. A handicap, due to these varying budget requirements, can completely prevent a firm from maintaining a position in a market segment because of its budget size limitation or its R&D experience. Further, high brand awareness might prevent some firms from adjusting consumers' perceptions through advertising. Also, if competitors have large budgets for advertising, the feasible share of voice of a firm with a limited budget could be too insignificant to show any impact. Finally, the costs of maintaining cost leadership are not only expenses for R&D budgets and expenses necessary to dominate a market—the most significant impact on profits might, in fact, be pricing, as a decrease in price causes a reduction in margins that might not be compensated for by a gain in sales. None of these costs should be ignored, because the choice of the basis for competing with other firms depends as much on their costs for maintaining an advantage as it does on the current position of a firm vis-à-vis its competitors.

ENTRY STRATEGIES

When a firm intends to market a new product or a new brand, it has to make a series of marketing decisions about when to enter the market, what mix of marketing variables to use, and how aggressive the introduction should be. The following decisions are, therefore, analyzed in this section: (1) the timing of the entry in terms of pioneering advantages, (2) the signaling of the entry to the competitors, (3) the brand introduction marketing mix allocation, and (4) the scale of the entry.

Pioneer Advantage

The empirical literature offers evidence of a general advantage of being first in a market. The arguments advanced for that inherent advantage are reviewed here. However, there are also risks associated with pioneering, which will be discussed next.

Monopolistic Profits. Being first means that there are no competitors in the market. Consequently, in theory, the single firm can realize monopolistic profits. The danger, however, is that high profitability will attract new entries, unless some types of barriers have been erected. In MARKSTRAT, a brand positioned by itself close to a segment ideal can be in that position because it satisfies the needs of that segment, and it could be difficult for competitors to develop a product at least as good. This implies, however, that the pioneer has taken advantage of the best opportunity for brand positioning. If, instead, the brand had been positioned some distance from the ideal point, a new brand could enter in a better position on the perceptual map and the advantages of the lack of early competition would disappear immediately. Nevertheless, depending on the extent of awareness established in the market, a residual advantage might remain. The first mover needs to possess a high awareness level and needs to spend advertising dollars to increase the later entrants' costs of gaining awareness and a position in the consumers' perceptual maps.

Distribution Support. Another, and possibly more sustainable, advantage may be derived from having an established distribution support system. If the pioneer brand sells and is supported by an appropriate advertising program, distributors might not have an incentive to carry the brands of later entrants. This advantage is achieved in MARKSTRAT by coordinating the marketing-mix program (i.e., thinking about the long-term impact of sales force allocation to the distribution channels).

Production Experience. Finally, the first mover benefits from a greater accumulation of experience in production, which gives it cost advantages over competitors. This would suggest adopting the largest scale of production possible to achieve the fastest learning effect possible.

These advantages are not, however, without risk. Going after a new market such as the Vodite market necessitates making decisions with limited information. It is difficult for consumers to express their needs when the product is not yet available. This is particularly true in the case of a completely new product (radical innovation), but it also holds for a segment of an existing market where there is no competitor. It is difficult to translate feasible physical characteristics of potential new products into preferences and to evaluate the relative impact of alternative strategies. This situation reflects the risks of innovating because of the limited information available for making decisions. One possibility is to introduce a new product and allocate limited marketing resources to investigate the market reaction to a given entry strategy. This is similar to performing a market test. It reduces the risk of engaging important resources for a given strategy, but it also gives competitors time to react more effectively.

Entry Signaling

The signaling of the entry can affect the long-term profitability of the introduction because it provides information (correct or sometimes misleading) to competitors, to distributors, and to consumers. In MARKSTRAT, consumers react to the product offerings and are not influenced beyond the marketing-mix variables. Distributors also behave according to industry practices that are not influenced by the behavior of an individual firm. Nevertheless, the simulation does consider the dynamics of market share, sales growth, and advertising support on the behavior of distributors. This issue is addressed in Chapter 8. Signaling in MARKSTRAT is the result of the behavior of competitors and occurs only through the decisions of each firm. Each firm tries to interpret the decisions of competitors to anticipate their strategies. Any information provided through marketing-mix decisions is likely to influence competitors' decisions. For example, heavy allocation of resources to a segment might be interpreted by competitors as an intention to focus on that segment, which might give the firm time to develop an R&D project directed at another segment. Launching an early Vodite could indicate an intention to allocate major resources to that market. This could deter smaller firms from entering the Vodite market.

Marketing Mix

New brands can be successfully marketed even though they are not first in a market. They need, however, to provide a differential advantage to consumers. Besides catching up with the existing competitors' awareness levels, late entries need to communicate the product benefits with heavy advertising expenditures, possibly beyond those of the existing competitive brands. The need for a large allocation of resources to advertising for late brand introductions is reinforced by the need to spend more on advertising to position the new brand effectively. The advertising message and, therefore, the perceptual objectives and advertising research play more important roles for late entrants than for the pioneer.

The size and the allocation of the sales force need not necessarily change when a new brand is introduced. These decisions depend on the distribution synergies of the new brand with the existing portfolio of the firm. If the shopping behaviors of the markets or market segments are similar to those of the segments already served by the firm, reallocation might not be necessary. Costs can therefore be saved by sharing the sales force and distribution costs.

Scale of Entry

When competitors sell similar products, a large-scale brand introduction may be necessary because of cost gains due to experience. If potential entries by other firms are a threat, largeness of scale gives the entrant a cost advantage that will deter new brand introductions by competitors. In addition, a large-scale entry can signal to existing competitors a commitment to the brand and the probability of a strong reaction if the introduction is challenged. A large-scale entry, therefore, can signal competitors to stay away.

A large-scale entry can, however, cause a strong reaction from existing competitors if they feel that their profits are threatened by this increased rivalry. If such a reaction is expected, a better entry strategy is to build the level of sales slowly and introduce the brand on a smaller scale that will not draw as much attention from competitors.

Another reason to prefer a small-scale entry is uncertainty about a new market. In a segment where there is no product offering or in a new market, such as the Vodite market, it may be prudent to introduce a brand on a small scale so as to test the market and learn from this initial period instead of committing resources that could be wasted if consumers did not respond as expected to the new brand. Similarly, in cases where competitors' reactions are difficult to predict, a market test (small introduction) should be done to evaluate how competitors are going to adapt to the new competitive environment.

DEFENSIVE STRATEGIES

In this section, first the decision variables that the firm can use to defend its position are reviewed. Then the factors that determine the effectiveness of defense strategies are discussed. These strategies can be called forth by a competitive entry or an aggressive existing competitor.

Elements of Defensive Strategy

The decisions that a firm needs to make when reacting to a competitor's threatening its position are (1) the direction of the reaction (e.g., attack versus retrenchment), (2) the marketing-mix variables that will change as part of the defense strategy, (3) the degree or size of the reaction, and (4) the market or market segment(s) in which the firm should react.

Direction of Reactions. Reactions can be categorized as four types: (1) retaliating, (2) accommodating, (3) ignoring, and (4) abandoning. Retaliating is a declaration of war, wherein the firm signals its intention to fight back. A decision to accommodate indicates instead that there is room for all players and that each might be better off if they cooperated. This strategy can be implemented by cutting back on the marketing effort. The decision to ignore means that the firm does not change its marketing-mix strategy, at least until it has learned more about the strategies of the competitors and their impact on sales, market share, and profits. Finally, abandoning means withdrawing the brand because it lacks competitive advantage in that market. Indeed, it might be more costly to fight back or stay in than to abandon the effort and concentrate on more attractive brands and markets.

Marketing-Mix Variables. The marketing-mix variables are all the decision variables offered in MARKSTRAT for a brand—price, advertising, sales force, repositioning, new brand introduction, etc. An interesting issue is which marketing-mix variable a firm should react with. Should it react with the same marketing instrument the attacking firm is using, or should it use a different one, reflecting the use of a strategy different from the attacker's?

Size of Reaction. A large early reaction from competitors can deter the aggressor and reduce its expectations in the market. Each firm should evaluate what it would take to convince the aggressor to slow down its attack. This might depend on the size of the reacting firm. A small reaction by a large firm could be a sufficient warning signal to the aggressor.

Domain of Reaction. In some cases, the strongest signal can be sent in a market or market segment other than the one in which the aggressor has attacked. This is the case, for example, if the defender could seriously hurt the attacker in another market but not in the market of the aggression.

Determinants of Choice of Defensive Strategy

In this section, we discuss which combination of the above defensive reaction decisions is most effective in a given situation. Four factors influence the choice of defensive strategy: (1) the strategy of the entrant, (2) the expected behavior of all the competitors, (3) demand factors, and (4) characteristics of the defending firm.

Entrant Strategy. Typically, when a new competitor enters a market, prices can be expected to go down because of the increased competition. This, however, assumes a price-elastic market. Thus, this behavior can be expected in only some MARKSTRAT segments. If the new brand or an existing brand competes on price, it might be more profitable to reposition and compete with a differentiated product in a different market segment where a product characteristic is a competitive advantage. Advertising can then be increased relative to its level before the aggression to cover the additional repositioning task. A large entry should generate a strong response, with all effective marketing instruments, to make the aggression unsuccessful if this is a likely outcome. If there is little chance of reducing the impact of the aggression, it might be better to abandon an already questionable position right away.

Expected Behavior of Competitors. It is clear that the success of a defensive strategy, like that of any other strategy, depends on how competitors react to it. Therefore, knowledge of competitors is extremely important in designing the proper defensive strategy. Given the difficulty of anticipating competitors' behavior in response to your firm's defensive strategy, which in most cases is peculiar to the specific situation, it is particularly useful to evaluate the impact of several types of competitive reactions on the effectiveness of the defensive strategy of your firm. Contingency plans can then be developed as certain behaviors emerge from the competition.

Demand Factors. Price retaliation has been recommended when the preferences in a given market are homogeneous. This is likely when a market is newly created, so consumers have not yet established strong preferences and the market is not yet fragmented. This could be the case also in the mature stage of the product life cycle, when competing products are similar (commodity like) and competition is based solely on price because of the high level of price sensitivity in these markets.

Accommodating by decreasing the marketing effort (advertising, sales force, etc.) is a more profitable strategy in a mature market, where competitive activity does not affect primary demand levels.

Firm Characteristics. In MARKSTRAT, small brands are in a worse position than large ones because of the experience curve effects on costs. Therefore, when market growth starts to slow down (and, more conclusively, when it becomes negative), the intensity of competition typically increases. In these environments, smaller brands will become unprofitable first. Hence, they should exit that market (segment) while they are still generating some cash.

CONCLUSION

In this chapter, competitive strategies have been considered. First, key elements of competitive analysis that help in designing a marketing strategy in MARKSTRAT were developed. Then the bases of competitive advantages and the environment in which each basis is most sustainable were discussed. Finally, the determinants of a strategy for introducing a new brand and for defending the position of a brand under attack were elaborated. For each of these situations, the factors to assess in a particular simulation of MARKSTRAT in order to design the most effective strategy were discussed.

CHAPTER 9 SUMMARY

Competitive Analysis

- Defining the set of relevant competitors
  - Product market analysis of perceptions and preferences
  - Industry segment analysis
- Assessing the intensity of competition
  - Structural factors
    Degree of threat to entry
    Threat of substitutes
    Barriers to entry: capital required, degree to which existing firms satisfy consumers' needs, marketing investment levels, coverage of key distribution channels
  - Economies of scale/experience
  - Competitive behavior
    Marketing expenditure trends
    Reaction functions and reaction elasticities

Competitive Strategies

- Cost leadership
  - Experience/cumulative production
  - R&D experience
  - Synergies with other products
- Product differentiation
  - Positioning of each competitive brand
  - Stability of consumer preferences
  - Mobility barriers
- Choice of basis of competitive advantage
  - Firm characteristics
  - Price elasticity of demand
  - Complementarity of bases of competitive advantage
  - Cost of achieving and maintaining basis of competitive advantage

Entry Strategies

- Pioneer advantages
  - Monopolistic profits
  - Distribution support
  - Production experience
- Entry signaling

— Competitors' decisions in key segments
— Signals to be read from these decisions
■ Marketing mix
— Allocation of resources to brands, segments, and marketing-mix variables before new brand introduction
— Marketing synergies between new brand and existing brands
■ Scale of entry
— Large-scale brand introduction as a deterrent to new competitive entries
— Expected reactions from competitors to large- and small-scale brand introductions

Defensive Strategies

■ Determinants of choice of defensive strategy
— Entrant strategy
— Expected behavior of competitors
— Demand factors
— Firm characteristics
■ Elements of defensive strategy
— Direction of reaction
— Marketing-mix variables
— Size of reaction
— Domain of reaction

10

Allocation of Resources

Marketing strategy concerns the allocation of resources to businesses that a firm wants to be in and the allocation of resources to the marketing-mix variables for each brand across businesses. In this chapter, methods of evaluating alternative strategies are discussed (1) in terms of the choice of markets/segments in which the firm can do business and (2) in terms of the amount of resources to provide for each of these markets/segments.

The chapter is divided into three sections that correspond to the three steps in the analysis leading to the allocation of resources decisions. The first section discusses how businesses, or products/markets, fit together in the concept of a "balanced" portfolio for the firm. The second section discusses the specific issue of evaluating new businesses in terms of their potential and their fit with the firm's strategy. Finally, the last section presents a list of determinants that guide allocation of resources within the portfolio.

EVALUATION OF PRODUCT/MARKET PORTFOLIOS

One approach to the analysis of product/market portfolios is to represent the various businesses in which the firm operates on a two-dimensional map. This map offers diagnostic information on the position of the firm and shows how the various businesses in which the firm is involved fit together.

To summarize this diagnostic information, each dimension is divided into a number of ranges so that each business belongs to a cell. Product/market portfolio matrix analysis consists of evaluating the businesses based on the set of cells in which the firm operates. In this section, two types of matrix approaches to product/market portfolio analysis—standardized and individualized—are discussed briefly, and their uses in MARKSTRAT are shown. The limitations of these methodologies are pointed out, and the methodologies are illustrated in the context of MARKSTRAT.

A Standardized Approach: The Growth/Share Matrix

The Boston Consulting Group has proposed using two dimensions to represent a portfolio of products: market growth and relative market share. The rationale for choosing these two dimensions is discussed first. Then the specific selection of the relative market share and market growth variables is discussed. Next, selection of the unit of analysis is considered. Examples are given of portfolios in MARKSTRAT. Finally, some of the issues raised by this methodology are presented.

Rationale for Matrix Dimensions. The motivation of the original portfolio analysis is financial. Basically, cash generation and cash usage are the two key elements in evaluation of a business or a set of businesses. Therefore, a business can be evaluated simply by how much cash it generates (or is expected to generate) and by how much of a cash investment is necessary. Assuming that capital can be generated only from within the firm, it is clear that some long-term equilibrium should be attained between businesses that generate cash and businesses that require capital investments. In MARKSTRAT, although additional budgets can be negotiated under certain conditions determined by the instructor, this assumption is correct. Budgets are to some extent a function of the net marketing contribution, and investments are permitted only within the constraint of the budget limit.

Figure 10.1 represents four businesses, corresponding to four extreme cases in terms of these dimensions of cash usage and cash generation. The horizontal axis represents the level of cash generated, and the vertical axis represents the level of investment required. Business A does not generate much cash, but does not require much cash either. From a financial point of view, it is not clear what use this business is to the company. Therefore, from a purely financial perspective, it should be eliminated. However, this business could have certain purposes. It could enable the company, because of its sales volume, to achieve greater economies of scale and/or benefit from greater experience (from an experience curve point of view). Consequently, it could reduce the cost of other businesses, which would become more attractive from this financial point of view. It could also be that this business contributes to the image of the firm or to its competitive position. The first example has to do with the interactions between businesses in terms of costs, or cost synergies. These cost synergies, in MARKSTRAT, do not concern

Figure 10.1

The Cash Basis of Portfolio Analysis

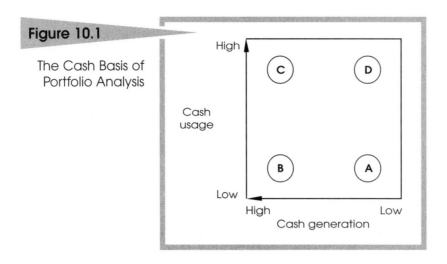

economies of scale in production or experience effects on production costs because each brand is manufactured on a different production line and follows a different experience curve, unless the brands share the same physical characteristics based on the same prototype. However, marketing cost synergies can exist in terms of sales force and distribution, for example.

The second type of synergy between businesses is on the demand side. There is little pure demand synergy in MARKSTRAT because each brand competes independently. Nevertheless, because of competition, a brand may play a role in a firm's competitive strategy. By remaining in a market, one firm can prevent another from generating cash to use in another market or business.

These examples illustrate some limitations of the purely financial view of a portfolio. Nevertheless, as indicated earlier, given that MARKSTRAT firms must strive to grow with their own resources, these firms must keep in mind when they plan that they have to generate their own resources for implementing their strategies in the long run.

Specific Variable Selection. The rationale for portfolio analysis described above is difficult to use because of the difficulty of measuring the cash generation potential of a business as well as the capital investment levels. Therefore, correlates of cash generation and cash usage are typically used to derive a portfolio map in terms of the cash dimensions underlying the financial portfolio rationale. The Boston Consulting Group has suggested that *market growth* is closely related to cash usage and that *relative market share* is a "good" indicator of cash generation. Low-growth markets, it has been argued, are typically mature markets requiring little cash, whereas high-growth markets necessitate high investments to develop the markets and to fight the increasing competition that is attracted to these markets. On the other dimension, relative market share has been used as an indicator of the ability of a business to generate cash. This relative market share is usually computed as the market share of a product divided by the market share of its largest competitor. The argument used to justify the relative market share variable (or market share in general, although different classifications result depending on the definition) is that a business with a higher share enjoys more experience in terms of cumulative production than its competitors. This enables it to produce at a lower cost and to generate higher margins. The rationale for the value of relative market share rests, therefore, on the existence of an experience effect. When the experience effect exists, as in MARKSTRAT, it is clear that, other things being equal, a relationship between relative market share and profitability should exist.

Therefore, these two variables—market growth and relative market share—have been typically substituted for cash usage and cash generation in the portfolio analysis, as indicated in Figure 10.2. The typical growth/share matrix defines two levels (low and high) for each variable and develops the four well-known cells of *cash cow* (high relative market share in low-growth market), *star* (high relative market share in high-growth market), *dog* (low relative market share in low-growth market), and *problem child* (low relative market share in high-growth market). The ideal portfolio, replicating the rationale of cash equilibrium explained above, suggests that a firm should not have any businesses in low-growth markets with small relative market shares

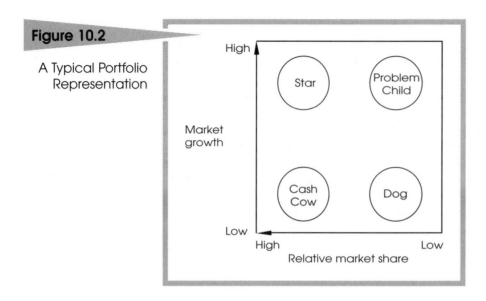

Figure 10.2

A Typical Portfolio Representation

(dogs). Instead, a firm should use the cash generated by businesses in low-growth markets with high relative market shares (cash cows) to invest in the problem children, the stars being self-sufficient. The assumption is that this investment, and therefore the allocation of resources across businesses, will enable businesses in high-growth markets to build their share and become stars. As the market matures and the growth rate slows down, the stars automatically become cash cows. Therefore, the "ideal" portfolio creates a dynamic process, which is self-perpetuating as long as there are new problem children to take over in the cycle and replace the once cash-generating products.

It should be pointed out at this point that the relationships between market growth and cash usage and between relative market share and cash generation are not without controversy. Indeed, it is not clear that low-growth markets generate cash, even when the business is in a high relative market share position. Low-growth markets are typically markets in the mature stage of the product life cycle. These markets are often fragmented, with multiple market segments of different values in terms of size and margin. They are also characterized by a high level of competition, and even though some competitors might exit when growth slows (as occurs with a shake-up of the industry structure), they might engage in escalation of marketing expenditures as a competitive reaction to each others' marketing decisions. Although such competitive behavior can help expand the market in the early stages of the product life cycle, the only outcome at such a late stage is a cut in margins.

In high-growth markets, it is assumed, in the rationale used for selecting market growth as an indicator of cash usage, that cash is necessary to fight new competitors and to develop the market. It is often the case, however, that some competitors benefit from the investments of other competitors (such as the pioneers). Cash consumption does not need to be high in such cases.

A similar problem occurs with the market share variable. The experience curve is not the only factor to consider, because other bases of competitive advantage can be more profitable and more sustainable in the long term. In addition, market share is only an outcome variable and is not under the control of the firm. Indeed, the more important question would be "What are the determinants of profitability?" There is no doubt that market share has a double role to play: on the cost side if there are economies of scale and experience effects and on the demand side because of the larger volume of sales generated. The main determinant of market share is the marketing-mix strategy. Therefore, beyond cost issues, in a causal sense market share does not generate greater cash per se. The issue is one of the relationship between the marketing-mix variables and market share or the costs involved in gaining the share, which can be represented by the marketing-mix elasticities.

The typical portfolio analysis assumes that it is easier (requires less investment) to gain share in a high-growth market because competitors' sales might still increase, even though their share decreases. This assumes that competitors are somewhat complacent, which can be true in high-growth industries. It is unlikely, however, that all competitors who strive for market share will be complacent if they believe that they can maintain and even improve their position because of different bases of competitive advantage that might be sustainable in the long run. Hence it is unlikely that they will give up easily and abandon the territory while they still have a chance. Therefore, it can also be quite costly to gain market share in high-growth markets. This is an area where the competitive notions developed in Chapter 9 can be used to evaluate the difficulty of gaining share and the extent to which high-growth markets are really preferable.

So far, we have assumed that the four cells in the matrix had been identified. Now let us consider the problem of assigning the cut-off delimiting the low and high levels of each variable (market growth and relative market share). There are several definitions of relative market share. One that is used frequently involves dividing the business market share by the industry leader's market share if the business analyzed is not the leader or, if it is, dividing the business leader's share by that of the next closest competitor (with the next highest share). In that case, a natural cut-off point is a relative market share of 1.0. However, this is rather constraining because only one competitor per industry will be in a cash cow or star position. Some companies prefer to use a lower cut-off point of 0.7 or 0.8. Opposed to this, other firms want to give a product a cash cow or star position only if it has a significantly dominant position and use a higher cut-off point of 1.2 or even 1.5.

For market growth, the cut-off point is usually determined on the basis of the average growth of the mix of markets in which the firm is present. One can, however, decide on a higher level to develop a more aggressive approach in the search for new market opportunities or a lower level to emphasize the possibility of growing with established products.

In fact, the cut-off for each variable is rather subjective. Therefore, the portfolio analysis should consider this issue, find a justification for the value selected in a given application, and compare different definitions.

Unit of Analysis. Another issue that arises in developing a portfolio analysis concerns the unit of analysis. What constitutes a business? In MARKSTRAT, two alternatives are possible. It is possible to consider the Sonite and Vodite markets in the aggregate. Each firm has a given market share in each of these markets. This, however, aggregates all the segments as if they were homogeneous when, in fact, each market segment has its own peculiarity in terms of market size, stage of development, competition, etc. So it is generally more appropriate for firms to evaluate their portfolios using each brand in each segment (e.g., in Figure 10.3, SEMI-Pr is brand SEMI in segment Professionals) as the unit of analysis. Because a brand can sell in multiple segments, even though it is positioned for a given segment, it could be appropriate to represent the brand in different locations in the portfolio to correspond to each segment in which it is sold. However, sales outside the segment for which the brand is positioned are usually relatively small, so the main segment for each brand might be sufficient to represent the firm's portfolio. The **Analysis** module of MARKSTRAT provides a tool that automatically generates growth/share portfolio matrices. The portfolio of each firm can be represented for each market or for the Sonite and Vodite markets combined. In Figure 10.3, the scope of the portfolio for Firm E was chosen to be "all markets."

Examples of MARKSTRAT Portfolios. In spite of the limitations of the growth/share matrix pointed out above, diagnostic insights (in particular, in terms of source of financing) can be gained from such a matrix representation. The main objective to keep in mind is the maintenance of the cash balance over time. Therefore, a portfolio where some cells would be empty should be carefully analyzed to determine whether the firm is heading into financial difficulties in the future. For example, Figure 10.4 presents a portfolio that must

Figure 10.3   A Portfolio Generated by the Analysis Module Option

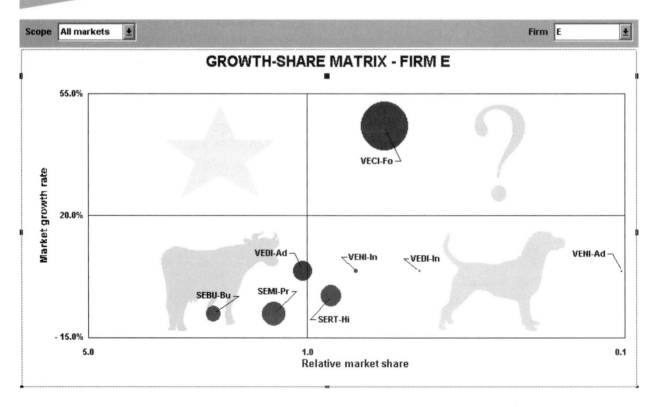

Figure 10.4

An Unbalanced
Portfolio

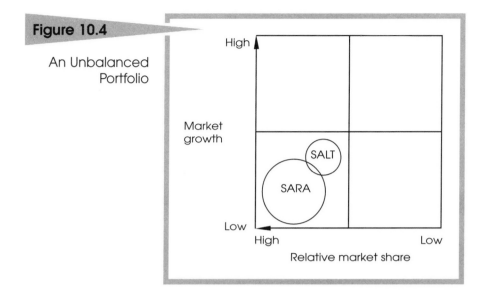

be very profitable currently, as evidenced by two products in leadership positions in low-growth markets (with large sales volumes, as indicated by the diameters of the circles). However, the future is compromised by the absence of new products to maintain sales and profitability in the long term. After the markets for SALT and SARA decline, there will be nothing to maintain the firm's position. This portfolio is typical of shortsighted profit maximization objectives.

Figure 10.5 presents another problematic portfolio. Although the firm has been successful with SULI and SUFA, three brands are positioned improperly. Given their lack of clear competitive advantage in their respective markets, resulting in a low share, SURO, SUNY, and SUMA probably should have been pruned from the portfolio. These brands require resources that might be better used in other markets. Therefore, even though these three brands may

Figure 10.5

A Portfolio
Representation of
Inability to Prune
Poor Performers

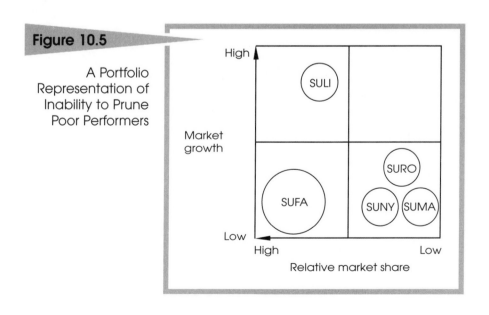

still generate some level of profitability, the portfolio representation should bring the team's attention to the fact that a reallocation of resources should be considered.

The example above does not always lead to a decision to exit from the market, as was proposed. In fact, Figure 10.6 shows a portfolio where it might be necessary to maintain the brand in a dog position. This firm markets two brands that are in growing segments and one that is in a low-growth segment. None of these brands dominates its respective segment, as they all have a small relative market share. This is relatively representative of a smaller firm with limited resources. In that case, SIBI, if profitable, should be maintained, because it does provide some profits that can be used to develop new products for the future. This strategy can be very effective, particularly when the competition in the low-growth segment is weak.

Issues with the Growth/Share Matrix. We have pointed out a number of issues in the use of the growth/share matrix. The discussion above does not exhaust the list of limitations of this methodology, although those described above are particularly appropriate in the MARKSTRAT simulation. Two major issues basic to this method are worth mentioning: the use of a single variable each for cash usage and cash generation and the normative implications of portfolio assessment.

It is clear that each of the financial dimensions is not appropriately represented by a single indicator. Therefore, errors are introduced if all the determinants of cash usage and market share are not used. The following discussion of individualized portfolios indicates how this problem can be partially remedied.

Even more basic is the problem of the implications of the portfolio assessment. The growth/share matrix provides a potentially useful diagnostic tool. It summarizes, simply, where the firm stands in terms of its relative market share position and in terms of growth within the segment in which it conducts business. It can even present some elements of the financial

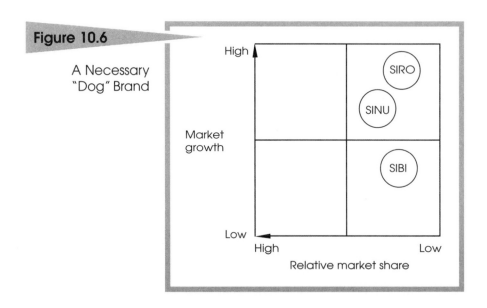

Figure 10.6

A Necessary "Dog" Brand

equilibrium situation of the firm. However, this type of portfolio analysis provides little information on how to reallocate resources across the brands/segments. This is due to the lack of information in this analysis about the opportunities for gaining share and about the costs of gaining this share. These opportunities and costs differ for different alternatives, even among those in the problem child cell. This issue is valid for the individualized portfolio as well and will be discussed later.

An Individualized Approach: The Attractiveness/Position Matrix

In the attractiveness/position matrix approach, the market growth variable is replaced with a more complicated construct of the attractiveness of an industry/market/segment. The portfolio that is derived thus loses its financial interpretation. Indeed, an attractive market does not necessarily use more or less funds than an unattractive market. However, if a market is attractive, it must be worth some level of investment. Therefore, resources should be allocated to the markets that are attractive. In addition, the better the competitive position (or potential position), the greater the competitive advantage and, therefore, the greater the resources that the firm should be willing to devote to maintaining or building this position.* Therefore, this attractiveness/position matrix indicates the position of each of the businesses of the firm and indicates which are worth investing in to maintain or build a position.

Figure 10.7 shows an example of such a matrix. The SEMI and SECU brands should not receive resources because the market segments they are in are not believed to be attractive. On the other hand, SELF and SELL are in attractive markets. The allocation of resources between these two brands depends on the cost of maintaining SELL's position and the cost of moving SELF from a weak to a strong brand position, if this is possible. It depends also on the relative benefits, as represented by the attractiveness dimension.

This issue illustrates the first aspect of the development of the individualized approach: What are the components of these two dimensions? The process that determines the attractiveness dimension is parallel to that which determines the position dimension. However, each has some peculiarities. Therefore, the process that leads to an attractiveness/position matrix is dealt with by discussing first the attractiveness dimension and then the position dimension.

Assessment of the Attractiveness of a Market. The attractiveness of a business can be assessed by the four-step process outlined below:

Step 1: Determine the relevant factors contributing to the attractiveness of businesses for the firm.

Step 2: Determine the direction and form of the relationship between each factor and the attractiveness measure, and assess the value of each business on each contributing factor developed in step 1.

---

*Note that this does not necessarily imply that greater resources are needed; however, if they are, the opportunity justifies the allocating of the resources.

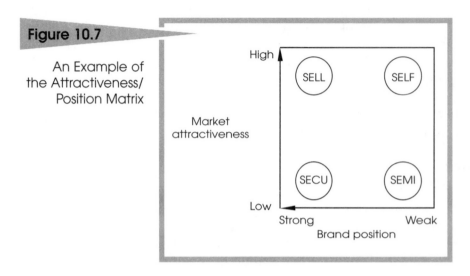

Figure 10.7

An Example of
the Attractiveness/
Position Matrix

Step 3: Determine the weight of each factor's contribution to the attractiveness measure.

Step 4: Compute the value of each business on the attractiveness measure.

This procedure is now illustrated for the MARKSTRAT firms, with a list of factors that are particularly relevant in MARKSTRAT.

Step 1. The following factors can potentially influence the attractiveness of a market:

- Market factors
  — Market/segment size, in units
  — Market/segment growth rate
  — Market/segment primary demand elasticity to price
  — Advertising elasticity (primary market/segment demand)
  — Shopping habits of consumers in market/segment
  — Demand elasticity to product features
  — Forecasting accuracy of market/segment size
  — Forecasting accuracy of market shares
- Competition
  — Number of brands competing in market/segment
  — Size of competitors (their available resources)
  — Marketing-mix strategy of competitors
  — Reactivity of competitors in market/segment
  — Positioning of competing brands
  — Threat of new brand introductions in market/segment
  — Extent of barriers for each competitor not yet in market/segment
- Financial factors
  — Contribution margins
  — Experience effects

Step 2. After the relevant factors have been selected from the list above, the firm must determine for each factor whether a high value of that factor leads to greater attractiveness or not, and by how much. This can be done by defining categorical levels for each factor. For example, it can be assessed that a market size below 1,000,000 units per year has a low level of attractiveness (to which a value of, for example, 0 can be assigned). A value of 1.0 can be assigned to a high level of attractiveness, which a market size of above 5,000,000 units per year might be considered to have. A value of 0.5 can be assigned to a medium level of attractiveness of between 1,000,000 and 5,000,000 units.

This step must be performed for each factor selected in step 1. This could result in the following data, assuming these factors were selected:

	Score
Market/segment size, in units	0.5
Market/segment growth rate	0
Number of brands competing in market/segment	1.0
Reactivity of competitors in market/segment	1.0
Contribution margins	0.5

Step 3. In this step, each factor selected in step 1 must be assigned a weight such that the total for all factors adds up to 1.00. The example below illustrates how the weights can be assigned.

	Weight
Market/segment size, in units	0.15
Market/segment growth rate	0.15
Number of brands competing in market/segment	0.30
Reactivity of competitors in market/segment	0.15
Contribution margins	0.25
	1.00

In this example, the number of brands already competing is the most important factor in determining the segment's attractiveness. This could be because it is difficult to perform well from both a marketing and a financial perspective in a market with many brands. This factor is twice as important as segment size or growth rate. This weighting scheme is clearly subjective and should represent the best judgments of the managers of the firm. It should be kept in mind, however, that these assessments are approximate, and a sensitivity analysis might be appropriate to check the extent to which final evaluations will change when the weights vary.

Step 4. In this last step, we compute the level of attractiveness of the market for which the factors have been assessed. The level of attractiveness is the weighted average of all the factor ratings:

	Score	*Weight*	*Value*
Market/segment size, in units	0.5	0.15	0.075
Market/segment growth rate	0	0.15	0
Number of brands competing in market/segment	1.0	0.30	0.3
Reactivity of competitors in market/segment	1.0	0.15	0.15
Contribution margins	0.5	0.25	0.125
		1.00	0.65

An attractiveness value of 0.65 is therefore assigned to this market segment.

Assessment of the Position of a Business. The procedure for assessing the position is similar to that for assessing the attractiveness of a market/segment:

Step 1: Determine the relevant factors contributing to the position of the firm's businesses in their respective markets/segments.

Step 2: Determine the direction and form of the relationship between each factor and the position measure, and assess the value of each business on each contributing factor developed in step 1.

Step 3: Determine the weight of each factor's contribution to the position measure.

Step 4: Compute the position of each business on the position measure.

Step 1. The following factors might contribute to the position of a business in a market/segment.

- Market factors
  - Market/segment share, based on units sold
  - Market/segment share, based on value
  - Sales volume of brand, in units
  - Sales volume of brand, in value
  - Growth rate of market share (based on units and value)
  - Growth rate of sales (based on units and value)
  - Brand price elasticity
  - Brand advertising elasticity
  - Brand sales force elasticity
  - Influence of brand on market/segment size
- Competition
  - Competitive advantage
  - Price elasticity of competitive brands
  - Advertising elasticity of competitive brands
  - Sales force elasticity of competitive brands
  - Cross-elasticities for marketing-mix variables
- Financial factors
  - Brand margin
  - Cumulative production versus that of competitive brands

Step 2. After the relevant factors have been selected from the above list, the firm must determine for each factor whether a high value of that factor leads to a better position of a brand or not, and by how much. This can be done by defining categorical levels for each factor. For example, it can be assessed that a market share below 0.20 constitutes a weak position (to which a value of, for example, 0 can be assigned). A value of 1.0 can be assigned to the very good position that might apply to a market share of above 0.70. A value of 0.5 can be assigned to an average position of between 0.20 and 0.70 market share.

This step must be performed for each factor selected in step 1. This could result in the following data, assuming these factors were selected:

	Score
Market/segment share	0
Brand price elasticity	0.5
Competitive advantage	0.5
Brand margin	0.5
Cumulative production	1.0

Step 3. In this step, each factor selected in step 1 must be assigned a weight such that the total for all factors adds up to 1.00. The example below illustrates how the weights are assigned.

	Score
Market/segment share	0.30
Brand price elasticity	0.20
Competitive advantage	0.30
Brand margin	0.05
Cumulative production	0.15
	1.00

In this example, market share and the competitive advantage are the most important factors in determining the brand's position. Price elasticity is also relatively highly weighted. This weighting could represent the fact that cost leadership is extremely important. Consequently, the market share and cumulative production reflect the position of the brand. At the same time, the brand price elasticity allows a firm to gain volume by lowering the price, which contributes to lower costs. Lower prices could, however, affect the margins, which are not very important in this case.

Again, this weighting scheme is clearly subjective and should represent the best judgment of the managers of the firm. Therefore, a sensitivity analysis might be appropriate to check the extent to which the final evaluations of the brand's positions will change when the weights vary.

Step 4. In this last step, we compute the strength of the position of the brand for which the factors have been assessed. The strength of the position of the brand is the weighted average of all the factor ratings:

	Score	Weight	Value
Market/segment share	0	0.30	0
Brand price elasticity	0.5	0.20	0.10
Competitive advantage	0.5	0.30	0.15
Brand margin	0.5	0.05	0.025
Cumulative production	1.0	0.15	0.15
		1.00	0.425

A value of 0.425 is therefore assigned to the strength of the position of this brand segment, reflecting a below-average position. Now that the market attractiveness and the strength of the position have been computed in terms of values that range between 0 and 1.00, it is easy to plot this business on a

Figure 10.8

The Attractiveness/
Position Map

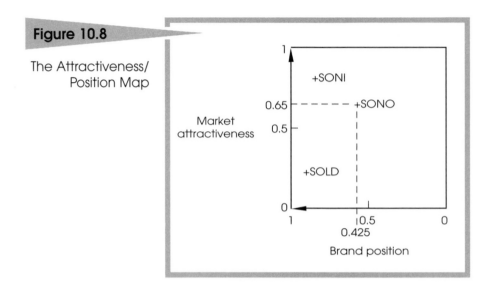

two-dimensional map. Figure 10.8 gives an example of such a map, including the point for which the values above were computed.

Factors Affecting the Allocation of Resources

In the example above, the portfolio of the firm is relatively eclectic. The SONI brand is well positioned. SOLD has a strong position, but in a not so attractive market. SONO is in an attractive market but with a relatively weak position. The position of SONI should be maintained, and resources should be devoted to this objective. At the same time, it might be possible to improve the position of SONO; with a strong position, SONO would improve the portfolio. Therefore, resources should be reallocated from SOLD to SONI and SONO. This approach is more complete than the growth/share matrix because it considers many more factors, including possible synergies, uncertainty in predicting demand, and elasticities of marketing-mix variables. However, these qualitative evaluations are insufficient to determine the level and the nature of resources required to build a business or maintain it in a desirable location in the attractiveness/position individualized matrix. Therefore, a better link between market share or sales and the level of marketing-mix activities is required to determine how much to invest in each marketing-mix variable.

Before we discuss these issues in greater detail, we assess a specific business—a new business in which the firm does not yet operate.

EVALUATION OF NEW BUSINESS OPPORTUNITIES

Is the evaluation of a new business different from the assessment of a business in which the firm already operates? Clearly, the attractiveness of a market can be assessed whether or not the firm is in this market. The only problem is that the evaluation of one factor of market attractiveness could depend on the characteristics of the firm with respect to that business. For example, a highly price elastic market is attractive only if the firm possesses a cost advantage. This point illustrates that the assessment of market attractiveness and business position can be very complex, as they are not always based on fully independent factors. Further, for a new business, assessing market attractiveness is more difficult because the firm does not yet have any market position. Consequently, the analysis must rely on the managers' evaluations of the potential position of the firm in that business. This can be partly accomplished by analyzing the factors discussed above that contribute to the business position. However, many factors can be evaluated only in terms of expectations. These expectations, in turn, depend on marketing decisions. Therefore, the major issue in the case of a new business is evaluation of the strategy (nature and extent of resources) necessary to build a competitive position in the market. This issue is indeed similar to the conclusion we have drawn from our discussion of portfolio analysis.

An analysis of a new business is concerned with two questions: Is the market worth investing in? If it is, how much should be invested? Analyzing the attractiveness of the market, as suggested before, and comparing it with the attractiveness of markets currently in the portfolio can provide the answer to the first question. The answer to the second question requires knowledge of two key factors: (1) the ability to gain a strong position and earn profits in this business and (2) the ability to establish barriers to protect a competitive advantage and, hence, the long-term profitability of that business.

The second factor was discussed at length in Chapter 9, on competitive strategies. The first factor, the ability to gain a strong position, rests on the opportunity and the costs involved in achieving this position. Assuming that the opportunity must exist because this business was judged attractive, one must establish the extent of the costs—that is, of resources necessary to establish a strong position in this market. This raises the basic question that is missing from typical portfolio analysis: How much investment is necessary to achieve a strong, sustainable position in this market? The complexity of this question is magnified by the inherent uncertainties in new market entry situations. Although uncertainty is also a factor in allocating resources to existing businesses, as briefly discussed above, uncertainties about new businesses are particularly crucial. Indeed, there are, typically, greater uncertainties associated with new businesses. The demand is more difficult to predict (particularly if the market is at the introduction stage of the product life cycle). Also, competitive reactions are difficult to forecast. These uncertainties should be critical to a risk-averse manager. However, perhaps more important is the risk of not investing while the firm can, a risk that has been called the missing-the-boat risk. This risk for new business is probably more important than the traditional sinking-the-boat risk because not only might the missed opportunity be expensive in terms of opportunity cost, but a competitor's taking advantage of that opportunity might in the long term affect the profitability of the businesses in which the firm operates. The importance of this risk depends on the length of the window of opportunity or the strategic window facing the firm.

DETERMINANTS OF ALLOCATION OF RESOURCES

The level of investment necessary to obtain a sustainable position in a market is not independent of the other markets and the levels of investment in other businesses. In addition, the allocation of resources decision is affected by the ability to gain share or sales. This factor differs across markets and depends on the relative effectiveness of the various marketing-mix variables, which also differs across businesses. Therefore, the allocation of resources decision depends on the relationship between the marketing-mix variables and market share or sales. It also depends on the margin of each product. As indicated earlier, synergies between businesses are the reason for a firm's desire to maintain a portfolio. These synergies are both on the demand side, in ability to affect demand in one business with marketing activities in other businesses, and on the cost side, in economies of scale, experience, or economies of scope. Finally, uncertainty surrounding the ability to relate market share or sales to the marketing-mix effort levels must affect the allocation of resources decision.

The Effectiveness of Marketing-Mix Variables

More resources should be devoted to brands exhibiting a high level of response to the marketing instruments than to those exhibiting a lower level of sensitivity because the former investment will be more effective. This is the case for advertising and sales force expenditures. The price decision, although not an expenditure, follows the same rationale and has a particularly important effect on the margin level. Therefore, the higher the demand elasticity of the brand's price, the lower the price (and, consequently, the margins) should be, everything else being equal. It is, therefore, essential for strategic decisions on the allocation of resources between multiple businesses to measure the effectiveness of the marketing-mix variables. Without going into detailed measurement models, the next section provides a conceptual framework for specifying such models.

Product positioning is clearly a strong determinant of market share and sales because it is related to the degree to which the product is perceived to deliver key benefits and therefore the degree to which the product satisfies the needs of the consumers. Although effects of a position on sales or market share can be assessed, the costs of achieving that position are more difficult to evaluate. We have discussed two approaches to repositioning a brand in MARKSTRAT. R&D, in particular, is a long-term endeavor that is difficult to relate to product positioning. Nevertheless, the effort required to reposition a brand (through advertising or R&D) should be related to the extent to which that repositioning will affect sales or market share. This extent should vary across market segments and firms, just as product requirements, R&D capabilities, and competitive activity differ across segments and firms.

Demand Synergies

As discussed earlier, demand synergies refer to the extent to which a marketing variable of one brand affects positively the demand for other brands in the portfolio. More resources should be devoted to brands that highly influence the sales of other brands. In particular, if these cross elasticities are especially high for some marketing-mix variables, greater emphasis should be placed on these variables. It is clear, however, that this cross-elastic, or synergistic, effect should be balanced with the regular elasticity effects in the allocation of resources decision. For example, if brand SARA has a low advertising elasticity but is greatly affected in a positive way (i.e., an increase in sales) by the advertising of SALE, more should be spent on advertising SALE than would be if it were not for the cross-elasticity effect. However, if SARA shows a greater response to its own elasticity, no more should be allocated to advertising SALE.

Cost Synergies

Cost synergies can result from different phenomena. They can be achieved in MARKSTRAT from economies of scope in marketing activities. They can also arise from economies of scale and experience from cross elasticities of demand. Both of these sources of cost synergies are particularly important, as they directly affect the unit margins. It is therefore crucial to exploit them efficiently.

Cost synergies arise from marketing activities, because advertising one brand can expand the primary demand of a market segment. Consequently, achieving sales objectives for two brands in the same market segment can be less costly in terms of advertising expenditures than if there were no synergy. More important, synergies can be achieved in terms of the sales force. Because all salespeople represent all the brands marketed by the firm, additional sales force might not be required to sell a brand sold through the same channel of distribution as others.

The unit base cost can be lower because of experience curve effects when cross elasticities occur. Therefore, more effort should go into marketing brands whose marketing instruments affect the levels of sales of other products for which cost per unit and experience are important.

Uncertainty and Risk

Finally, uncertainty in predicting demand—in particular, the degree to which the marketing-mix strategy predicts performance—should be a strong indicator of the degree of investment in a brand. The greater the uncertainty, the smaller the amount of resources a risk-averse manager will allocate to a brand. This allocation rule should recognize, however, that behind this inaccuracy of prediction might be an opportunity for a high level of sales or market share, generated by a given marketing-mix strategy. So, when faced with uncertainty, marketing managers should balance a recognition of opportunity with risk aversion.

CONCLUSION

This chapter has discussed the factors to consider in allocating resources to the various brands and market segments. Several approaches, including the matrix type of portfolio analysis and individualized portfolio evaluation, were discussed and evaluated. In particular, the benefits as well as the limitations of such approaches were pointed out and their applications illustrated in the context of MARKSTRAT. Finally, additional factors to consider in making allocation of resources decisions for marketing strategy purposes were discussed. These include explicit recognition of the relative effectiveness of the marketing-mix variables for each brand or market segment combination, the evaluation of demand as well as cost synergies between products/markets, and the formal assessment of uncertainties and risk associated with each market.

Evaluation of Product/Market Portfolio: The Growth/Share Matrix

- Premises
  - High market share generates cash revenues.
  - High market growth uses more cash resources.
- Guide for the growth/share matrix in MARKSTRAT
  - The unit of analysis is the brand/segment combination.
  - Multiple definitions of market share are used.
  - The market segment growth rate cut-off depends on the market segments in which the firm has products.
- Issues in the growth/share matrix approach
  - Market growth is not the only factor related to cash usage.
  - Market growth is not necessarily related to cash usage.
  - Market share is not necessarily related to cash generation (it ignores the cost of gaining share and could overvalue the effect of the experience curve).
  - There are multiple factors leading to profitability.
  - Cash is not the only consideration in evaluating a portfolio.
  - Internal cash balance is not always desirable.
  - Cut-off values are arbitrary.
  - The unit of analysis depends on the level of analysis.

Assessment of Market Attractiveness

- **Step 1:** Determine the list of relevant factors contributing to the attractiveness of businesses for the firm.
- **Step 2:** Determine the direction and form of the relationship between each factor and the attractiveness measure, and assess the value of each business on each contributing factor developed in step 1.
- **Step 3:** Determine the weight of each factor's contribution to the attractiveness measure.
- **Step 4:** Compute the value of each business on the attractiveness measure.

Factors Leading to Market Attractiveness

- Market factors
  - Market/segment size, in units
  - Market/segment growth rate
  - Market/segment primary demand elasticity to price
  - Advertising elasticity (primary market/segment demand)
  - Shopping habits of consumers in market/segment
  - Demand elasticity to product features
  - Forecasting accuracy of market/segment size
  - Forecasting accuracy of market shares
- Competition
  - Number of brands competing in market/segment
  - Size of competitors (their available resources)
  - Marketing-mix strategy of competitors
  - Reactivity of competitors in market/segment
  - Positioning of competing brands
  - Threat of new brand introductions in market/segment
  - Extent of barriers for each competitor not yet in market/segment
- Financial factors
  - Contribution margins
  - Experience effects

Assessment of Business Position

- **Step 1:** Determine the list of relevant factors contributing to the position of businesses for the firm in their respective market/segment.
- **Step 2:** Determine the direction and form of the relationship between each factor and the position measure, and assess the value of each business on each contributing factor developed in step 1.
- **Step 3:** Determine the weight of each factor's contribution to the position measure.
- **Step 4:** Compute the position of each business on the position measure.

Factors Contributing to Business Position

- Market factors
  - Market/segment share, based on units sold
  - Market/segment share, based on value
  - Sales volume of brand, in units
  - Sales volume of brand, in value
  - Growth rate of market share (based on units and value)
  - Growth rate of sales (based on units and value)
  - Brand price elasticity
  - Brand advertising elasticity
  - Brand sales force elasticity
  - Influence of brand on market/segment size

- Competition
  - Competitive advantage
  - Price elasticity of competitive brands
  - Advertising elasticity of competitive brands
  - Sales force elasticity of competitive brands
  - Cross elasticities for each marketing-mix variable
- Financial factors
  - Brand margin
  - Cumulative production versus that of competitive brands

Important Factors Influencing Resource Allocation That Need to Be Explicitly Recognized

- Demand synergies
- Cost synergies
- Uncertainties and risk

APPENDIX A

Installing MARKSTRAT3

COMPUTER REQUIREMENTS

The minimum computer configuration required to operate MARKSTRAT3 is the following:

- IBM-compatible personal computer
- Intel 486 or Pentium processor
- 4 megabytes of memory
- Hard disk with at least 6 megabytes of available storage
- Windows 3.1 or Windows 95
- Laser or ink-jet printer

INSTALLING MARKSTRAT3

This section describes how to install MARKSTRAT3 on a stand-alone computer. To install MARKSTRAT3 in complex environments with network servers and/or remote workstations, please contact your instructor. Complex installation procedures are fully described in the Instructor's Manual.

Start the MARKSTRAT3 setup utility by performing the steps in the table below.

Windows 3.1	*Windows 95*
Insert the **Team** diskette in the disk drive.	
Select the **Program Manager** by pressing Alt-Tab a number of times until it appears.	Click on the **Start** button.
In the **File** menu, select **Run . . .**	In the **Windows95** menu, select **Run . . .**
Type **A:SETUP** in the **Command line** box, and click on **OK.**	Type **A:SETUP** in the **Open** box, and click on **OK.**

In a short time, a dialog box will ask you to choose a language for the instructions. Then the main dialog box of the setup utility will pop up, as shown in Figure A.1. A number of choices must be made.

- *Where do you want MARKSTRAT3 to store private data files?* MARKSTRAT3 needs a directory on a local or remote disk unit in which to store your private data files. For a stand-alone computer, this directory must be located on a local disk unit, usually C or D. We suggest that you use the default directory suggested by the software.
- *Where do you want to install the MARKSTRAT3 application?* You must specify where MARKSTRAT3 read-only files (executable files, images, sounds, etc.) will be installed. For a stand-alone computer, select the first choice, *install it on this computer*, and enter the complete path of the directory in the box below. This directory will be created if it does not already exist. We suggest that you use the default directory suggested by the software.
- *How will you transfer data between the instructor and team?* For a stand-alone computer, data transfers must be done by diskette. Select one of the first two options: *By diskette—Drive A* or *By diskette—Drive B.* Note that only the relevant drives appear on the choice list.

Figure A.1   MARKSTRAT3 Setup Utility

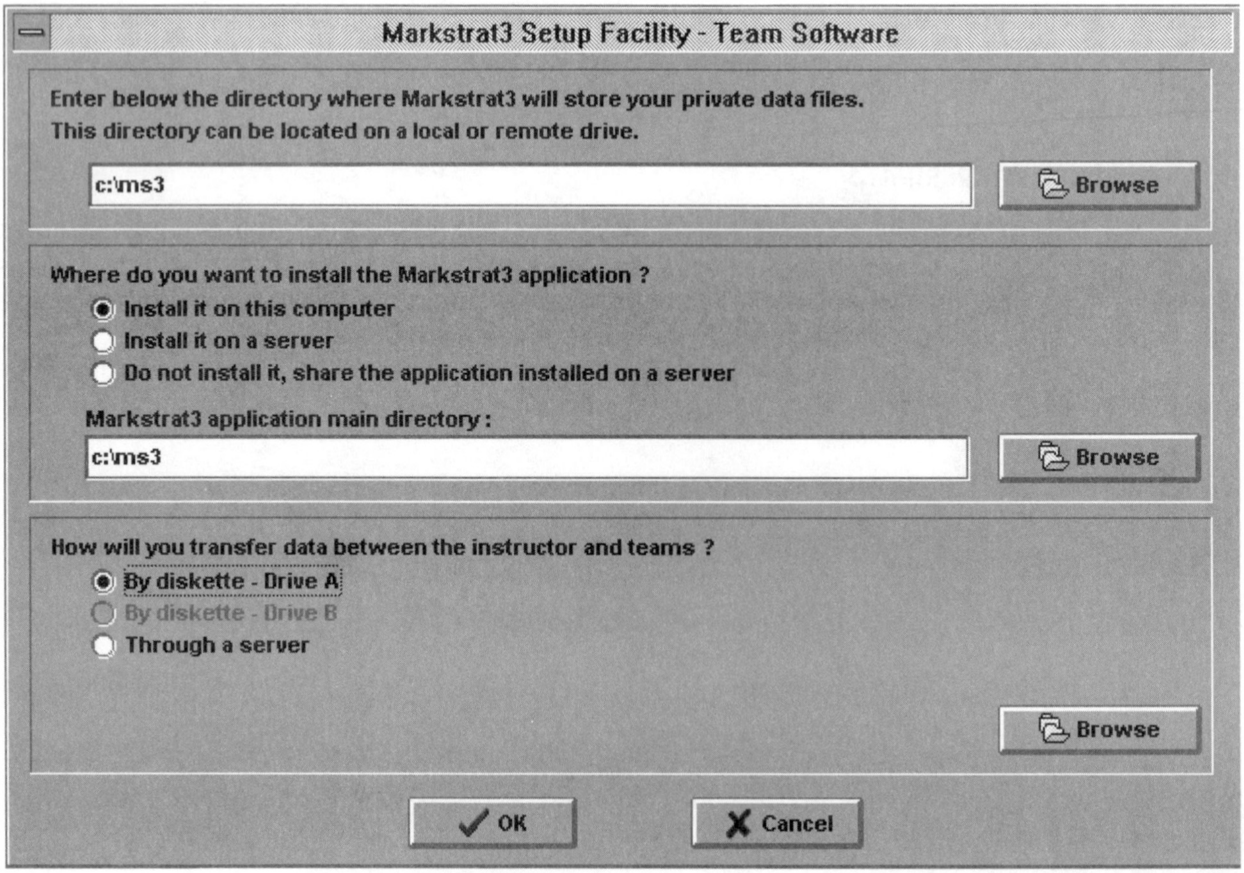

Once the choices have been made, you may proceed by clicking on **OK**. The setup utility will create the required directories, decompress the MARKSTRAT3 files, and place them in the appropriate locations. At some point, you will be requested to insert the **Library** diskette. Finally, the setup utility will create an icon in a program manager group called **MARKSTRAT3—By Strat*X.** In Windows 95, an entry is added to the Windows 95 list of programs.

Printing Documents

M ARKSTRAT3 documents can be printed on any Windows-compatible printer. However, high quality and high printing speed will be obtained only with ink-jet or laser printers. Dot-matrix printers should be avoided whenever possible.

The MARKSTRAT3 printing facility is activated by clicking on the small printer button 🖨 in the top right-hand corner of the screen. MARKSTRAT3 documents are grouped in three categories: team reports, decision-related reports, and data tables or graphs. Depending on the module in which you are currently working, pressing the **Print** button will let you print different documents.

- From the **Interface** module, print your team report.
- From the **Decisions** module, print decision-related documents (Summary of decisions and budget, Detailed budget, Marketing plan).
- From **Other** modules, print the currently displayed graph or data table.

PRINTING TEAM REPORTS

Team report printing can be done by the instructor or by the team itself, by clicking on 🖨 *while in the* **Interface** *module.* The dialog box shown in Figure B.1 will pop up; a number of options must be specified, as explained below.

- *Number of copies.* Specify the number of copies to be printed.
- *Content.* The team report includes three separate documents: the Company Report, the Newsletter, and the Studies. Each document contains several sections, as shown in Figure B.1; in the case of the studies document, each study is composed of two sections, one for the Sonite market and one for the Vodite market. Check the documents and the sections you want to print; the five buttons on the lower right-hand side will help you select complete documents.
- *Purchased studies only or all selected studies.* The option of printing all selected studies is reserved for the instructor and so is not activated in the team software. You can print only the studies that you purchased at the beginning of the period. If you need one of the other studies, ask

Figure B.1   Printing Team Reports by Selecting Options

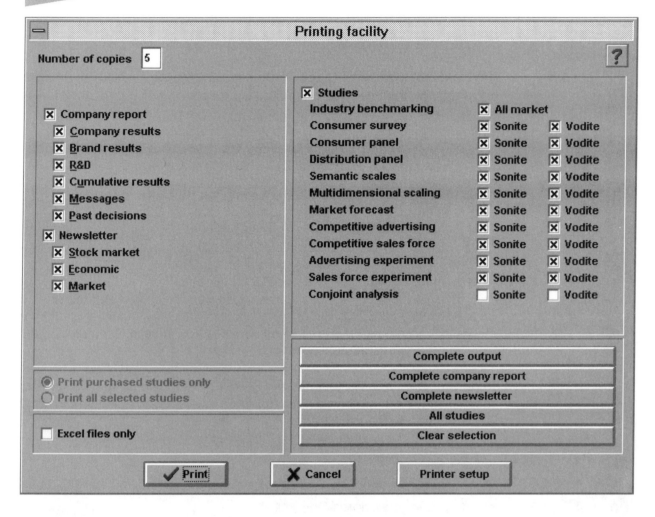

your instructor for a copy; he or she will probably agree to print it for you, at a reasonable price. . . .

■ *Excel files only.* Each time a document is printed, MARKSTRAT3 produces an Excel 4–compatible file containing the document image. When the *Excel files only* option is checked, the Excel files are produced but the documents are not sent to the printer. You can implement mathematical or statistical models within your favorite spreadsheet package and then use these files to analyze MARKSTRAT3 data without having to key in all numbers. The Excel files are located in the private directory; their name is of the form IIIICT99.XLS, where

— IIII are the first four letters of the industry name;

— C is a one-letter code:

    N = Newsletter,

    R = Company Report,

    S = Studies, . . . ;

— T is the team initial: A, E, I, O, U, or Y;

— 99 is the period number.

For instance, A-MMSU04.XLS is the team U study document of industry A-MMII in Period 4.

PRINTING DATA TABLES OR GRAPHS

Any data table, graph, map, or portfolio matrix can be printed by first displaying it and then clicking on the printer button. A self-explanatory dialog box will pop up.

PRINTING DECISION-RELATED DOCUMENTS

While making your decisions, you can print the following documents:

- *Summary of decisions and budget.* This three- to five-page document provides a clear view of the current decisions and of the current expenditures, loan amounts, and allocated budget.
- *Detailed budget.* This two-page document provides a detailed view of the current expenditures, loan amounts, and allocated budget.
- *Marketing plan.* This two-page document provides projected results for next period, based on the sales forecasts that have been entered in the marketing plan tool.

To print one of these documents *while working in the* **Decisions** *module*, click on the printer button, select the document in the dialog box (shown in Figure B.2), and click on the **Print** button.

Figure B.2   Printing a Decision-Related Document

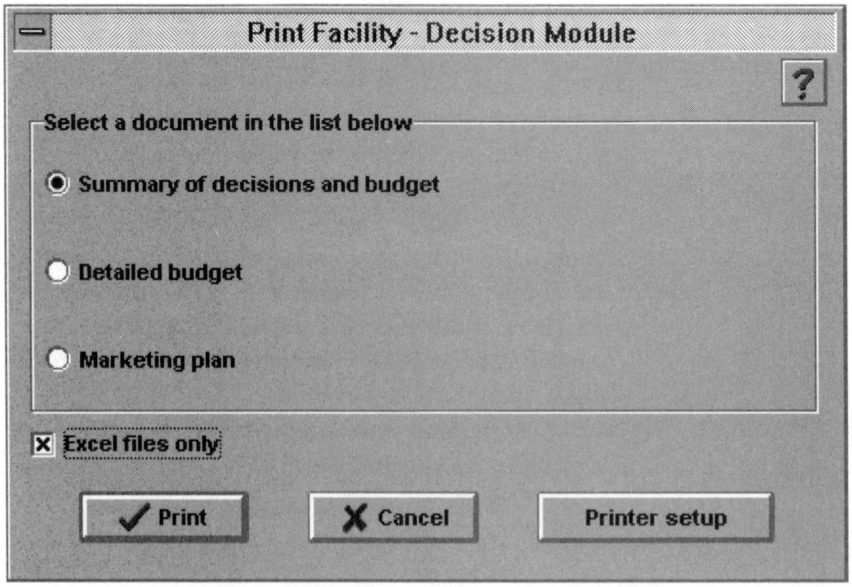

Software Configuration

The MARKSTRAT3 configuration is normally specified at installation time, but it can be partially modified by clicking on the small toolbox button 🔧 located in the top right-hand corner of the screen. The dialog box shown in Figure C.1 pops up. The configuration includes the following elements:

- *Program directory.* This is where MARKSTRAT3 read-only files are stored: executable files, images, and sounds. The program directory may be located on the local computer or on a remote one. *The program directory can be changed only by reinstalling the software.*
- *Private directory.* This directory, on the local or remote computer, is where private data files are located. The private directory can be changed by modifying the properties of the program manager icon in Windows 3.1 or the properties of the shortcut in Windows 95. You may also reinstall MARKSTRAT3 and specify a new private directory.
- *Instructor/team exchange directory.* This directory specifies how you will transfer data to and from your instructor. If the exchange directory is A:\ or B:\, then data transfers are done with team diskettes. If the exchange directory is located on a disk drive of a network server, then data transfers are done through the network. *We suggest that you not change the value of this directory unless you are requested to do so by your instructor.*
- *Language.* This is the language used in the simulation. There are currently two languages available: English and French. Future releases of MARKSTRAT3 are likely to offer additional languages such as German, Italian, and Spanish.

Figure C.1   Modifying the Software Configuration

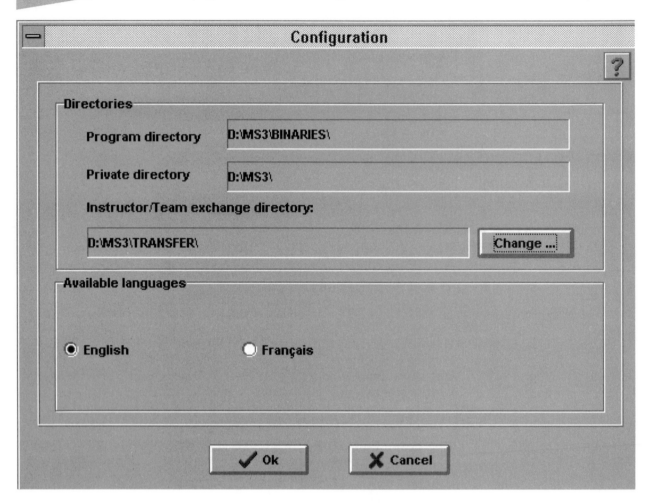

INDEX

Abandonment, 171, 181
  of R&D project, 129
Accommodation, 171
Administrative errors, 9
Advertising
  budget for, 21–22, 58, 101
  competitors', 32, 42, 161
  decisions about, 22, 52, 58
  expenditures for, 14, 21–23, 42, 45, 152, 170, 172, 192
  objectives of, 21, 58, 124–125
  as reaction, 162
Advertising experiment, 45
Advertising research, 22, 42, 58, 123
Allocation
  budget, 22, 123
  marketing mix, 3, 168
  resource, 3, 142, 155, 170, 177, 180, 183–185, 190, 192–193
  sales force, 170
  time, 9, 21, 59–60
Analysis
  competitive, 3, 157–158, 163
  conjoint, 47
  consumer, 3
  environmental, 3
  marketing, 3
  product/market, 3, 158, 177
  regression, 107, 115
  trend, 108
Artificial accuracy, 10
Assessment of perceptions/preferences, 103
Asymmetries, 153
Attacks, 157, 171, 172
Attractiveness, 105, 153, 154, 185–187
Attribute, 103, 105, 114, 129, 143, 151, 152, 164–165, 166
Availability
  of product, 17, 80
  of project, 55, 80
Awareness
  brand, 20, 21, 22, 32, 109, 136, 150, 151, 152, 153–155, 169
  consumer, 13

Barriers
  to entry, 21, 106, 130, 159–160, 166, 191
  mobility, 152, 164, 166
Brand
  availability of, 154

  awareness of, 20, 21, 22, 32, 109, 136, 150, 151, 152, 153–155, 169
  characteristics of, 17–18, 23, 85, 114, 128, 130, 143, 169
  demand for, 109–110
  introduction of, 18, 54, 134, 163, 168, 170
  modification of, 18, 55, 115, 136
  perception of, 104
  positioning of, 41, 103–105, 109, 116, 122, 154, 163, 192
  preferences for, 105, 107, 152
  repositioning of, 21, 31, 58, 124, 153, 172
  withdrawal of, 55–56
Brand choice, 150–151
Brand names, 17, 18, 23
Brand portfolio, 53–54
Budget
  additional, 24, 129, 131, 132, 133–134, 172, 178
  advertising, 21–22, 58, 101
  changes in, 14, 67–68, 70, 76
  cuts in, 68, 101
  exceeding of, 66
  marketing, 14
  maximum, 14, 75
  minimum, 14, 18, 75, 134
  R&D, 23, 24, 66, 110, 131–132, 139, 142–144, 161, 169
Buffs, 19

Cannibalization, 105, 109
Cash cow, 79, 181
Code names, 128
Communication objectives, 58, 124, 170
Company report, 8, 51, 71–72, 81, 112
  brand results, 76, 112
  company performance, 14, 73–76, 78, 99
  company results, 72
  company scorecard, 72, 83
  cumulative results, 51, 80, 112
  decisions, 51
  messages, 80
  past decisions, 82
Competition, intensity of, 9, 42, 155, 159, 161, 163, 168, 171–172, 187
Competitive advantage, 161, 163, 164, 166–168, 170–171, 181, 183, 185, 186, 189, 191
  complementarity of bases of, 158, 167
  through cost leadership, 164
  through product differentiation, 165, 166, 167
Competitive analysis, 3, 157–158, 163

Conjoint analysis, 47
Consumer, 18
    perceptions of, 37, 104, 136, 153, 168
    preferences of, 42, 153, 166
Consumer survey, 32–33, 151
Contingency strategies, 142
Contribution
    after marketing, 75
    before marketing, 74
    net, 14, 75
Cost
    base, 16, 22, 23, 62, 79, 110, 113
    extraordinary, 56
    of goods sold, 15, 74
    of inventory disposal, 74
    of inventory holding, 16
    manufacturing, 24
    of market research, 85
    minimum realistic, 130, 144
    production, 165
    and productivity gains, 139
    transfer, 14, 16, 24, 74, 110
    unit, 23
Cost advantage, 110, 165, 167–168, 170, 191
Cost leadership, 164
Cost reduction, 64, 131, 138–140
Cost synergies, 178, 193
Cumulative expenditures, 79
Cumulative results, 80, 112
Cut-off point, 181

Decision module, 52, 80, 82, 93, 124, 134
Defensive strategies, 171
Demand
    forecast, 46
    price elasticity of, 167, 192
    primary, 21, 150, 155, 172, 186, 193
Demand synergies, 178, 192–193
Differentiation, 138, 164, 165, 166, 167
Diffusion, 109
Distribution channels, 19, 20, 35, 58, 154
Distribution margins, 20, 96
Distribution mix, 96–97
Dog, 179
Downgrading, 130

Economic environment, 26
Economic variables, 84
Economies
    of scale, 105, 160, 178, 181, 192, 193
    of scope, 192
Entry
    and marketing mix, 170
    scale of, 170
    signaling of, 169
    strategies for, 168, 172
Environmental analysis, 3

Evolution
    of market, 107, 108
    of preferences, 107, 150, 153
Exceptional cost, 75
Exceptional profit, 75
Expenses, 14, 44
Experience curve, 25, 110–111, 112, 131, 139, 140, 165, 167, 180, 193
Extraordinary cost, 56

Feasibility studies, 62, 131, 140–141, 143, 144
Firm characteristics, 167, 172–173
First mover's advantage, 168
Forecasting
    of demand, 108
    of market share, 109
    procedure for, 112–113
    of sales, 108
    transfer cost, 113

Gross national product, 26
Growth rate, 19, 21, 84, 108, 181, 187–188
Growth/share matrix, 184

High earners, 19

Ideal point, 37, 41, 104, 106–107, 152–153, 166
Ignoring, 171
Inflation, 16, 20, 24, 25, 26, 62, 84, 112, 113–114, 133, 134
Instructor, role of, 5, 7, 10, 13, 14, 51, 66, 81, 82, 178
Inventory
    disposal of, 57, 74
    holding of, 14, 16, 74
    obsolete, 74, 136

Learning, consumer, 151
Learning curve. *See* Experience curve
Loans, 67, 76

Management responsibility, 31
Margins, 20
    channel, 74
    distributor, 96, 130
    percentage, 20
Market research, 22, 31–32, 51, 61
    cost of, 14, 85
Market share, 35, 78, 86, 176, 179
Marketing department, 14–15, 26
Marketing mix, 31
    effectiveness of, 161, 192
Marketing-mix variables, 171
    elasticity of, 163, 181
Marketing plan, 93–94, 101
    inputs to, 95
MARKSTRAT monetary unit (MMU), 13, 57
Mass communication. *See* Advertising

Messages, 80–81, 98, 150, 152
   error, 9, 70, 98
   warning, 66, 70, 98
Mobility barriers, 152, 164, 166
Module
   analysis, 107, 115, 117, 182
   decisions, 52, 80, 93, 124, 134
   interface, 7
   marketing plan, 94, 101
   newsletter, 82
Monopolistic profits, 168
Multidimensional scaling study, 39–42, 103, 105, 107, 114, 117, 125, 154, 158

Newsletter, 21, 22, 51, 82, 84–85, 133

Optimal brand position, 105
Others (consumer group), 19

Password, 8
Perceptual map, 39, 103–104, 119–120, 124, 154, 165, 169
Perceptual objectives, 58, 124, 170
Physical characteristics, 17–18, 119, 143
Pioneer advantage, 168
Portfolio
   financial, 179
   product, 26, 69
Portfolio analysis, 178–179, 181–182, 191
Positioning, 3, 105–106
Preferences, 39, 42, 103, 152, 153, 166. *See also* Ideal point
Price, 57
   average retail, 73
   average selling, 20, 73
   discount, 20
   recommended retail, 20
   variation in, 20
Price elasticity, 167, 188
Problem child, 179
Product. *See also* Brand
   differentiation of, 137, 165, 166, 167
   life cycle of, 150, 160, 172, 180
Product characteristic, 130, 142
Product portfolio, 26, 69
Production experience, 169
Production level, 16, 57, 69, 112
Productivity
   analysis of, 3
   gains in, 25–26, 110, 139
Professionals, 19
Profit. *See* Contribution
Projections, financial, 97–98
Purchase intentions, 32, 109, 149–150, 152, 153–155. *See also* Preferences

Reaction, 171–172
Reaction elasticity, 162, 163
Regression, 107, 112, 115–119

Research and development
   additional investment in, 24, 80
   base cost of, 62
   budget for, 23, 24, 66, 110, 131–132, 139, 142–144, 161, 169
   expenditures for, 14, 24, 165
   feasibility studies in, 62, 131, 140–141, 143, 144
   on-line query in, 24, 62–64, 132
   request for, 22–24
   results of, 78–79
   unit cost reduction and, 131
Resource allocation, 14, 190
Retaliation, 171
Retrenchment, 171
Revenues, 14–15, 44, 74, 130
Risks, 9, 105, 133, 168, 169, 193
   of missing the boat, 191

Sales force, 21
   allocation of, 21, 58–61, 170
   competitors', 32, 42
   expenditures for, 14, 192
Sales force experiment, 45–46
Saturation level, 108, 152
Scope of targeted market, 164
Segmentation, 3, 19, 103
Semantic scales study, 35–39, 103, 114, 115, 154
   versus multidimensional scaling study, 39, 105, 114, 117
   optimal positioning with, 114
   versus perceptual mapping, 105
Signaling, 169
Simulation, 1, 2
   MARKSTRAT, 1, 2–4, 51
Singles, 19
Sonite, 16
Star, 179, 181
Stock market. *See* Newsletter
Stock price index, 73, 82
Strategic analysis, 3, 142
Strategic group, 158
Strategic window, 191
Strategy
   advertising, 21
   contingency, 142
   growth, 15
   marketing, 21, 142
   positioning, 105, 106
Stuck in the middle, 106
Study. *See also* Multidimensional scaling study, Semantic scales study
   conjoint analysis, 47–48
   consumer panel, 34
   distribution panel, 35
   industry benchmarking, 44
   market forecast, 46–47
   R&D product feasibility, 62, 131, 140–141, 143, 144

Synergy
    cost, 178, 193
    demand, 179, 192
    distribution, 165, 170

Test marketing, 120
Threat of entry, 158
Time allocation, 21, 59–60
    by MARKSTRAT groups, 9

Transfer cost, 14
    forecasting, 110
    minimum feasible, 62
Trend line, 107, 108

Uncertainty, 1, 10, 127, 132, 191, 193
Upgrading, 130

Vodite, 18